The Global Debt Crisis: Forecasting for the Future

The Global Debt Crisis: Forecasting for the Future

Edited by
Scott B. MacDonald,
Margie Lindsay
and
David L. Crum

Pinter Publishers
London and New York

First published in Great Britain in 1990 by
Pinter Publishers Limited
25 Floral Street, London WC2E 9DS and
PO Box 197, Irvington, New York.

British Library Cataloguing in Publication Data

A CIP catalogue record for this book is available from the British Library
ISBN 0 86187 742 X

Library of Congress Cataloging-in-Publication Data

The Global debt crisis : forecasting for the future / edited by
Scott MacDonald, Margie Lindsay and David Crum.
p. cm.
ISBN 0–86187–742–X
1. Debts, External – Developing countries. I. MacDonald, Scott B.
II. Lindsay, Margie. III. Crum, David.
HJ8899.G56 1990
336.3′435′091724–dc20 90–34581
CIP

Filmset by Mayhew Typesetting, Bristol, England
Printed and bound in Great Britain by Biddles Ltd., Guildford and Kings Lynn

Contents

About the authors

Uwe Bott works in the Plans and Programs Department of the Inter-American Development Bank in Washington, D.C. He holds degrees in law and economics from the University of Frieburg in West Germany and was a Fulbright scholar at Georgetown University. He has travelled extensively through the Caribbean and is the author of a chapter on the sugar industry in the Dominican Republic in *The Politics of the Inter-American Sugar Trade* (edited by Scott B. MacDonald and Georges A. Fauriol and forthcoming in 1990).

David L. Crum is an assistant vice-president at American Security Bank, N.A. in Washington, D.C. He received his M.A. from the Johns Hopkins University's School of Advanced International Studies in Washington, D.C. and joined the bank as an international economist. He co-authors a monthly column for the *International Trader of Northern Virginia*, has published in *Export Today* and *Journal of Modern African Studies* and has travelled to Africa.

Michael Hobbs is a Ph.D. candidate in economics at Yale University in New Haven, Connecticut. He has a M.A. from the University of London. He also interned at the Office of the Comptroller of the Currency in 1988.

Jane Hughes is a professor of economics at Brandeis University, in Waltham, Massachusetts. She received her M.A. in International Affairs from the Johns Hopkins University's School of Advanced International Studies and a Masters of Business Administration from New York University. She has worked for Political Risk Services, a division of International Business Communications, USA, and is a former vice president with Manufacturers Hanover in New York. She has also published a major study on Latin America with Euromoney Publications.

Margie Lindsay is Editor of the *Financial Times* Newsletter, *East European Markets*. She is an expert in East European affairs, contributing to the BBC World Service and a frequent speaker on business in Eastern Europe and the Soviet Union. She is also the author of *International Business in Gorbachev's Soviet Union* (Pinter Publishers, 1989).

Scott B. MacDonald is the International Economic Advisor at the Office of the Comptroller of the Currency in Washington, D.C. Prior to that position, he was the Chief International Economist at Maryland National Bank and before that he served at both American Security Bank and Connecticut National Bank. He received his Ph.D. in Political Science from the University of Connecticut and his M.A. in Area Studies from the University of London's School of Oriental and African Studies. He is the author of *Trinidad and Tobago: Democracy and Development in the Caribbean* (1986), *Dancing on a Volcano: The Latin American Drug Trade* (1988), and *Mountain High, White Avalanche: Cocaine and Power in the Andean States and Panama* (1989) and was a co-editor of *The Caribbean after Grenada: Revolution, Conflict and Democracy* (1988). He also has published in *Middle East Insight*, *The Journal of Interamerican Studies and World Affairs*, *SAIS Review*, and *Export Today*.

David Maslin is a vice president at Morgan Guaranty in New York. He works on the Philippines and other Asian countries and has travelled extensively through the region.

Richard O'Brien is the editor of the *Amex Bank Review* and a senior vice president and chief economist at the American Express Bank in London.

John Roberts is currently an analyst for *Oil Daily Energy Compass* in London. Through the years, he has worked with Reuters, Inter-Press Service in Beirut (1978-80), the Middle East Economic Digest (MEED) in London and Washington (1981-8) and as the Washington correspondent for *Al-Hayat* (1988-9). He also worked with the *Financial Times* Newsletters between 1985-1989. Mr Roberts has travelled extensively in the Middle East.

Preface

The global debt crisis has been like a trip with Alice through Wonderland. Things have gotten stranger and stranger. Financial Mad Hatters and Cheshire Cats have flitted in and out of the world's capitals seeking to conjure up sweeping solutions to the interrelated problems of indebtedness, poverty and, in some cases, maintaining popular support for newly-restored democratic governments. The debt crisis has sidetracked development aspirations, led to political turmoil and, worst of all, refused to go away.

For all the well-intentioned solutions advanced, none seem to fit the magnitude and scope of the problem. At the end of the 1980s, a substantial number of countries were destined to stagger into the next decade burdened by past commitments, often impossible to meet. In many cases the situation is complicated by political factors: political turmoil in Eastern Europe which has exasperated economic reform; ethnic tensions; the struggle to maintain new democratic institutions in Latin America and the Caribbean.

This book examines the global debt crisis region by region. Eight chapters have a specific geographical focus: Latin America; Central America and the Caribbean; North Africa and the Middle East; Sub-Saharan Africa; South Africa; Asia; Southern Europe and Eastern Europe. The remaining chapters examine the historical evolution of the crisis and the proposed solutions. A concluding chapter pulls the various strands together and forecasts what the future may bring for each region.

This book is meant to be an accessible and comprehensive guide to the history, current status, and future direction of the global debt crisis. Although the theme is economic and financial, emphasis has been placed on the equally important political and social dimensions, which in many cases are indivisible from the problems facing debt repayment.

Like Humpty Dumpty on his wall, the players in the continuing drama that is the world debt crisis have been in peril of tumbling to their destruction, but thus far, none has been irretrievably broken. With wisdom and compassion, the world's policy makers can move forward from this stalemate into a lasting solution in the 1990s.

Acknowledgements

This book would be the less without some thanks on the part of the editors to those that lent a hand. All three editors thank Frances Pinter for her patience. Scott MacDonald wishes to thank Dr Ahmet Imre, Chief Economist at Dişbank, Istanbul, Dr Sharif Ghalid, the Director of Africa/Middle East Department at the Institute of International Finance in Washington, D.C. and Leon Tarrant, Chairman of ICERC, at the Office of the Comptroller of the Currency for their willingness to discuss the debt issue in its many shapes and forms. Appreciation is also extended to Philip Osburn and Loren Cain at the Office of the Comptroller of the Currency for their kindly reading of various chapters and suggestions. Above all, Scott MacDonald thanks his wife, Kateri, for her patience and support.

David L. Crum also wishes to thank Donna M. Nemer, now with Citicorp's Latin American Investment Bank, for helping him get his start in banking and finance; Dr I. William Zartman, of the Johns Hopkins University's School of Advanced International Studies, who encouraged him to begin writing about Africa; and, most of all, his fiancée, Indira Jhappan, for all her support, advice and forbearance.

Although there were many hands that helped this book along the way, the editors and authors take sole responsibility for the book.

Chapter 1

Introduction — a perspective on debt*

Richard O'Brien

The Less Developed Countries (LDC) debt crisis is now eight years old, close to the average maturity of most of the original banks loans. The saga of LDC lending and the growing relationship between private banks and LDCs however started in earnest some twenty years ago. The purpose of this chapter is to provide the debate with some historical perspective, to put the crisis itself into context. A great deal of ink has been used on LDC debt since the crisis broke, but a great deal happened before the fateful 'Mexican Weekend' of August 1982.

This chapter describes nine phases of the LDC-banking relationship: it is tempting to suggest nine lives of lending, though that metaphor suggests, rather uncomfortably, that time is running short.

Phase one (1970–3)

Phase one was the two- to three-year period to 1973, up to when the first oil shock happened. At that time the Eurocurrency markets were beginning to flex their muscles and banks were getting into the habit of looking for international lending possibilities. At the same time developing countries' creditworthiness was being given a tremendous boost by the commodity price boom, which was not thought to be a one-off phenomenon - unlike the 1950s boom following the Korea War. Rather, it was seen as a long overdue correction in favour of the producers of raw materials. The view that commodities were now a valuable asset was given a psychological boost by the Club of Rome (a private study group) report published in 1972. This warned the world of the rapid depletion of its natural resources. Metals and minerals producers looked stronger - one of the star borrowers and early casualties was the copper-producing country of Zaire, whose earnings

---

* This chapter draws upon an earlier paper written by Richard O'Brien which identified seven phases of lending. 'Banking Perspectives on the Debt Crisis' was published in the *Oxford Review of Economic Policy*, Spring 1986. Mr O'Brien is grateful for permission to re-publish a considerable part of that earlier work.

rose by 120 per cent in two years and almost halved in one year. Ten years after the boom, Zaire's exports were only 8 per cent higher than the 1974 peak.

Lending to developing countries offered attractive rewards (spreads were up to 2 per cent over the base market interest rates, Libor or the London inter-bank offered rates), and occasionally even above 3 per cent over Libor. Lending seemed to carry low risk. Very few LDCs had much in the way of commercial bank debt and even some experiences in the 1960s of rescheduling official debt at the Paris Club (official debt negotiations held under French Treasury auspices) did not deter private lenders.

Phase one was brought to an abrupt end on 6 October 1973 when the Yom Kippur War triggered the first major oil price rise. Oil prices, having taken hesitant steps upwards in the preceding eighteen months, were quadrupled by the end of the year. The oil crisis, especially when allied to the initial oil embargo and physical shortages leading to 'gas lines' in the United States seemed to confirm the Club of Rome prognosis and showed cartel producer power at its strongest. However, as most commodity producers were importers of oil, their creditworthiness was severely damaged. Other commodity prices came off their peaks, often in a spectacular fashion. By 1975 Zaire was seeking a debt rescheduling.

Phase two (1974–75)

Phase two was a period of retrenchment and rethinking in the Eurocurrency market. Confidence was generally at a low ebb with the 1975 recession and stock market collapses (most spectacularly in Britain where the Financial Times 30-share index fell to just 30 per cent of its previous peak). Confidence in the new offshore global financial market was given a massive shock in June 1974 when the small private German bank, I.D. Herstatt, collapsed. For the first time there was a severe contraction in interbank activity in the Euromarket and thus fears for the market's liquidity. The failure later in 1974 of the twentieth largest bank in the United States, Franklin National Bank, added to the sense of market instability even though its bankruptcy was due to its own mismanagement problems and excessive expansion.

At the same time, the Bank of England had to push out its 'lifeboat' to support the secondary or fringe banks following the collapse in the United Kingdom property companies and prices. Like the LDC debt crisis, the property companies, to which the secondary banks had lent large amounts of funds, were hit by the simultaneous rise in interest rates and fall in asset values, themselves a function of the violent reversal of liberal monetary policy (the so-called 'Barber Boom'). The collapse of the US real estate investment trusts (REITs), which had raised a great deal of money in the form of syndicated Eurocredits, was a further negative factor.

As a result of these crises, those who saw the Euromarket as an unregulated, unstructured and uncontrolled pyramid of credit had plenty of anecdotal evidence to draw upon in 1974. In the event, the major casualties of the 1974 crises were the consortium banks (banks owned by a consortium of other banks) and the severe jolt given to confidence in the international banking system.

Japanese banks in particular had a difficult time in 1974–5. First the oil was thought to be bad news for Japan; Japanese banks had to pay substantially higher rates for funds in the interbank market due to the relatively protected nature of their market. Other aspects of this phase were the debt crisis of Zaire, followed in mid-1975 by the collapse of the Indonesian oil company, Pertramina, where debts were taken over by the state to prevent a major debt crisis from destroying the creditworthiness of the country.

Phase three (1976–9)

Phase three started with the economic upswing in 1975–6 following the 1974–5 mini-recession. At that time several of the major developed countries decided to reflate their way out of trouble. The big Euroloans of the mid-1970s were for Britain and Italy. The rise in oil prices was followed by a rapid increase in manufactured export prices. As a result, the huge oil deficits began to be reduced. Oil prices were stable and the dollar began to fall rapidly (much to the concern of the Organization of Petroleum Exporting Countries or OPEC, which saw its hard-won price gains of 1973 diminishing in real terms and its financial investment depreciating). Nevertheless, the Euromarket regained its confidence, deposits were easy to come by with the oil producers as major depositors and the sense of well-being allowed spreads on Euromarket loans to diminish by 1978.

Phase four (1979–81)

Phase three ended and phase four began with the second oil crisis in June 1979. This second major rise in the price of oil probably averted more country-related financial disasters than it initially caused. Mexico had been in deep trouble following the 1976 peso devaluation and subsequent period of austerity. Indonesia was still picking up the pieces after the Pertramina debacle. Nigeria had turned its massive \$4.9 billion current account surplus of 1974 into a \$3.8 billion deficit by 1978. Gabon, having recently borne the costs of hosting the annual Organisation of African Unity (OAU) conference, was facing the prospect of financial problems; its few Eurobonds were trading at a deep discount. Peru had sought rescheduling in 1976, but the arrival of higher oil prices just as oil began to come out of its new wells in the Amazonian jungle gave the country a welcome breathing space.

At first banks seemed to be taking a cautious line on lending after the second oil shock. The volume of syndicated lending activity fell by 16 per cent in 1980. In part, this was due to particular circumstances in specific countries. Brazil under the tutelage of the then Finance Minister, Antonio Delfim Neto, was attempting to avoid going to the International Monetary Fund (IMF) trying to keep spreads low. Bankers wanted higher spreads on Brazilian risk and an IMF programme. By December 1980 it looked as if Brazil would indeed swallow the IMF pill, as its foreign currency reserves had been heavily depleted due to the slow down in borrowing. However, in early 1981 Brazil announced a new programme of economic measures, regarded as very similar to an IMF programme. A modest rise in spreads then saw lenders come back in 1981. South Korea was also taking a cautious line in 1980, following the assassination of President Park Chung-Hee in 1979, which led to a reassessment of economic and political prospects.

In 1979, four months after the second oil price rise and on the sixth anniversary of the first oil shock, an equally significant event occurred – the announcement by the then chairman of the US Federal Reserve Board, Paul Volcker, of a new US monetary policy. This set the scene for a rapid rise in nominal and real interest rates over the coming decade. Initially it was not clear whether this new determined and concerted attack on inflation would succeed, or would be sustained in the United States. The then US president, Jimmy Carter's on-off credit squeeze in 1980 suggested a lack of conviction that real interest rates would stay high for long. During this time there was a boom in new commitments of loan monies to LDCs without such loans being drawn down. The build-up of these commitments, often in the form of short-term facilities, planted some of the seeds for the later short-term debt crisis.

By 1980 the market had grown substantially and a wide range of banks were active. US banks were still the leaders in LDC lending, although their share had fallen from 54 per cent in 1975 to 38 per cent by 1980–81. Of US banks' international assets, 28 per cent were in OPEC and non-oil LDCs. Most other banking groups were slightly less concentrated in the LDCs, with French, German, British and Japanese banks in the 20 to 25 per cent range and with most other groups below 20 per cent. The newest entrants to the market were the Arab banks, which were increasingly lending to borrowers outside the group of Islamic countries. The figures at this point could be read two ways: either non-US banks still had some room to increase their LDC portfolios given their lesser relative concentration on LDCs, or, given the growing perception of risk in lending to LDCs, they might not wish to raise their LDC portfolio to the level reached by US banks.

Phase five (1981–2)

Despite these initial concerns the reassessment period of phase four lasted barely a year. Phase five started in 1981 with syndicated Eurolending beginning again in earnest, and borrowers, who had been cautious in 1980, coming back into the market. A curious and worrying development was the continuous contraction of spreads. Given the obviously growing risks in the markets and the increasing borrowing requirements, it seemed logical for spreads on Eurocurrency loans to LDCs to widen as the LDC credit risk increased. This, however, did not happen as the competition for lending intensified. Yet in 1981 appetite for long-term lending was slowly diminishing, at which point the trend switched to borrowing on a short-term basis. To a degree, there was a hidden upward pressure on spreads. Mexico, for example, followed a policy of sacrificing longer maturities to maintain a low spread. The interest spread had long been regarded as the mark of a country's creditworthiness. One leading banking magazine even assessed risk ratings according to a formula based on spreads. In syndicated loan negotiations it was an accepted negotiation tactic to trade spreads against maturities. While Brazil, anxious to keep as long a capital repayment schedule as possible, accepted a rise in spreads, Mexico played the opposite hand. Spreads did not rise for Mexico, but maturities shortened.

The increase in short-term lending was so swift (occurring mainly in 1981) that it was not until early 1982 that the danger signs could be seen in the data. Once noted, reaction was fast, with the debt crisis hitting in full force five months later. In part, this short-term lending was possible as countries drew down commitments arranged in earlier, better times. Lending to LDCs' banks in the interbank market also had grown. Traditionally, interbank lending was thought to be less subject to country risk considerations, until it became clear that several LDCs were using their own banks as key fund raisers. Where the LDC banks' assets were primarily lent to the parent country (rather than having a global mix of assets) the LDC bank immediately had difficulties when the country rescheduled.

Bankers traditionally regarded short-term exposures as being of lower risk than term exposures. The rationale for this is twofold: first, by making a short-term commitment the bank, in theory, gives itself the option of non-renewal of the facility at an earlier date than would be possible with a term loan; secondly, many short-term facilities are truly trade-related and do carry a greater degree of security than long-term loans. The loan provides short-term bridge finance to cover cash flow needs, or merely credit prior to delivery of payments for goods delivered. But neither of these degrees of comfort could stand up to a massive boom in short-term lending. The option not to roll over the short-term facility disappeared with debt moratoria and the good short-term loans were brought down by the bad.

The atmosphere of crisis in Latin America heightened in April 1982 with Argentina's invasion of the Falklands (Malvinas). Argentina was already in economic crisis and the war with Britain prompted bankers to reassess the risks. The degree of solidarity shown by other Latin American countries (such as Venezuela which switched deposits out of London banks), encouraged reassessment across the continent. Given that most countries' liquidity and debt positions were not in good shape, this reassessment revealed weaknesses which led to a general downgrading of credit ratings throughout the region.

The fifth phase came to an abrupt halt in August 1982 when Mexico sought its debt moratorium; this became known as the Mexican weekend. Brazil soon followed Mexico. Brazil had spent most of the year putting off any application to the IMF pending important elections due in November. But eventually its monthly borrowing requirement of $1 billion became too much for the market to stand and any interruption of flows proved dangerous.

Phase six (1982–5)

The ensuing sixth phase ran up until late 1985. From then until the present banks' reaction to the debt crisis has been to stop lending to LDCs unless forced to do so. There were small rises in assets held in both rescheduling countries and those not in financial difficulties, but the growth in lending has been nothing like the pre-crisis days - even though the small rise in exposure somewhat underestimates activity, as it incorporates some write-downs of loans, the calling of government guarantees on export credits and other adjustments. At the same time, banks have faced other credit problems. A concerted effort by regulators to improve the ratio of capital to assets (capital adequacy), has led to a need to increase capital and to curtail asset growth.

Phase six also saw banks lending in tandem with IMF programmes. In the long run, for banks to ally too closely their credit decisions with those of another institution is to risk a dilution of banks' central responsibility for assessing credit risk. In this case the purpose has been to ensure some adjustment and to coordinate the rescue packages. Large banks have generally been in favour of this approach in order to keep smaller banks in the game. Small banks with less exposure often have had the ability to write-off the loans, but such write-offs have the effect of shifting the new lending burden on to the larger institutions.

However successful the concerted effort to rescue countries' finances has been, there are major differences between different financial institutions' objectives. Not only are there differences between small and large banks in terms of their level of exposure, but also the regulatory and tax differences across countries means that different nationalities of banks have a variety of options.

Most noticeable has been the many West German banks favouring interest capitalisation (which reduces their income stream), while US banks tend to favour new lending programmes to sustain interest income.

Seventh phase (1985–7)

The seventh phase began in October 1985 with the announcement by the then US Treasury Secretary, James Baker, of his plan at the IMF/World Bank meeting in Seoul, South Korea. The Baker Plan (as it became known) was greeted as a welcome initiative. The plan called for private banks to increase their lending to those LDCs facing debt problems and for the World Bank and others to increase their support. In return it called upon on LDCs to increase efforts to adopt supply-side policies and to encourage private sector and foreign investment. Overall the plan was designed to allow economic growth, recognising that the austerity implied by IMF programmes (phase six approach) could only be applied temporarily. The Baker Plan confirmed an official acceptance of the view that growth is economically essential to solve debt problems, as well as being politically important. IMF programmes are designed to correct the worst of countries' imbalances and to encourage financial reforms. But such correction inevitably means austerity. Cutbacks in imports are the quickest way of reducing borrowing requirements. Short, sharp policy shocks try to set in motion some of the basic structural reforms. If, however, such a programme does not work after two to three years, then new growth-orientated solutions must be put in their place.

The timing of the Baker Plan was appropriate: the degree to which countries faced problems of solvency rather than merely illiquidity was becoming clearer. It was also clear that some countries were close to insolvency, while at the same time some countries' stock of currency reserves (liquidity) had been rebuilt. Many initial liquidity problems derived from low levels of foreign exchange reserves and excessive short-term debts. If short-term debts are measured against the normal levels of trade financing requirements (somewhere between three to six months equivalent of imports), then excessive short-term debts had been more than halved since 1982. At the same time foreign currency reserves had been rebuilt due to new lending by banks and the IMF. As a result most countries' liquidity positions were in much better shape than in 1982. Nevertheless, even with these improvements a number of countries still faced high debt burdens. Even with capital repayments rescheduled, many countries still faced the need to use up over 30 per cent of their annual foreign exchange earnings to pay interest. Most importantly for lenders' strategy, the idea of providing new money to finance interest payments was looking less and less sensible.

Phase eight (1987–9)

The end of phase seven can be dated from the February 1987 announcement by Brazil of a moratorium on debt servicing. Phase eight began with the major debt provisioning by the banks (begun by Citibank soon after the Brazilian move). Brazil called a moratorium on interest to try and cut its debt service payments, which continued to be onerous. In practice, Brazil found its moratorium backfiring as short-term lines of credit arrangements were cut. But the shift to greater provisioning was probably to everyone's benefit. The phoney way of assuming that all the loans were worth 100 cents on the dollar began to face up to some sort of reality. However, the price of LDC debt in the secondary market - where LDC debt is sold off at discounts - fell sharply, to the point where loans probably became underpriced when compared to countries' true ability to pay. One test of how far the banks believed the secondary market prices to be the Mexican zero-bond deal: the results of that deal suggested that the banks did not believe a large discount was acceptable, especially when interest payments - which are the source of banks' current earnings - were still at risk.

During phase eight banks sought ways of reducing their exposure and designing new forms of exit bonds. These are a means for lenders to exit from the position at a discount. The Mexican exit bonds tied to US Government zero coupon bonds - bonds carrying no interest cost but aimed at a large discount to reflect that zero interest - were the first major attempt. But during this period the fall in secondary market prices and the rise in provisioning had a serious impact on banks' earnings and certainly undermined the view that the muddling through approach was really working. Banks were losing money, the countries' investment levels were stagnant (thereby reducing growth and export earnings prospects) and the apparent value of assets - as indicated by the secondary market - was plunging. The climate encouraged new plans and ideas to surface in the market in early 1988; some were old ideas reworked. Central to the debate was the extent to which the US Administration should step in to break the deadlock. The US line has been consistent: that the problem is one for the banks and the countries to resolve and that the emphasis should be on new money and the right economic policies. Even though the monies called for under the Baker Plan were provided, neither monies - nor policies - had been forthcoming in a sufficiently positive way, such as the failed Cruzado Plan in Brazil.

In the new debate during this period, Japan has made a number of attempts to create a new momentum, although the suggestions made by that country at the 1988 IMF/World Bank meetings in West Berlin were not backed up with concrete proposals. The absence of the then Finance Minister Kiichi Miyazawa, at the time - due to the illness of the Emperor - made it easy to maintain a certain ambiguity with respect to these 'new' initiatives. US policy was firm throughout 1988, which was an election year.

Phase nine (1989–00)

The ninth phase began in March 1989 with the announcement of the Brady Plan. Although the initial announcement of the plan left a lot of questions unanswered and lacked detail, the plan began a phase of a serious attempt to reduce debt. Debt reduction was a phrase first heard in official circles at the 1988 IMF meetings. Although all agreed that the idea of debt reduction was a good one, no one knew how it was to be achieved. At the West Berlin meetings, for example, great pains were taken - and still are - to ensure that debt reduction is not taken to mean debt forgiveness, even though forgiveness is one possible way of achieving reduction. The first official estimates of the possible impact of the plan were that it could reduce debt by over 20 per cent - $70 billion - over a three-year period, with interest paid to be cut by $20 billion over the same period. Given the size of the existing debt burden, if this were to be the case, it should bring the level of debt down closer to a serviceable level. If LDC country debts are reduced to a level that could be serviced - for example, an interest to export earnings ratio of no more than 20 per cent- then that ought to be the best guarantee of future repayment. During the debate the banks have been keen to ensure that, if debt relief were to be given, that the remaining assets would then be fully serviced. That assurance could be provided by a multilateral institution if it took over the remaining debts, which itself sought repayment from the country, and which offered the banks bonds at the value of the discounted debt. So far banks have had to hope that IMF programmes would succeed, but if they fail, lending to support an IMF programme is shown to offer little more than comfort from that IMF linkage (albeit the only comfort available). But ultimately the solution is likely to involve the debts being reduced to a level which countries can service on their own, without guarantees having to be offered amongst creditor parties.

Since the election of the US President, George Bush, in November 1988, the markets and the LDCs had been awaiting a new initiative from the US Administration. The Baker Plan, which ran for three years, needed a follow-up plan. The amounts called for under the Baker Plan were provided. For the banking community, for example, the Baker Plan called for a net inflow of new capital of $20 billion from the banks, which barring a final $700 million, was done by mid-1988 - despite Brazil's moratorium in the interim. There was still a net outflow to banks when the interest payments due were taken into account, but this was the inevitable result of the slowdown of the growth of debt. It is mathematically impossible to stop debt from rising and not to have a net flow of funds to creditors, unless there is debt reduction of some kind.

The fact that the cast of characters had changed, offered the chance and excuse for a new approach. Some also have looked to the presence of Mr Baker himself in the State Department under the Bush Administration to start pushing for a more politically-orientated and politically-sensitive solution. In the Latin American region, 1989 also started with new presidents in Mexico and Venezuela and there were also major elections in Argentina, Brazil, Chile and Uruguay. Despite the riots in Argentina and Venezuela after announcements by the respective governments of new austerity programmes, a new and different way forward appears to be in place.

The main characteristic of the latest phase in likely to be a new realism. This new realism predates the Brady Bretton Woods speech in March 1988 that launched his debt plan, having come into play with the loan reserving policies in 1987 - the start of the eighth phase - and gathered pace in 1988 with the new debt debate opening up in part as a result of proposals from the marketplace. Instead of new money being the only solution, with those wanting to opt out of being pressured to stay in, the attempt has been underway to find a way for banks to choose between new money and debt reduction. It is recognised that debt-for-equity swaps, while helpful are of marginal benefit. Swaps cannot go too far without having some serious monetary effects on the domestic economy - as the debt is swapped, not reduced.

Any solution needs to have two important ingredients. First, if debt reduction is agreed, lenders will want to feel that the remaining assets will be fully serviced and that one debt reduction will not be followed by another or that the breathing space given will be used effectively by the countries. Second, the free-rider problem of certain banks that do not provide new money or debt reduction and expect repayment must be dealt with, so that lenders either put in new funds or accept some debt reduction at a fair price. The other Brady Plan ingredient - a review of regulatory aspects - should help to encourage this.

The Japanese connection

Japan is clearly set to play an increasingly important role. In the 1980s, the Japanese financial system has made rapid advances and by the end of the decade, the world's largest banks in terms of assets are Japanese. Moreover, Japan is probably the premier creditor nation in 1989 and saddled with an enormous external debt and budget deficit like the United States. So far Japan has been content to play a supporting role, from time to time urging action, but prepared to await for US initiatives. The so-called Miyazawa Plan for debt reduction itself, although never formally presented, can be seen as a signal from Japan that something more ought to be done, but that Japan would not force the issue prematurely if the US wanted to wait. Japan has occasionally disappointed the international community by announcing new lending or aid plans which turn out to be part of already agreed plans, put forward by another country or body. In contrast, the US approach tends to be to announce a new approach and then try to organise the financing to make it work. As the world moves into the 1990s, the greater responsibilities facing Japan as a leading financial power will force it to play a more activist role.

Relationships - banks and LDCs

Whatever happens it is clear that banks have reassessed the real underlying business reasons for banks to be involved in developing countries. While banks will continue to do business in LDCs, the relationship between LDCs and private banks is likely to incorporate a much smaller amount of long-term loans as a result of the damage done by the debt crisis. However, business will continue on other fronts. First, developing countries are themselves depositors with international banks whether they are private, governmental or corporate sector depositors. In many cases the deposit relationship is the first major area to be established and often the first point of contact. Secondly, international banks have developed considerable correspondent banking networks with developing country banks, using this to help finance trade and other activities. Banks remain the major financiers of international trade. This area of business - including confirmation of Letters of Credit (LCs), refinancing of LCs and other trade facilities - is profitable and is likely to continue. With developing countries becoming a force in international trade, international banks are bound to compete for this business. Thirdly, banks have built up branch and representative networks worldwide. While some have been closed down, most banks do not let go of hard won banking licences lightly. Through these branches banks often work with LDCs to service their industrial country clients, such as multinational companies. Often the support of clients' business opportunities in LDCs is essential if a bank is to offer a full global service to its major clients.

All these areas of business are important to banks. What may be in doubt, however, is the idea of international banks lending medium- or long-term money to developing countries. The growth in medium-term syndicated credits was a new phenomenon of the late 1970s. While banks did not take an explicit interest rate risk because of the floating rate nature of credits, the extension of large medium-term loans was generally a departure from traditional banking practices. The natural reaction of banks in the face of crisis is to cut back longer term lending as their international asset growth policy is reassessed.

At the same time there are major changes in the nature of banking itself. Securitisation of international domestic finance - where traded bonds and instruments replace bank loans - challenges the whole concept of international banking based on asset growth and profits derived from net interest income. This securitisation and the accompanying restructuring develops both from changes in national financial industries, particularly in the US, and from changes in global balance-of-payments flows. Instead of the 'recycling' of funds from OPEC to LDCs in the 1970s, the principal payments imbalance is between

Japan, West Germany and other surplus industrial countries, and the US deficit. In the 1970s OPEC's risk aversion favoured risk-free deposits with international banks. LDCs could not raise funds in securities markets as they were by and large unknown quantities in investment markets and hence banks relied upon bank credit. In contrast, in the 1980s Japanese pension funds and other international investors from industrial countries were willing and capable of purchasing securities from, for example, US Treasury instruments and others so that the Japan-to-the-United-States 'recycling' can be done via the securities markets, bypassing the banks.

As a result, international financial intermediation and investment is increasingly taking place in the securities and equity markets, where the financial intermediaries obtain their income from fees, from corporate advisory work and other investment banking activities. Placement of issues in securities markets depends on creditworthiness as assessed by non-banks as well as by banks, which makes this source of finance less accessible to a wide range of developing countries.

As this shift occurs, the mix of loan assets available to banks might decrease in quality, as in theory only those unable to tap securities markets will be looking for loans. A number of LDCs will continue to be important trading and business partners. The idea which gained credence in the 1970s, that countries such as Brazil and South Korea were the industrial country of the future, was not merely a banker's fantasy, even though it is taking longer to come to fruition than some may have hoped. South Korea and Taiwan may be lonely success stories, but they are successful and can expect to graduate to a new economic status over the coming years.

As the debt crisis resolves itself, the LDC-banking relationship should slowly return to business as usual. Banks can be expected to want to service traders, investors and corporate clients. This will mean taking on some short-term exposures. Correspondent banking services to LDC banks will continue to be offered.

Banks may not return to the medium-term sovereign lending business for a long time, however. The 1970s lending boom may prove to have been a remarkable aberration with respect to LDC financing. It was born of extraordinary payments imbalances combined with the emergent Eurocurrency market and other factors. The conditions happened to be ripe for increased international banking activity. But there is no reason to suppose that another payments shock of the extent of the oil shocks will hit the LDCs (like the reverse oil shock hitting Mexico and others at the end of the 1980s), or that a sudden emergence of a new group of inexperienced savers (like OPEC) will emerge. Therefore, there is no reason to expect large amounts of medium-term bank lending to LDCs. This term was not only an aberration from normal banking practices, its results have shown it is not the best way to finance development.

Another characteristic of the new business climate is likely to be a change in the current links between official and private money flows.

The debt crisis has seen a coming together of official and private lending decisions which would seem to be in direct conflict with the difference in objectives between profit maximising private banks and multilateral economic management institutions. The collaboration has been necessary to solve the crisis, but it should not be seen as a long-term proposition. Also, it would not seem logical to push for more official guarantees of private flows. Rewards are there to warrant inflows or they are not. One area of guarantees used has been in trade credit and losses by official trade credit agencies are making the agencies wary of extending too much cover to private trade risk-taking lenders.

The optimal way for private capital to enter LDCs is via risk-taking direct investment and project lending. A mythology has been built up over the years discouraging LDCs from using direct foreign investment. Fear of foreign control over the country is the typical obstacle cited, although foreign investors have just as much to be concerned about expropriation. In the 1970s direct foreign investment was swamped (in size) by borrowings and the untied nature of loans made them more attractive than foreign investments. But if LDCs are serious about using foreign capital, then a healthy contribution of risk capital ought to be a vital ingredient. Just because the flows so far have been small, it does not mean that with the right climate, the flows will not occur. The unprecedented 1970s boom in bank lending to LDCs ought to prove that almost anything can be achieved.

The nine phases of the debt crisis

Phase one: before the oil shock (1971–73)

Volume: $7.3bn of LDC syndicated loans in 1973 of which $4.6bn for non-oil LDCs
Spreads: usually ¾ to 1½ per cent over Libor
Maturities: almost half have maturities within six to ten years; only 8 per cent less than six years

Phase two: post oil shock reassessment (1974–5)

Volume: up to $7bn–$8bn for non-oil LDCs; oil producers back in market in 1979
Spreads: rising to 1¼ per cent to 2 per cent over Libor
Maturities: 75 per cent below six years by 1975

Phase three: recovery and boom (1976–9)

Volume: rising steadily in 1976–7, tripling by 1979 to $33bn for non-oil LDCs
Spreads: falling to below 1 per cent in 1979
Maturities: lengthening, especially in 1978–9

Phase four: post oil shock hesitation (1980)

Volume: falls for the first time on record
Spreads: average spread rises from ¾ per cent to over 1 per cent
Maturities: lengthening to concentrate in seven-ten year range

Phase five: the last hurrah (1981–2)

Volume: recovery to record level (almost $40bn for non-oil LDCs in 1981)
Spreads: rising a little
Maturities: a little shorter (alongside a boom in short-term borrowing outside syndicated credit market)

Phase six: the debt crisis (1983–5)

Volume: rapidly falling (all LDCs down to $14bn in January-September 1985)
Spreads: rapid rise in 1983 to 1¾ per cent (alongside reschedulings), but back below 1 per cent by 1985
Maturities: lengthening, to just below nine years on average

Phase seven: The Baker Plan (1985–7)

Volume: a little new money, with additional official funds
Spreads: little change
Maturities: rescheduled, or standard terms, for creditworthy borrowers

Phase eight: Brazil's moratorium and bank reserving (1987–9)

Volume: Baker Plan amounts completed but little voluntary lending
Spreads: little change
Maturities: rescheduled, or standard terms, for creditworthy borrowers

Phase nine: the Brady Plan (1989–)

Volume: debt reduction is the aim
Spreads: standard terms or subsidised
Maturities: standard terms or rescheduled

Chapter 2

Latin America

Jane Hughes

Introduction

It has become a truism, but is none the less true, that the 1980s were the 'lost decade' for Latin America. In terms of virtually every indicator - economic growth, investment, social progress and quality of life - the region stood still or backpedalled over the course of the decade. While not the only culprit, the debt crisis and resulting negative capital flows were a major force behind the disaster, as Latin America transferred abroad an average $20 billion a year since 1982, or 3 per cent of its GDP.

Clearly debt has gone from being a symptom of failed economic policies, to a serious disease in itself. Many observers argued in 1982 that the debt crisis would do the world a great service, by highlighting domestic economic policy failures in Latin America and mandating corrections. While this may be true, the debt crisis in itself now appears to many as a malaise without correction.

To generalize, however, a feeling of calm, even complacency, regarding the Latin American debt situation now prevails - in stark contrast to the near-panic of 1982. Most important, it is evident to all that the international banking system has survived intact.

Large commercial banks have returned to profitability. In recent US Congressional testimony, three leading bank regulators indicated that US banks are no longer threatened by the global debt crisis. Despite the launching of the Brady Plan, in March 1989, the Baker Plan is still more or less in place as a 'successful' test case under the new Plan's debt reduction guidelines eluded creditors and debtors; at the end of 1989, neither the Mexican nor the Costa Rican rescheduling agreement had been finalized. Recent economic summits of the Group of Seven leading industrial countries have focused more on self-congratulation at the robustness of the world economy and relative stability of currency levels than on the Third World and debt.

Nevertheless, many observers doubt whether this complacency is justified. To examine the Latin American debt situation at the end of the 1980s versus 1982, it is best to begin by taking snapshots of various indicators at the two points in time, later focusing on analysing the two points from the perspective of the major actors - individual debtor countries, the International Monetary Fund (IMF), the US government and commercial banks. Finally using this it is possible to look forward and make a few forecasts and recommendations for a future course of action.

Economic progress

The 1980s have clearly been the lost decade in terms of economic growth for Latin America. The region's economy grew less rapidly than did its population in the 1980s for the first time in twenty years. Real income per capita in the middle-income developing countries, or less developed countries (LDCs - which would include Argentina, Brazil and Mexico) has tumbled by 8 per cent since 1982. More specifically, some data on average annual growth in 1983-8 in the major Latin American countries present a dismal picture.

Table 2.1 Average annual growth 1983-8 (%)

Argentina	1.5
Brazil	3.8
Chile	4.2
Mexico	0.0
Peru	0.2
Venezuela	1.0

Source: All data are the author's estimates, and should be treated with corresponding caution

Despite the better than average performance of Brazil and Chile, it is clear that the picture for the region was discouraging. Data on inflation are even less promising.

Table 2.2 Average annual inflation 1983-8 (%)

Argentina	370
Brazil	295
Chile	21
Mexico	92
Peru	221
Venezuela	16

Source: IMF, author's estimates

With regard to both growth and inflation, these average annual figures actually are rosier than the current situation, as 1988 data were especially depressing. GDP for Latin America and the Caribbean as a whole was up a scant 0.7 per cent for the year, while per capita GNP was down by 1.5 per cent. According to a preliminary report by the United Nations Economic Commission for Latin America (ECLA), the economic crisis of the region, then in its eighth year, was at its most acute state yet. This fear would certainly be borne out by inflation figures for 1988: Argentina ended the year at 420 per cent, Brazil at 934 per cent and Peru at 1722 per cent. The figures for 1989 for all three countries threatened to be worse.

Table 3.2 Economic indicators

	Real GDP growth (%)		CPI inflation (%)		Trade account ($bn)		Current account ($bn)	
	1982	1988	1982	1988	1982	1988	1982	1988
Argentina	−4.9	1.0	164.7	350.0	2.8	3.0	−2.4	−2.5
Brazil	0.9	1.0	98.0	685.0	0.8	19.0	−16.4	4.0
Chile	−14.1	6.0	9.9	10.0	0.1	2.0	−2.4	−0.6
Mexico	−0.6	0.4	58.9	110.0	6.8	4.9	−6.4	−3.1
Peru	0.9	−8.4	64.4	774.0	−0.4	0.2	−1.8	−1.4
Venezuela	0.7	2.0	8.3	27.0	2.9	0.7	−4.9	−1.6

Source: IMF, author's estimates

Turning to the external accounts, there are a few positive developments although the overall picture is still not bright. The happiest news is from Brazil, which is currently running the world's largest surplus on trade, estimated at close to $20 billion for 1988. Chile and Colombia, too, improved their current account performances since 1982. However, the major oil exporters (Mexico and Venezuela) have, not surprisingly, witnessed a major deterioration in their current accounts although Mexico has made great strides in improving its non-oil exports performance.

Indebtedness

The data on indebtedness indicate a heavier debt burden virtually across the board than in 1982 when the crisis first erupted. Despite the death of the new syndicated loan market for Latin American borrowers, restructurings of new loans to finance debt service, plus stagnant growth have combined to substantially swell the indebtedness and debt servicing burdens of most countries in the region. Total foreign debt of Latin America and the Caribbean totalled about $400 billion at the beginning of 1989, as compared with $290 billion in mid-1982.

The region as a whole has been making net transfers abroad of about $20 billion, or 3 per cent of its GDP, since the debt crisis began in 1982. This figure was even higher in 1988 at $29 billion or 4 per cent of GDP, representing a huge commitment of resources to debt servicing over the 1980s.

Table 2.4 Selected countries: debt indices

	Brazil 1982	Brazil 1988	Argentina 1982	Argentina 1988	Mexico 1982	Mexico 1988
Debt/GDP (%)	32	40	77	82	53	63
Debt/exports (%)	365	350	446	573	332	357
Total debt ($bn)	85.7	115	43.6	63	91.2	107

Source: IMF, author's estimates

Table 2.5 Debt indicators

	Total external debt ($bn)		Total debt/ GDP (%)		Debt service exports (%)		Total debt exports (%)	
	1982	1988	1982	1988	1982	1988	1982	1988
Argentina	43.6	63.0	77	82	102	63	446	573
Brazil	85.7	115.0	32	40	89	46	365	350
Chile	18.0	17.4	74	88	69	28	349	350
Mexico	91.2	107.0	53	63	70	42	332	357
Peru	11.3	18.8	56	51	52	45	271	528
Venezuela	34.0	34.7	43	56	34	41	169	275

Source: IMF, author's estimates

The only bright spot here is that the total indebtedness of the region actually declined slightly in 1988 (from $410 billion to $401 billion), thanks to debt/equity conversions, mainly in Brazil, Chile and Mexico. Even so, it is clear from any indicator chosen that the debt burden is heavier now than ever in terms of GDP, exports and debt service requirements.

Political developments

With regard to Latin America's political geography, the region has undergone a major transformation since 1982. The changes can be summarized as a shift away from military and authoritarian regimes toward democracy and, more recently, a further shift leftward among the populace. By the end of 1988 a further factor - the increasing fragility of these democracies - was becoming more evident, too.

It is perhaps surprising, or counter-intuitive, that the debt crisis should have been accompanied by a wave of democratization, most notably in the shift from military to civilian power in Argentina and Brazil, the birth of a credible opposition in Mexico, and even the departure of Chile's General Pinochet. (Pinochet, in fact, will remain as the commander-in-chief of the armed forces for eight years after he leaves the presidency in March 1990.)

The debt crisis - despite stagnant growth, massive transfers of resources abroad and continuing internal redistribution of wealth - has generated neither revolution nor authoritarianism at home. However, on closer examination it becomes clear that the debt crisis and the wave of democratization in Latin American politics are not uneasy bedfellows at all. On the contrary, a relationship begins to emerge.

The military's role in producing the crisis to begin with helped to strip these regimes of their legitimacy, while at the same time heightening their eagerness to turn over power to civilians as the morass deepened. Witness Argentina and Brazil, even the decline of the Institutional Revolutionary Party (PRI) in Mexico, to see how the debt problem helped grease the decline of the status quo or military regime, perhaps even more quickly and painlessly than would otherwise have been the case.

Another trend that is even more closely related to the debt crisis is the dramatic swing to the left in these nascent democracies of Latin America - even in the long-established political systems like Mexico. Elections are being held by Argentina, Brazil, Colombia, Peru and Uruguay in the 1989-90 period. In each country parties well to the left of the present discredited government are heavily favored to win.

In each case, debt management is a key political issue, with populist and opposition parties promising radical revisions in existing debt agreements or even outright moratoriums to ease the burden of debt service on the populace. Mexico and Venezuela completed elections in 1988 with the victors promising wide-ranging renegotiation of debt accords following campaigns in which foreign debt figures as a major, if not the major, issue exploited by the opposition.

These factors were particularly evident in the meteoric rise of the leftist Cardenista opposition that very nearly unseated the PRI in Mexico's presidential election. Local elections virtually throughout the region in 1988 indicate that voters often identified with the views of leftist oppositions, as in Argentina, Brazil and Mexico.

Nevertheless, the trend toward democratization in Latin America is probably the most encouraging development of the last decade, especially when weighed against the fear of riots and revolutions that never occurred in response to the debt crisis. It is also possible to say Latin America has demonstrated an admirable, and perhaps surprising, degree of political and social resilience when put to the test. But it is impossible to ignore the fragility of these new democracies - a factor that is increasingly gripping the imagination of the US government.

While fears of Mexico becoming the next Iran or the first domino are almost certainly laughable, a number of serious questions remain: Will Latin militaries, especially in Argentina and Brazil, stand for the increasing radicalization of electoral politics? Will Pinochet really allow a civilian government to emerge in Chile? Can Mexico's PRI maintain its legitimacy after a disputed presidential election that it may not even have won? Can Peru and, to a lesser degree, Colombia avoid that social anarchy and political disintegration that seems to be threatening?

These and many other pressing concerns have created fears that without a set of new debt initiatives designed to reverse the net transfer of resources northward, a wave of radicalization seems poised to engulf the fragile democracies of Latin America. While the past decade suggests that the new civilian regimes are certainly tougher than one might have expected, fears about the future are certainly legitimate.

Quality of life

There is very little to debate with regard to social concerns and quality of life issues in Latin America since 1982. Even the most casual observer can see the results of the economic deterioration that marks an abrupt end to the social progress of the 1960s and 1970s.

With the plunge in per capita income comes high unemployment and a sharp decline in real wages and living standards for most Latin Americans. Even more distressing, it is becoming increasingly evident that the biggest losers are those whose economic advancement occurred during the recent period of dramatic growth in 1960-80 - the lower classes and emerging middle class.

In an especially painful reminder of the social costs, a recent UNICEF report charges that children are bearing the brunt of the Third World debt crisis. According to the report, throughout Africa and Latin America, average family incomes are down by 10 per cent to 25 per cent since the beginning of the decade while malnutrition and disease levels are soaring.

Table 2.6 Social indicators

	GDP per capita ($)		Unemployment (%)*	
	1982	1988	1982	1988
Argentina	1,955	2,391	4.6	6.0
Brazil	2,110	2,138	5.5	5.5
Chile	2,110	1,553	19.6	8.5
Mexico	2,375	2,079	9.4	4.2
Peru	1,110	865	10.6	9.5
Venezuela	5,019	3,305	7.1	8.5

* Unemployment figures refer to official statistics; unofficial estimates, particularly of urban unemployment, may be substantially higher.
Source: IBC Political Risk Services, Inc. and author's estimates

Throughout Latin America, government spending on social services such as health and education as well as investment and development projects has been slashed to help finance the net transfer of resources abroad to service the debt.

Better or worse?

Most of this highlights the price of the debt crisis for Latin America in terms of economic stagnation, staggering debt service costs and rising social tensions. The inevitable conclusion appears to be that the debt crisis is now more acute than ever.

But the question whether the debt problem in Latin America has really deteriorated or improved since 1982 finds an answer depending on perspective. Who are the different players on the debt field and what progress has been made, from each player's point of view, in tackling the crisis since 1982 and - if indeed it is still a crisis. The key players - the US government, IMF, commercial banks, and the individual debtors - each require their own analysis.

By dividing these players into success stories or failures - actors whose management of the debt crisis since 1982 may be considered a success or failure - it is possible to examine those players for whom success has been achieved in one way or another on the debt issue since 1982 and for whom the issue is probably no longer a crisis.

However, there are two major caveats. First, the debt problem has been accompanied by an astounding and never-ending metamorphosis in the roles of each player. Most notable, commercial bankers have been transformed from affable, overeager salesmen to irascible collection agents and reluctant creditors. As this transformation process is still ongoing and alive, the role of any actor may change imminently.

Second, the highly subjective classification of debtor countries into successes or failures in dealing with the debt problem is embarrassingly time-sensitive. Inconsistent economic policies and the vagaries of world events (such as oil and commodity prices), as well as political developments, means that one country can move from success to failure and vice versa with astonishing speed. Today's success is tomorrow's basket case. These classifications may well change, and so can only represent each country's position and prospects at the beginning of 1989.

Success: the commercial banks

Those players which have been relatively successful in managing the debt crisis are the commercial banks. Through an agile mix of policies aimed at augmenting capital and limiting new Latin American lending to 'involuntary' packages, the banks have made huge strides in reducing their vulnerability to Latin American credits. As US bank regulators recently told Congress, commercial banks on the whole no longer have a debt crisis.

Nevertheless, there is no doubt that in 1982 banks faced grave problems, as it became clear that major Latin American borrowers could not service their debts. The high degree of exposure and concentration of profits in a few large Latin American countries posed a severe threat to major US banks. Latin American exposure averaged twice the capital base for major banks, while totalling fully 7 per cent to 10 per cent of assets and profits for Chase Manhattan Bank, Chemical Bank, Citibank and Manufacturers Hanover Trust.

Banks moved quickly (too quickly, critics would argue) to distance themselves from the problem. Essentially 'red-lining' all of Latin America, the bottom dropped out of the market for new credits in August 1982. New financing since then have been almost entirely 'involuntary' - at the prompting of the IMF and western central banks as a precondition for IMF funding. During the eighteen months before August 1982, total new lending to Latin America by commercial banks totalled $42 billion; in the next 18 months, this figure plunged to just $9 billion.

Banks also reduced their vulnerability by increasing capital and reserves via a series of aggressive actions. Through these steps, plus the steady erosion of credits to Latin America through selling, swapping, writing off and writing down such loans, the banks are now heavily cushioned against any new shocks from the Latin American borrowers.

Table 2.7 World's top hundred banks ($bn)

	1982	1987
Net profit	16	30*
Equity capital	146	300
Latin American exposure	182	237
Bank provisions	0	65
Net exposure equity (%)	125	57

* Estimate
Source: IBCA Banking Analysis, appearing in the *Financial Times* (London), 5 January, 1989

Accordingly, the big banks had returned to profitability by 1988. In fact many enjoyed a record-breaking fourth quarter in 1988 because Brazil's official end to its eighteen-month moratorium allowed them to declare income on those interest payments. Bank stocks were generally strong in 1988, with the greatest recovery seen in the stock of those banks with the greatest exposure to Third World debt. Manufacturers Hanover stock, for instance, shot up by 38 per cent in 1988, suggesting that the market was rethinking its earlier downgrading of banks with heavy Latin American exposures.

At the beginning of 1989, it is clear that although Latin American debt continues to occupy a great deal of bank management's time and energy - and is responsible for countless headaches and irritation - it is no longer capable of destabilizing the commercial banking system or even any individual banks, as seemed eminently possible in 1982.

US policy

The US government, too, probably deserves a place in the list of successes in terms of the debt management strategy. When the debt crisis broke in 1982, the US had ample interests at stake to justify its close involvement with subsequent developments. With respect to direct economic interests, before 1982, Latin America took 20 per cent of US exports and approximately the same level of its foreign direct investment. According to one estimate by Ellen S. Goldberg and Dan Haendel, a debt moratorium by Brazil would cause a $25 billion drop in the US GNP and claim 400,000 jobs.

The US government was equally concerned with maintaining the integrity of the international banking system in the face of fears that such a moratorium would spread through the system, leading to possible insolvency of major international banks with unthinkable global consequences.

The government identified three major goals that prompted it to take action in 1982: to protect the investment of US banks, to maintain the stability of the international banking system, and to uphold US economic and security interests in Latin America.

These goals led the US government to spearhead efforts to provide short-term financing for Brazil and Mexico when the crisis erupted in mid- to late-1982, and have kept it on the leading edge ever since then.

With Latin American indebtedness worse and the political situation fragile at best, why call US debt management a success? The answer is that it is a qualified success, as the US government has more or less achieved two of its three goals. Commercial banks have been restored to profitability and the stability of the international banking system seems assured. Despite the fact that the task is clearly not over, the government has reason to be relatively pleased with its efforts to date when measured against the yardstick of its own, admittedly limited, goals.

The government's primary instrument to achieve these goals has been the Baker Plan, which was really nothing more than a restatement of existing strategy: the US would encourage debtors and creditors to renegotiate long postponements on repayment of principal while mandating economic adjustment programs in debtor countries in exchange for new money from commercial banks.

Whether it is intended to or not, the Baker Plan has worked almost entirely as a saviour of commercial banks. It has shielded banks from writing off much Latin American debt as uncollectable (stretching generally accepted accounting practice to its utmost limit in the process), while expecting debtors to make huge interest payments abroad in exchange for very little new money. Nevertheless, the Baker Plan has provided the international financial system with a framework for negotiations, and in doing so helped prevent a breakdown in relations between debtors and creditors.

However, the Baker Plan's failure to address the need for growth and development in the Third World has created a growing feeling that the Plan is bankrupt, leading to new challenges to US leadership on the debt issue from around the world. The Bush administration's Brady Plan was launched on March 1989. Key elements of the new Plan were debt reduction and a reaffirmed emphasis on structural adjustment. Something was also supposed to be done about capital flight, but actual procedures remained vague. Although Mexico and Costa Rica have come under the Brady Plan's umbrella, only Chile presented a rapidly resolved debt reduction deal in 1989. At the close of the decade, US strategy has succeeded only in the sense that it has achieved most of the US government's goals as codified in 1982, rather than in the sense that it has noticeably advanced global goals of economic and social progress in Latin America.

The US government has also succeeded in what was probably its key goal in 1982: ensuring the stability of the international banking system and of major commercial banks. So, it is fair to call US strategy a qualified success, even as the government begins to inch forward in a new direction: toward the economic and political security of Latin America.

A success: Chile

Chile clearly deserves to be in the success category in terms of its economic progress during the past decade. Despite major crises in 1975 and again in 1982, the country is at the top of the Latin American league in terms of economic prosperity. As a result of unremitting application of market-orientated economic reforms, Chile has achieved sustainable real growth of 5 per cent to 6 per cent a year in recent years while exports are booming, employment exploding and investment rising. Moreover all of this has been possible despite a low inflation rate of under 20 per cent a year.

On debt management, Chile's total indebtedness in early 1989 was no higher than in 1982, and down substantially from the peak level of 1986 due to Latin America's most aggressive program of debt reduction through equity swaps. As a result, Chile today boasts easily the best debt picture in the region. All of its foreign debt has been restructured and the country has steadily serviced all international obligations since 1982.

Also, Chile has simple trade lines available and its payment profile through the early 1990s appears to be manageable. In fact, the senior debt negotiator, Hernan Somerville, resigned in late 1988 after five years on the job, explaining that his mission was accomplished.

The question now becomes, how did Chile accomplish this miracle, and why has its model not been exported to the rest of Latin America? Chile achieved its success primarily through the application of market-orientated reforms, which freed the business sector to become the most open and dynamic in the region. The budget deficit has been slashed to under 1 per cent of GDP (an enviable record by US standards) as hundreds of state enterprises have been privatized and over 200,000 jobs slashed from the public payroll. A set of clear and consistent rules encouraged debt/equity swaps and new foreign investment, while dramatic cuts in import tariffs forced industry to become competitive on world markets.

However, this progress has not come without cost. The sudden end of industrial protection was a major factor behind the devastating recession of 1982 in which several large industrial groups collapsed while the economy shrank by nearly 15 per cent in one year alone. Drastic real wage cuts coincided with high unemployment and a wave of bankruptcies; minimum wages are still among the lowest in Latin America.

Despite the steady growth since 1982, Chile is still struggling with the need to distribute its poverty more equally. The country is deeply divided between the desperate poverty of its many slums on the one hand and newfound wealth of the upper and middle classes on the other. Reforms and growth in the macroeconomy have brought little benefit to the poor: the rate of extreme poverty is somewhere between 15 per cent (official estimate) and 40 per cent (opposition estimate) of the population.

Even more important, the Chilean miracle is not exportable to the rest of Latin America because it was achieved in a political vacuum. The government had no need to wrangle with business groups, labor unions or congress over these policies. Strikes were banned, for instance, while public protest over debt/equity swaps (which has arisen in Brazil and Mexico in particular) was simply not possible in the repressed political environment. It is likely that the fragile democracies of Latin America could not sustain the extreme austerity conditions imposed by the Chilean government leading to the conclusion that the Chilean model can only provide limited lessons to the region as a whole. Moreover, the new Christian-Democratic led government which came to power with the December 1989 elections will have a difficult act to follow in meeting expectations and cooling an economy expected to have expanded by 8 per cent in 1989.

Another success: Mexico

The second country seen to be a success story is Mexico. While Mexico is not as clearly a success in terms of its debt management as Chile, it can still be tentatively placed on the plus side of the ledger. Mexico will always deserve special consideration as it is generally deemed to be the instigator of the debt crisis with the infamous Mexican weekend of August 1982, and because of its special geopolitical significance to the US. These factors have endowed Mexico with a set of undeniable advantages in the debt arena, as we shall see.

It is clear that Mexico has made economic progress since 1982. In fact international bankers now view Mexico more favorably than most of the Latin American countries especially Argentina and Brazil. Since 1982, the country has embarked on an economic adjustment program and made great strides, coming far from the inward-looking economy of the 1970s.

The government has slashed tariff rates, bringing the highest tariff down from 100 per cent to 20 per cent while stimulating a sharp rise in non-oil exports. State companies are also being sold off (about 400 state businesses have been sold, merged or liquidated since 1985), contributing to a major decline in the state's operating budget. While the basic foreign investment law is still in place, de facto application of restrictions has been much less inhibiting to investors than in the past.

Mexico has probably managed its relations with creditors better than any other Latin American country except Chile. Bankers rate Mexico as the least confrontational of the major creditors, while acknowledging that the Mexicans have played the US card with great skill (for example, extracting a $3.5 billion bridging loan from the US administration on the eve of the US presidential election to ensure stability during the Mexican political transition).

The Mexicans have also played a leading role in developing debt-reduction technology. In particular, Mexico led the way with the Aztec bonds in early 1988 which were collateralized with US Treasury bonds and could be exchanged for discounted bank debt.

Mexico's president, Carlos Salinas de Gortari, represents continuity in economic policy and as such is a popular figure with the international financial community. Salinas' peaceful transition to power has engendered a cautious feeling of optimism. If he can keep Mexico's restive population at bay just a little longer, he will be able to build on a new foundation and thus resume sustainable economic growth in the 1990s, thanks to the country's economic reform effort and the continuing support of the US.

However, the Mexican model is also not particularly exportable to the rest of the region. First, the US card has been a remarkably potent weapon. The US government's fears of instability on its border have been invaluable in helping Mexico obtain financial support both directly from the government, and indirectly from bankers after prodding from the US administration. Consequently, there was no surprise when Mexico was advanced as the first country to come under the Brady Plan's debt reduction program. Although an agreement in principle was hammered out in 1989 that aimed at 35 per cent debt reduction, the final signing of the new deal was not accomplished by the end of the year.

Second, Mexico boasts a particularly idiosyncratic political system which was also instrumental in allowing the government to implement reform. Until recently, the ruling PRI completely controlled virtually every sector of critical importance to the government, ranging from peasant groups to labor. This control muted opposition to government policies - certainly not as thoroughly as in Chile, but - enough to maintain political stability despite the country's economic woes. While this helped Mexico in its period of austerity, it was a peculiarly Mexican system and offers little as a model for other Latin American countries.

Failure: Argentina

The list of failures in Latin America's debt management is much longer, topped by Argentina, a spectacular failure by any standards. Argentina has emerged as 1989's most intractable debt problem, with little hope for resolution in sight.

The Argentine economy is stagnant, while inflation is over 400 per cent a year. By early 1989, the country had built up nearly $2 billion in arrears to bank creditors amid fears that arrears could reach $6 billion before any improvement will occur. Argentine economic history since 1982 has been one long economic crisis characterized by chronic hyperinflation, political instability, capital flight and devaluation - and punctuated by a series of ill-fated 'plans' such as the Austral Plan in 1985 and the Primavera Plan in 1988.

The extent of the disaster is especially surprising given the enormous potential of Argentina. In the 1930s, Argentines enjoyed virtually the same standard of living as West Europeans; by the 1980s, the country had slipped firmly into the Third World.

Argentina's problems centre around its legendary political instability. By early 1989, three military rebellions plus one armed rebellion by (presumably) leftist attackers since President Alfonsín took office in 1983 underlined the country's political fragility as presidential elections approached. The Peronists' victory in the May 1989 elections brought Carlos Menem to office. Despite his adoption of tough austerity measures and vows of halting the inflationary slide, the new president entered 1990 confronted by rising inflation, labor unrest and cabinet changes. Menem did manage to obtain an IMF loan due to his new programs, but serious questions continue to dog the Argentine leader.

Even without such steps, the country's chronic inability to meet IMF targets for its economic adjustment program (especially on the intertwined problems of inflation and government spending) spell serious trouble between Argentina and its creditors. The inescapable conclusion is that there is little hope for Argentina to become a successful debt management case any time in the next few years.

Another failure: Brazil

A much more debatable case, but one still deserving a place on the failure side of the ledger, is Brazil. In some ways, it will be surprising to many that Brazil is listed as a debt management failure. After all, Brazil recently ended the infamous debt moratorium that it declared in February 1987 amid general recognition - especially in Brazil - that the move had been a blunder. The country has completed a financial package allowing it to erase all interest arrears and collect $5.2 billion in new money. Moreover, foreign debt actually declined by about 5 per cent in 1988 thanks to interest payments and debt/equity swaps.

Why then is Brazil considered a failure? In fact, debt structure is the only part of its current economic management to look promising. Since debt strategy ultimately is an outgrowth of domestic economic actions, this bodes ill for future debt policy.

Brazil ended 1988 with inflation running at an annualized rate of 2,000 per cent. The embattled administration of lame duck President Sarney announced its sixth emergency economic package designed to cut inflation, but most observers agree that the drastic actions needed are not being taken. A review of the Brazilian economy reveals sharp declines in living standards, rising corruption, a near-breakdown in many public services and a crippling wave of strikes. In this environment, the new wave of austerity demanded by Brazil's economic problems, particularly with regard to budget cuts, is unlikely.

Moreover, presidential elections are also approaching in Brazil and a shift to the left presages a rout for the ruling party. Rising populist and nationalist sentiment is evident in the country's new constitution, which among other things codifies limits on foreign investment. Opposition to debt/equity swaps on nationalist grounds is also growing, creating serious doubts about Brazil's future foreign investment climate.

Political pressures probably ensure that significant reforms will not be undertaken in the next few years to halt Brazil's slide into hyperinflation and to improve conditions for foreign investors. As the country violates its spending and inflation targets set with the IMF and bank creditors, the latest debt agreement will be seen as a temporary lull in hostilities rather than a permanent solution.

Furthermore, the $5.2 billion in new money only covered Brazil's financing needs through mid-1989. Negotiations with creditors, however deteriorated once again when Brazil missed commercial bank payments in September 1989. On top of that, the presidential elections, which took place in two rounds in November and December, clearly occupied the country's leadership. The question faded as a pressing issue. The new president-elect, Fernando Collor de Mello, due to be inaugurated in March 1990, inherited an economy out on a limb with its creditors, inflation running at over 40 per cent a month, and growth remaining low at around 1 per cent for 1989.

Another failure: Peru

While Brazil is debatable, there can be doubt about the classification of Peru as a failure in debt management. Currently mired in its worst economic crisis of the century, the country is in a state of virtual economic collapse. Peru is suffering through a devastating recession accompanied by a huge decline in real wages, food shortages, widespread strikes and inflation that reached 1,722 per cent for 1988 and is currently estimated to be running at an annualized rate of 20,000 per cent.

Its debt strategy is bankrupt. The policy of limiting debt service payments to 10 per cent of exports since 1985 has made Peru a pariah in the international banking community. It has joined a very select group of countries (which includes Vietnam and Sudan) that are ineligible for World Bank and IMF loans because of its arrears, currently put at over $6.6 billion.

Peru's problems, however, come not so much from its debt service ceiling as from the use to which the government has put these resources. The president, Alan García, used the resources freed up to promote a burst of economic activity through increased government spending and wages. Price controls helped fuel a surge of consumer spending rather than productive investment, creating a very short-lived boomlet with devastating long-run consequences.

Once the boom turned to bust, the attempts of the embattled president to cope have been incoherent and incomplete at best; at worst, incompetent. Current political pressure for a more 'realistic' debt policy and discreet government contacts with officials of the IMF and World Bank give some hope; however, little progress is expected soon despite small payments to the World Bank late in 1989.

More failures: Colombia and Venezuela

Most will be astounded to find Colombia and Venezuela listed as failures. Although these countries are not failures in terms of their debt management strategy in an orthodox sense, they serve to highlight the failure of the system to deal with them properly. Colombia and Venezuela have been Latin America's best debtors consistently since 1982.

Colombia is the only Latin American country besides Paraguay to have avoided rescheduling since 1982, and has made substantial interest and principal payments steadily as the cost of significant economic activity at home, where all but the wealthiest are feeling the pinch. Moreover, both countries have achieved reasonable growth levels and inflation under 30 per cent for most of the period. Their moderate economic performances and timely interest and principal payments should make Colombia and Venezuela Latin America's most creditworthy borrowers.

However, it is evident that the system has failed to reward these two countries appropriately. Colombia and Venezuela actually pay slightly higher margins on their debt than do Argentina and Brazil. Their access to new voluntary lending is still a pipe dream, while even 'involuntary' financing is not easily achieved. Commercial banks were $150 million short at the beginning of 1989 on a $1.85 billion loan sought by Colombia to cover its financing needs for 1989-90. The money will be found, but the process is not easy, as Colombia's threat of a rescheduling if the entire package is not funded makes clear.

Not surprisingly, both countries are increasingly disillusioned over the lack of reward for their conservative debt strategies. Colombia announced at the beginning of 1989 that it will delay principal payments in the first quarter of the year as part of its new loan agreement. More strikingly, Venezuela (where recent elections saw the elevation of debt policy to a major national issue) has announced it will halt principal payments on some public sector debt. While both moves are limited in scope and not at all threatening to international banks, they illustrate the failure of the debt crisis management system over the past six years.

Mexico as a failure

Mexico, which appears as a success and a failure, earns this dubious dual position because its economic progress has been accompanied by enormous political consequences too great to ignore. The 1988 presidential election witnessed what will probably prove to be the permanent end of PRI hegemony over Mexican politics. The PRI candidate squeaked into office with barely 50 per cent of the vote, and even this dismal performance was with the aid of some election fraud. While the PRI still has a majority in congress, leftists within the ruling party may side with the opposition on some issues against Salinas, as pressure from a leftist opposition increasingly becomes part of the economic debate. All of this has created a sense of political anxiety much higher than in 1982, and is undoubtedly behind the US eagerness to extend its bridge loan in 1988.

These political changes illustrate, more than anything else, the costs of implementing even a moderately conservative economic adjustment program and debt strategy. Mexican living standards, real wages, and consumer buying power have all plunged by any measure since 1982 as the country has struggled to satisfy its creditors. Debt servicing cost fully $9 billion in 1988; Mexicans transferred abroad 6 per cent of their GDP to foreign creditors. The potency of these facts as a political weapon in the hands of a leftist opposition cannot be underestimated, as Cuauhtemoc Cárdenas proved to the PRI's dismay.

Moreover, Mexico is posing some new and especially difficult challenges to the debt management system. Like Colombia and Venezuela, Mexico believes it has seen few rewards for its relatively good behavior. (Mexico has in fact been more favored than the other two, but without the US card it probably would have seen no reward at all.) Bankers praise Mexico's economic policies lavishly, but are not at all anxious to lend the country any more money. Its last loan package, completed in 1987, took nine months to arrange and required the US government to pressure banks into participating in the end. Salinas now needs to promote growth, not austerity, and will need the cooperation of the US bankers to do so.

Thanks to the special US interest in maintaining a stable Mexico, Salinas will probably muddle through. But again, this illustrates the failure of the system to promote economic adjustment without producing agonizing social and political pain as a byproduct, and its inability to reward properly for good behavior in the absence of special geopolitical involvement.

IMF failures

The last player seen as a failure is the IMF. When the debt crisis first erupted in 1982, it initially produced a massive increase in the power, prestige and influence of the Fund. The world turned to the IMF as a white knight, or *deus ex machina*, perfectly positioned to manage the international debt crisis. The IMF was seen as an international law enforcement officer who could save the day by whipping the recalcitrant debtor countries into shape.

Today the IMF itself has become a sort of international whipping boy. It is a dirty word throughout Latin America, while even commercial bankers are deeply resentful of IMF prodding to participate in new credits and western governments are increasingly distrustful. Economists the world over have challenged the Fund's orthodox economic policies as inflexible and inappropriate. The IMF is even seeing a challenge from the World Bank, which recently concluded an agreement with Argentina before an IMF seal of approval was in place.

The path between these two points is a tortuous one. First it is clear in retrospect that too much was expected of the IMF at first, and that the Fund was handed too much power too abruptly. With its new-found ability to approach international creditors and insist on fresh lending before the IMF would grant credit, the Fund's once limited resources were implicitly swelled far beyond their actual constraints.

This created a situation in which the IMF has been dubbed a 'global capitalist planner', responsible for steering the world through the debt crisis. As the IMF seal of approval was routinely needed before the rest of the financial community would lend, the Fund became the police officer of the international financial system. By 1988, much of Latin America was operating under an IMF program.

Paradoxically, at the same time that the IMF was exerting this enormous power over the developing world, it had too little control over the set of developed world conditions that were instrumental in creating the debt crisis, such as oil prices; industrial countries' growth, trade, and interest rate policies; commodity prices; and currency fluctuations.

This led the IMF to focus solely on domestic and individual adjustments by each debtor country.

However, many economists have charged that the IMF prescription was highly inappropriate in these circumstances. First, devaluation was unlikely to improve a country's trade balance when industrial world growth was negative. At any rate, simultaneous devaluation by an entire region - which eventually occurred - would be likely to have a set of unexpected and largely undesirable consequences. Second, the IMF's recommendation of cuts in real wages and the fiscal deficit may have been reckless in the face of a global slowdown. Third, the removal of trade and capital controls has been challenged by studies suggesting that one reason why Asian economies adjusted to the economic crisis of the 1980s so much better than the Latin countries was because capital controls in the Asian nations prevented large-scale capital flight.

The conclusion, according to many observers, is that the IMF stressed a set of domestic adjustment policies that fit poorly with one another and especially with the global conditions prevailing at the time.

Table 2.8 Latin America under the IMF

	Annual average 1968-80	Annual average 1981-6
Real GDP growth	5.8	0.9
Per capita real GDP growth	3.4	−1.3
Inflation (weighted average)	32.4	95.1

	1981	1982	1983	1984	1985	1986
Trade balance ($bn)	−3.2	7.2	28.7	37.0	33.6	26.9
Current account ($bn)	−42.6	−41.1	−10.3	−3.6	−4.3	−6.7
Basic transfer* ($bn)	22.9	−1.4	−20.5	−26.8	−36.8	−32.8
External debt ($bn)	287	329	341	356	368	382
Debt/GDP (%)	36.2	43.1	48.2	47.3	46.2	47.0

*Basic transfer equals net capital inflows less interest payments abroad.
Source: Manuel Pastor, Jr, *The International Monetary Fund and Latin America: Economic Stabilization and Class Conflict*, p. 163

It is impossible to separate the 'IMF effect' from the general effect of the debt crisis. Even so, the IMF has become an international lightning rod, taking much of the blame as a massive reaction against IMF austerity in the Third World has set in. Latin American and OECD governments alike now tend to agree that the IMF years were ineffective at resolving the crisis. Both North and South - the developed and developing worlds - seem prepared to move beyond the IMF and explore other alternatives to debt management. But while the leadership role of the Fund is increasingly being called into question, it is more unclear than ever just what mechanism could replace it.

Looking ahead

What lies ahead for Latin American debtors? If the Baker Plan system of international debt management is bankrupt - the system failed to reward good debtors and is in danger of a complete breakdown - and the IMF has lost its luster in the role of debt manager, then what will emerge?

It is interesting in this context to examine the changes in conventional wisdom on the Latin American debt question between 1982 and 1989 - how the accepted set of general beliefs and guidelines was transformed in the 1980s.

Austerity versus growth

The first of these beliefs to undergo transformation relates directly to the foregoing discussion of IMF prescriptions of austerity. In 1982, it was generally accepted that 'austerity' policies were the answer to the Latin American debt crisis. If widely and consistently applied, austerity would produce leaner and meaner debtors better able to service debt and face a competitive world economy.

Austerity was very much in the eyes of the beholder, but generally was considered to include cuts in the budget deficit and inflation along with economic liberalization efforts such as the removal of trade and capital controls, a free exchange rate market and the abolition of subsidies.

Now austerity has joined the IMF as one of the two most hated terms in Latin America. Even for some very conservative banking and government officials and economists worldwide, austerity has lost its allure. Concerned that economic austerity would increased left-wing power south of the border, even the US president, George Bush, has noted the need to resume growth, replacing austerity as the conventional wisdom policy prescription for Latin American debtors.

Since 1982 in fact, much progress has been made by Latin American debtors on some basic economic reforms. The public sector deficit as a proportion of GDP has declined from 14 per cent to 6 per cent in Argentina, and from 12 per cent to 3.8 per cent in Brazil. However, the social and political pain that has resulted, plus the dawning realization that these reforms have spelled very little overall improvement, has led to the recognition that austerity is very far from the solution.

Also, a greater understanding has been gained of the costs of these policies in terms of deteriorating social services such as housing, health, schools and public services. The sharp decline, even virtual disappearance, of productive investment during the austerity period in

Latin America has resulted in a number of countries that are 'eating their infrastructure', an ominous sign for the future.

Finally, the world has learned a great deal about who exactly pays for austerity. In the crunch after 1982, Latin American governments squeezed the private sector first and themselves last. While the public sector deficit declined, most state enterprises managed to continue expanding so that the share of the public sector in terms of overall bank credit increased. Accordingly, domestic credit cuts fell heavily on the private sector, producing sharp declines in investment and real wages while unemployment and bankruptcies soared.

Moreover, studies increasingly have concluded that private sector workers, wage earners, the unemployed, and the underemployed have borne the brunt of austerity. All of these factors combined - an awareness of the social and political costs of austerity, plus a growing realization that the economic gains are less than supposed - has created a backlash against austerity and an increasing recognition of the need to resume growth in Latin American rather than undergo still more austerity.

Liquidity versus solvency

The second set of general beliefs that has undergone a major transformation centers around the very nature of the debt problem itself. In 1982–4, it was generally believed that the problem represented a temporary liquidity squeeze. Since the debt crisis was fundamentally related to worldwide economic conditions (declining oil prices, industrial country recessions, high interest rates), it was assumed that the debtor countries could muddle through until rescued by recovery in the industrial world. Various projections prepared by well-respected forecasting groups indicated that if industrial countries grew at a real rate of 3 per cent a year, interest rates remained below their 1983 levels (about 10 per cent for six-month Eurodollars), and capital inflows continued, then most of the major debtors could resume debt service and growth by the middle of the decade.

The IMF noted in its 1984 *World Economic Outlook*:

> Assuming moderate rates of growth in the industrial countries, some fall in real interest rates and unchanged terms of trade, and assuming also that the non-oil developing countries continue their present adjustment policies, the conclusion is reached that most groups of these countries can achieve adequate rates of growth of GDP (although somewhat below the rates attained during the 1960s and 1970s), while maintaining a manageable position with respect to their current accounts and debt service ratios (quoted in Griffith-Jones and Sunkel).

With hindsight such complacency seems remarkable. Such projections completely misread the very nature of the crisis. More important, however, is the fact that no one believes this any longer.

After a post-1984 period of solid economic growth in the industrial countries and oil price stability, the debt problem is far more intractable and long-term in nature than anyone ever thought at first. It is, in the words of a January 1989 *Financial Times* [London] editorial, 'a long-term disease of economic development', rather than a temporary liquidity problem. From a view of debt as a symptom of world economic malaise as in 1982, it is now seen as a disease in itself. This is truly a global debt crisis, and not a series of related cases of debt difficulty.

Another facet of this shift in beliefs is the evolution from expecting that debt will be repaid eventually, albeit over a longer period of time, to a general (if unsaid) understanding that much of the debt will never be repaid. Creditors have virtually no prospect of ever recovering the full amount of their loans. This is the tacit meaning of a secondary market where Latin American debt trades at less than $0.50 on the dollar, and of creditors' increased willingness to engage in debt reduction programs.

In 1982, most bankers believed the solution was to convert short-term obligations into long-term obligations; today the solution appears to be 'take what you can get'. In general, we can characterize this shift in beliefs as a change from expecting that the problem does have a solution over the long term in 1982, to a feeling that problem is intractable in 1989. While this probably does reflect a more realistic assessment of the nature of the crisis, an unfortunate byproduct is the despair that this shift has brought, both on the part of debtors and creditors. No party at this point even hopes for a return to general prosperity in Latin America, and this hopelessness is a dangerous sign for the future.

Debt crisis management

Given these major swings in conventional wisdom, it even more surprising that basic debt crisis management strategy and structures have remained in place throughout the period with remarkably little change. By the close of 1982, a three-part process for rescheduling was well-established. First, the country adopts a stabilization program. Second, this program is blessed by the IMF. Third, creditors reschedule and/or lend new money in support of this program.

This process was christened the Baker Plan in 1983 (three years after it had become standard operating procedure), and nothing has really changed since then except for the addition of debt reduction options. The basic structures in place to deal with the debt problem - the IMF, commercial bank steering committees, etc. - have also undergone almost no formal alteration since 1982.

While the international financial institutions have certainly been reorganized several times, their basic mandate and mode of operation have changed very little. The public debate on the need to pass from debt crisis management to a search for fundamentally new international financial strategies goes on, but no such strategies are even close to acceptance.

It is remarkable that the crisis management phase has lasted so long as the international financial community continually reacts to the latest problem debtor rather than moving pro-actively to avert new crises. While the conventional wisdom about the very nature of the debt problem has changed radically, management techniques to deal with the problem are essentially the same as in 1982.

New initiatives

It in not at all remarkable, therefore, that the quest for new approaches to debt management has intensified over the past two years. A host of new initiatives has been put forward by interested parties ranging from Fidel Castro to the Japanese Ministry of Finance. The proliferation of such initiatives has heightened the perception that creditors and international institutions are now ready to consider unconventional solutions.

With all of these initiatives now on the table, two basic trends have emerged. First, there is a pressing need for debt relief and debt reduction. Second, most proposals either implicitly or explicitly address the need for a shift away from the US/IMF leadership axis on Latin American debt management.

On debt reduction, banks, official lenders and debtors have been finding a mutual interest in voluntary debt reduction techniques such as the debt/equity swap. In 1988, the World Bank called for changes in world debt strategy to place greater emphasis on voluntary debt reductions and the latest financial packages with major debtors, such as Brazil, have included a wide variety of debt reduction options.

However, voluntary debt reduction through equity conversions - while intellectually pleasing and highly fashionable at present - is only a limited weapon at best. For one thing, it appears to heighten inflationary pressures in the host country by artificially swelling the local currency money supply. (Chile's experience may not be representative given the country's tight control over monetary policy - hardly a norm in Latin America.) While the jury is still out on the magnitude of this effect, it is clearly a concern given Latin America's vulnerability to hyperinflation. For another, equity swaps have run head-on into nationalist opposition based on fears that the country's best industries are being sold off to foreigners at a discount. Finally, the opportunities for (relatively) blue chip equity investment of the sort that would attract most commercial creditors are limited in Latin America.

An even thornier issue is that of debt relief. While a general consensus has emerged (even in the US government) that debt relief is appropriate for the poorest countries of sub-Saharan Africa, most creditors have no intention of conceding this point with regard to the middle-income debtors of Latin America. The real battleground will be Argentina, Brazil and Mexico. Despite calls for debt relief from several western governments, official agencies and the Soviet president, Mikhail Gorbachev, debt relief for Latin America is staunchly opposed by the US government, which will probably prove an intractable stumbling block for such plans.

There were hints of a shift in the official US attitude in late 1988. Increasingly driven by fears of political insecurity in the region, particularly in Mexico, the Bush administration has signalled its intention to take a more flexible stance which was outlined in the Brady Plan. The US had been stung by a crescendo of complaints from allies like Japan and West Germany, from international institutions like the World Bank and United Nations, from debtors themselves and from Democratic legislators in the US Congress, all charging that US leadership in Latin American debt management is bankrupt. Accordingly, the Brady Plan was advanced with the clear intention to ending the debt crisis. This meant some form of debt forgiveness, although it was not called that.

To counter perceived leftist trends in Latin America (which have been most cleverly highlighted by Mexican negotiators), the Brady Plan will permit more growth incentives and less austerity in the 1990s. Moreover, the US and IMF will have to cede power to a new axis that will involve the Japanese as well as other western governments. The US will be forced to pay more attention to new initiatives. Among the most intriguing is a suggestion that debt reductions be tied to economic progress, as opposed to past practice in which progress spelled expectations of higher debt service capabilities as in Colombia and Venezuela.

New development money

But while some promising new ideas are now on the table, it is dismaying that so little attention is being devoted to the regeneration of new development in Latin America. Considering the region's stagnation - if not regression - since 1982 with respect to per capita income, social development, investment and living standards, it becomes abundantly clear that Latin America needs financing for new development if it is to begin regaining lost ground. There is an internal contradiction between this requirement and the progress cited above in regard to debt reduction and debt relief.

If a creditor is willing to write off 50 per cent of a country's debt through a discounted equity swap or debt relief program, he is certainly not willing to lend that country more money at the same time. Renewed and sustained growth will require new investment. Various groups estimate that a new inflow of $20 billion a year is needed to reinvigorate Latin American growth (compared to a net outflow of $29 billion in 1988). However, it is unlikely that this inflow will be forthcoming from traditional sources in the near future.

The most important lesson of the past six years is that the Latin American debtors will need both rational economic adjustment policies and new financing to begin moving on to a healthier footing. They need that interplay between domestic adjustment and the international financial markets - an interaction which has not yet occurred. Colombia, Mexico and Venezuela, for example, have implemented more or less rational and consistent economic adjustment programs. But they are still as deeply mired in the debt crisis as ever, thanks to the absence of new financial inflows.

Latin America will need to see a period of rational domestic policies aimed at reducing the fiscal deficit and increasing the role of market-orientated economic forces, combined with a major readjustment of the international financial system that will reward good debtors with debt reduction as under the Brady Plan and new development capital. Unless both of these goals are achieved, the region will be condemned to another decade of 'muddling through' on debt while development continues to regress.

References

Balassa, Bela, Gerardo M. Bueno, Pedro-Pablo Kuczynski, and Mario Henrique Simonsen, *Toward Renewed Economic Growth in Latin America*. Washington, D.C.: Institute for International Economics, 1986.

Bergsten, C. Fred, 'Can We Prevent a World Economic Crisis?', *Challenge*, January-February 1983, pp. 4-13.

Dale, Richard S, 'International Banking is Out of Control', *Challenge*, January-February 1983, pp. 14-19.

The Economist, 'Bottomless Debt', 11 December 1982, pp. 11-13.

The Economist, 'Latin America: The Breaking of a Continent', 30 April 1983, pp. 17-24.

The Economist, 'Latin America: The Trembling Earth', 7 May 1983, pp. 21-6.

Financial Times (London), 'Debt and Mr Bush', January 1989.

Financial Times (London), 'IBCA Banking Analysis', 5 January 1989.

Fishlow, Albert, 'Revisiting the Great Debt Crisis of 1982', Kwan S. Kim and David F. Ruccio (eds), *Debt and Development in Latin America*. Notre Dame, Indiana: University of Notre Dame Press, 1985.

Goldberg, Ellen S. and Dan Haendel, *On Edge: International Banking and Country Risk*. New York: Praeger, 1987.

Griffith-Jones, Stephany and Osvaldo Sunkel, *Debt and Development Crises in Latin America: The End of an Illusion*. Oxford: Clarendon Press, 1986.

Kuczynski, Pedro-Pablo, 'Interview: Why the Music Stopped', *Challenge*, January-February 1983, pp. 20-30.

Kuczynski, Pedro-Pablo, 'Latin American Debt: Act Two', *Foreign Affairs*, vol. 61, no. 2 (Winter 1982/83), pp. 344-64.

Kuczynski, Pedro-Pablo, 'Latin American Debt: Act Two', *Foreign Affairs*, vol. 62, no. 1 (Autumn 1983), pp. 17-38.

Latin America Bureau, *The Poverty Brokers: The IMF and Latin America*. London: Latin American Bureau, 1983.

Pastor, Jr, Manuel, *The International Monetary Fund and Latin America: Economic Stabilization and Class Conflict*. Boulder, Colorado: Westview Press, 1987.

Petras, James F, *Latin America: Bankers, Generals, and the Struggle for Social Justice*. New Jersey: Rowan and Litchfield, 1986.

Chapter 3

Central America and the Caribbean

*Uwe Bott**

The human species, according to the best theory I can form of it, is composed of two distinct races: the men who borrow and the men who lend. Charles Lamb

Introduction

In autumn of 1988, two of the most powerful hurricanes of this century, Gilbert and Joan, went on a rampage in the Caribbean Basin killing more than 500 persons, wiping out residential areas and annihilating much of the productive capacity of the agricultural sector. Edward Seaga, then Prime Minister of Jamaica, whose country had been hit the hardest by Gilbert, was reported as saying: 'It looks like Hiroshima after the A-Bomb.' In fact, damage repair in Jamaica alone was estimated at $1 billion, one and a half times the value of Jamaica's 1987 exports. Some of the material damage, such as the virtual deracination of banana, citrus and coffee crops is expected to have long-lasting effects on the Jamaican economy.

In Nicaragua, Gilbert's evil sister Joan caused similar devastation. At least 50 people were killed and some 300,000 were left homeless. The city of Bluefields, home to about 60,000 inhabitants, was reported 90 per cent destroyed. But Gilbert and Joan did not come alone. On their backs swarms of voracious African desert locusts were sucked into the Caribbean posing a serious threat to sugar and banana crops. Although no extensive crop damage was reported, the battle against the locusts had an adverse effect on the region's agriculture. But the natural disasters of 1988 were only the latest of a string of such events that rocked the regions during the 1980s. An earthquake, measuring 7.5 on the Richter scale, shook San Salvador, capital of the El

* Mr Bott is an official of the Inter-American Development Bank. The views expressed in this chapter, however, are solely his views and do not purport directly or indirectly to represent the official or unofficial views or policies of the Inter-American Development Bank.

Salvador, in October 1986. It took the lives of more than 1,000 persons and caused material damage of more than $2 billion. Finally, throughout this decade civil wars in Central America have killed and maimed between 100,000-200,000 men, women and children, while having displaced millions who fled their countries in order to save their lives or in search of a better future.

It is almost incomprehensible for the onlooker to imagine the extent of human suffering brought upon large segments of the population in Central America and the Caribbean during the 1980s. The history of the region with its wars, hurricanes, earthquakes and its economic decay reads like a modern version of the book of Job who endured his afflictions with fortitude and faith. However, unlike Job, the faith of the people of Central America and the Caribbean is beginning to fade. There is no time for divine intervention. Instead, secular action is required to restore their confidence in a future with dignity.

This chapter is set out to analyse the extent, development and consequences of external debt on the economies of Central America and the Caribbean in the 1980s. It will focus on economic indicators, but would not be complete if it ignored the social impact of the crisis. The first section of the chapter will attempt to answer the question, why the developing world, in general, and the Caribbean Basin, in particular, have arrived at today's crisis. Sections two and three will elaborate in greater detail on the debt situation of the Central American and Caribbean subregions. The final section, then, will sum up what has been learnt and what appears to be required to resuscitate the suffocating economies of the Caribbean Basin.

Four development decades: one step forward and two steps back

A brisk stride through the past forty years of economic development in the Third World serves an analytical rather than historical purpose. It provides an explanation for the depth and length of the economic crisis in the developing countries during the 1980s. It also demonstrates that external debt, essentially a development problem, is the product of economic development policies conceived and pursued during the past four decades rather than the cause for today's calamities.

The 1950s Decade of import substitution

Led by Argentine economist Raúl Prebisch, many developing countries became convinced that their economies were being short-changed by continuously deteriorating terms-of-trade. According to Prebisch, there was a

> tendency toward a foreign constraint on development resulting from the low income elasticity of demand for imports of primary products by the centers, compared with the high income elasticity of demand at the periphery for manufacturers from the centers.

Consequently, import-substituting industrialization (ISI) was the key to development. In order to protect nascent domestic industries from foreign competition, Less Developed Country (LDC) governments erected higher tariffs, lower import quotas, and applied other administrative controls. They also provided incentives to local producers through domestic subsidies.

Import-substituting industrialization, in essence, taxed agriculture and reallocated resources toward industry, and was geared for the internal market at non-durable consumer goods. It was this internal market that would define the growth potential and limitations of import substitution. In the absence of economies of scale, import substitution soon lost steam. Moreover, it created many highly protected, inefficient and non-competitive industries craving for imports of intermediate and capital goods, and hence aggravated balance-of-payments deficits in developing countries which it originally had been designed to avert. Finally, import substitution produced an environment of inwardness and state interventionism, still prevalent three decades later in many Latin American countries.

The small developing countries of Central America and the Caribbean, however, could not reallocate resources towards ISI as readily as the larger Latin American states. In fact, they pursued ISI less vigorously and remained relatively open economies throughout the 1950s. Therefore, they grew at a slower pace during that decade than most of their Latin American neighbors. By the same token, they were also less affected by those negative side-effects of ISI.

The 1960s Decade of regional integration

As ISI had reached the confines of the domestic markets, integration, essentially a regional expansion of the import-substitution model, seemed the next logical step to many Latin American countries. Central America joined this era by establishing the Central American Common Market (CACM) in 1960 and the Central American Bank for Economic Integration (CABEI) in 1961. Initial success was promising. Tariffs on 98 per cent of all dutiable items within Central America were eliminated by 1966. The value of trade among the members of the Common Market increased almost eightfold between 1960 and 1968. It was estimated that initially about one percentage point of Central America's annual growth rate was due to the formation of the Central American Common Market.

In the Caribbean, the integrational movement led to the creation of the Caribbean Free Trade Association (CARIFTA) in 1968 and the Caribbean Development Bank (CDB) in 1969. This was not the first integrational effort of the Caribbean. In fact, the failure of the West Indies Federation in 1962 after four years of existence was responsible for the region's reluctance to enter into yet another integrational initiative. However, many countries of the Caribbean had become independent since, and were willing to reconsider integration as a means to reach economic independence, while retaining their newly gained national identities.

Some 90 per cent of intra-regional Caribbean trade was freed from import duties and quotas right from the start. As a result, intra-regional imports rose by 98 per cent between 1967 and 1971, or at an average of 19 per cent a year compared to 6 per cent annual growth rates prior to the establishment of CARIFTA.

The 1970s Decade of disruption and disintegration

The initial successes of integration proved to be short-lived. Both integration movements suffered one important short-coming: unequal distribution of benefits. In Central America, Honduras effectively withdrew from CACM in December 1970, by reintroducing tariffs on imports from its Central American neighbors. In combination with the political differences between El Salvador and Honduras which had resulted in a brief border conflict in 1969 (the so-called Football-War), this development made CACM for all practical purposes inoperative.

In the Caribbean the process of disintegration proved to be more protracted. The least developed countries within CARIFTA (such as Dominica and Grenada) had feared from the start that the absence of effective distributive mechanisms could result in economic losses. Their fears were confirmed when they realized that trade among the economically stronger countries, i.e. Barbados, Guyana, Jamaica, and Trinidad and Tobago had increased from 60 per cent of regional trade in 1967 to 69 per cent in 1971, while trade among the least-developed countries had declined from 1.9 per cent to 1.4 per cent of total regional trade during the same period. After painful negotiations, the Caribbean countries replaced CARIFTA by establishing the Caribbean Common Market (CARICOM) and the Caribbean Investment Corporation (CIC) in 1973.

The Caribbean integration movement had been granted a reprieve. However, in 1977 Guyana and Jamaica reimposed import-restrictions, plans for a joint smelter project between Guyana, Jamaica and Trinidad and Tobago fell through, and a number of CARICOM members began to pursue bilateral arrangements with extra-regional countries at the expense of regional cooperation. The decade of disintegration in the Caribbean came to a close with the de facto cessation of CIC by 1980.

Regional disintegration and domestic political instability was compounded externally by the two so-called oil shocks which should prove to have long-lasting effects on the world economy. In 1970, a barrel of oil cost about $2. By the end of 1980, this price had risen to approximately $41. In 1974 alone, oil prices increased by 300 per cent, with subsequent hikes of 150 per cent between 1979 and 1981. To finance ever increasing import bills and the ambitious development plans designed in the euphoria of the commodity price surges of 1970–73, the developing countries had to step up borrowing, while the oil-exporting countries flooded industrialized countries' banks with almost $400 billion in deposits of so-called 'petrodollars'.

Since the developed countries had neither will nor wallet to cover the increasing balance-of-payments deficits of the developing countries through equally increasing amounts of foreign assistance, the so-called 'recycling' of petrodollars to the developing countries via commercial lending, seemed to be the ideal solution to all parties. Commercial banks participated in a competitive spirit seeking profit-maximization and a US Treasury Assistant Secretary was quoted as saying: 'recycling the vast export earnings of the oil-producing countries back to the importing countries are relatively good'.

The 1980s The lost decade

The events of the previous decade had a devastating effect on the developing countries. In Central America total long-term debt had increased from roughly $1 billion in 1970 to $8.7 billion in 1980. Hence, Central America was almost nine times as indebted in 1980 as it had been in 1970. Caribbean long-term debt increased from $1.6 billion in 1970 to US $4.7 billion in 1980. Terms and conditions of lending also deteriorated. While lending had shifted from official to private sources, repayment schedules were shortened and interest rates increased.

Much had been achieved during the 1950–70 period in terms of economic growth in the developing countries, but some of the structural imbalances of their economies had been ignored. In fact, it could be stated that much of the growth of the developing world which exceeded industrialized countries' growth rates during those years might have been achieved in spite of these imbalances. For example, little progress had been made with regard to income distribution, trade, production and consumption patterns, agricultural productivity as opposed to agricultural production, the role of the state and increasing urbanization. The new economic realities of the 1970s and 1980s would relentlessly expose these imbalances and deepen a crisis triggered by external shocks.

Central America: From Guate-Mala to Guate-Peor

Guatemala owes its name to an Indian word undetermined in its derivation and meaning. Some hold the original to mean 'land of trees'. However, the last four letters of its name - by coincidence - correspond to the Spanish word for 'bad'. 'De Guate-mala a Guate-peor' has therefore become a colloquial expression for many Latin Americans to explain something that has gone from bad to worse (the ending 'peor' standing for worse). This is a very fitting description of the state of Central America in the 1980s.

For purposes of this chapter, Central America includes Costa Rica, El Salvador, Guatemala, Honduras, Nicaragua and Panama. Total external debt (EDT) of these countries' region, that is short term as well as long-term debt has more than doubled since 1980, increasing from $11.4 billion to $25.2 billion in 1987 (see Table 3.1). In 1986, total debt amounted to more than 100 per cent of the regional gross domestic product (GDP). Of course, the size of Central American debt is dwarfed by comparison to the figures for the entire Latin American region of $442.5 billion in 1987. It is the magnitude of debt accrued by Brazil and Mexico, for example, that catches our attention.

Table 3.1 Major indicators of Central American indebtedness

	1970	1975	1980	1981	1982	1983	1984	1985	1986	1987
Major flows (in US$ m)*										
Total external debt (EDT)	992	3,007	11,432	13,325	15,686	18,334	19,815	21,918	23,125	25,232
Total debt service (TDS)	178	410	1,261	1,366	1,449	1,759	1,615	1,608	1,648	1,390
Net transfer with Nicaragua	106	552	606	654	744	401	180	230	−129	−225
Net transfer without Nicaragua	85	447	422	450	613	167	−135	−324	−700	−686
Current account	−241	−843	−1,682	−1,636	−1,616	−909	−1,328	−1,069	−345	−1,140
Principal debt ratios (in %)										
EDT/GNP	15.7	25.7	48.3	58.5	68.0	74.3	74.2	80.4	89.6	91.9
EDT/Exports (XGS)	58.2	74.6	84.4	88.1	111.9	153.4	172.6	196.6	207.0	170.8+
EDT/XGS without Panama	60.9	79.6	145.5	191.0	255.4	298.6	312.6	354.7	363.0	274.5+
TDS/XGS	7.2	6.9	6.9	7.1	8.8	13.3	12.6	13.6	13.8	12.1+
TDS/XGS without Panama	7.0	7.3	8.1	11.2	13.3	23.7	18.3	23.0	21.3	19.2+

* 1970 and 1980 figures are for long-term debt only
+ Excludes Nicaragua
Source: World Debt Tables, Washington, D.C., World Bank, 1988-9
Note: Since Nicaragua is in 'passive default', its inclusion in net transfer data is distorting, therefore these data were calculated also without Nicaragua. Since Panama's exports, according to World Debt Tables, exceeds those of the rest of Central America combined, its inclusions distort EDT/XGS and TDS/XGS ratios, therefore these ratios were also calculated under the exclusion of Panama

It is also true, however, that each of the large debtors has a per capita income that exceeds that of every Central American nation except Panama. Additionally, the former have a bigger cushion to soften the blow of crisis and austerity than the latter. Honduras, Nicaragua and El Salvador, for example, have per capita incomes of below $1,000 and rank among the poorest countries of the Western Hemisphere (see Table 3.2). Between 1980 and 1987, per capita income, already low in Central America, dropped by 13.5 per cent compared with a decrease of 5 per cent for all of Latin America. Also, while Central America accounts for 5.7 per cent of all Latin American debt in 1987, its combined GDP makes only 3.8 per cent of the region's total.

Nicaragua's high debt/capita ratio in combination with its low income/capita ratio is the most worrisome case. During 1980 to 1987, Nicaragua more than tripled its external debt, a record surpassed in Latin America only by Barbados. At least 20 per cent of its current debt stock of $7.3 billion is due to accumulated interest arrears, since the country has virtually defaulted against many loans. Consequently, there have been almost no new commitments from multilateral lenders since 1983. Obviously, political circumstances are the reason for a meager $24 million of lending commitments from private creditors since 1981.

It is important to recall the tremendous destruction of productive capacity and infrastructure with which the current Nicaraguan government was confronted when it took power in July 1979. Its debt/gross national product (GNP) ratio was twice as high then as that of all of Latin America. At the time, about 50 per cent of the country's debt was owed to private banks. The debt rescheduling that occurred between the new Nicaraguan government and the commercial banks resulted in an agreement in 1981 with an interesting twist, since it based its terms on the perceived ability of the country to pay rather than on market conditions. The most innovative feature of the agreement was an interest rate cap of 7 per cent for the first five years. Any exceeding difference was to be capitalized and to be repaid following the expiration of the grace period.

Unfortunately, even those very attractive terms found Nicaragua at a loss, with constantly rising current account deficits, and with an inflation rate ranging anywhere between the official 26,000 per cent and the guestimated 50,000 per cent in 1988. Nicaragua's fiscal deficit was reported at 27 per cent of GDP. Its per capita income decreased by 17.5 per cent between 1980 and 1987 and is now lower than in 1960. Nicaragua ranks twenty-first in per capita income terms out of twenty-five Latin American nations, and third among those nations in terms of debt per capita. It is the only Central American country in which per capita debt exceeds per capita income.

While the Nicaraguan government has not agreed to an IMF stabilization program and, in fact, would be ineligible for financing because of its current arrears, it has begun to address some of the economic

Table 3.2 Debt/capita and income/capita in Latin America (1987, in US$)

Country	Debt/capita	Rank	Income/capita	Rank
Panama	2,341	1	2,549	8
Barbados	2,300	2	3,532	3
Nicaragua	2,083	3	879	21
Venezuela	1,999	4	4,107	2
Jamaica	1,860	5	1,704	13
Argentina	1,825	6	2,745	6
Chile	1,694	7	2,213	11
Costa Rica	1,693	8	2,011	12
Trinidad & Tobago	1,574	9	2,900	5
Uruguay	1,385	10	2,733	7
Guyana	1,301	11	669	24
Mexico	1,299	12	2,423	10
Ecuador	1,052	13	1,326	19
Bahamas	1,007	14	10,430	1
Brazil	876	15	2,428	9
Peru	871	16	1,517	15
Bolivia	824	17	721	23
Honduras	706	18	782	22
Paraguay	624	19	1,402	16
Colombia	568	20	1,581	14
Dominican Republic	550	21	1,401	17
El Salvador	357	22	900	20
Guatemala	335	23	1,376	18
Haiti	131	24	300	25
Suriname	n.a.	n.a.	3,257	4
Latin America	1,091	2,223		
Central America	948	1,285		
Caribbean	720	1,306		

Sources: Debt = Total External Debt, *World Debt Tables 1988–1989*, volume II, World Bank, 1989. Population + Income per Capita: *Economic and Social Progress in Latin America, 1988 Report*, Inter-American Development Bank

problems of the country during 1988. Thus, a drastic austerity program of mass devaluations, lifting of price controls, removal of subsidies, and restrictions of credit was imposed. However, without any substantial foreign assistance and after the terrible devastation caused by hurricane Joan which destroyed the country's two major export crops, coffee and cotton, causing $840 million of damage, there is little hope for an improvement in the near future. In fact, as one observer put it, with everything having failed so far, 'Nicaragua has entered the ethereal realm of experimental economics.'

Costa Rica is another interesting case in Central America. By early 1978, Costa Rica was a prosperous country. The economy was growing at an annual rate of almost 10 per cent, unemployment measured only 3.5 per cent, and inflation was down to 4 per cent per annum. Much of this growth had been supported by record coffee export prices in 1975 and 1976.

Massive government spending in spite of declining merchandise of trade indices from a base of 100 in 1977 to 82 in 1978, and finally 67 in 1981 in combination with the oil-price and interest rate hikes during that period, left a gaping hole in the country's treasury. By mid-1981 foreign exchange reserves were depleted. In August 1981, one year before the 'Mexican rescue', Costa Rica suspended principal and interest payments to commercial banks. What developed demonstrates the complexity of debt rescheduling negotiations. There were basically two different sets of private lenders involved in the Costa Rican debt negotiations: commercial banks and bondholders. The bondholders received preferential treatment and were being paid despite the Costa Rican moratorium. Commercial banks demanded *pari passu* treatment from the Costa Rican government, i.e. for all private lenders to be treated equally. When the bondholders perceived that the Costa Ricans might be swayed by the commercial bank to stop paying them as well, their lead manager sent an angry telex to San José) in February 1982 threatening that

> if your commercial bank creditors insist on forcing you to violate this code of obligations [to pay to bondholders] and if you accede to this pressure, we shall campaign vigorously to ensure that you become ineligible for any financing from multilateral institutions.

While the issue was settled amicably in June 1982 - incidentally commercial lenders did not receive *pari passu* treatment of bondholders - it proves how intertwined debt negotiations can be. A simplistic distinction between official and private lenders does not even begin to grasp the complexity of the negotiating process and the pressures to which a debtor government is exposed.

Under three successive administrations, (President Rodrigo Carazo 1978–82, President Luis Alberto Monge 1982–86, and President Oscar Arias since 1986) Costa Rica has now been absorbed with debt rescheduling negotiations. Each administration had a different approach to its creditors. While President Carazo declared the debt moratorium and had to deal with private creditors up in arms against each other, President Monge had a more conciliatory approach, and reached an IMF stand-by agreement of SDR (special drawing rights) 92.2 million in December, 1982. Painful adjustments were made. Inflation was brought down and the economy registered a moderate 2.9 per cent growth in 1983 and a vigorous 8 per cent growth in 1984. President Monge also rescheduled the country's commercial debt on two separate occasions.

Still grappling with its payment problems, President Arias limited Costa Rica's interest payments to $5 million per month causing arrears of more than $200 million by June 1988. He also introduced a debt conversion program, under which some $153 million of Costa Rican debt was swapped during 1986 and 1987. While the program was temporarily suspended by the end of 1987, it was revived in 1988 and took on a new and innovative dimension.

Concerned about the environmental impact of the pace of current deforestation, which is estimated to leave the country without trees by the year 2015, the Arias government introduced a debt-for-nature program in August 1987. Under the program conservationists were permitted to buy Costa Rican debt of up to $5.4 million on the secondary market. Costa Rica then exchanged these papers, bought at 17 cents per dollar, into bonds in Costa Rican colones at 75 per cent of the face value. The non-tradeable bonds had a maturity of six years with an average interest rate of 25 per cent. Only the interest payments were immediately available to expand, manage and protect many of Costa Rica's parks, crucial to tourism. Principal on the bonds would begin to be paid in the second year. By March 1988, the $5.4 million debt-for-nature swap had been completed. The government approved a second quota by the end of 1988, and in January 1989 the Nature Conservancy, an international membership organization committed to the global preservation of natural diversity, reported to have bought $5.6 million of Costa Rican debt for a total of $784,000 from American Express Bank to protect 355,000 acres of forest. The conditions of that conversion were similar to the first transaction. In early 1989, Costa Rica began to consider an expansion of the program, not only in size, but also in scope incorporating other developmental goals; hence, adding yet another category to debt conversions, that of debt-development swaps.

As innovative as the Costa Rican government has been during the second half of the 1980s in its attempts to reduce its debt stock, it remains that debt conversions alone will not be able to resolve its payment crisis. New financing and additional debt reduction will be needed. By the end of 1989, it appeared that Costa Rica had reached an agreement with its private creditors to reduce its debt by US$1 billion through debt buybacks and capitalization of past interest payments. This development would have to be regarded as a major breakthrough for that country.

There are two characteristics of the Central American debt situation, which are of particular concern. First, between 1984 and 1987, Central America (except Nicaragua) exported capital of almost $2 billion to its creditors. This negative net transfer of capital depressed domestic investment below 1960s levels when measured as a percentage of GDP in all countries but Costa Rica. It is easy to imagine the future impact of such declining investment figures on economic growth. Second, throughout this decade Central America continued to battle with chronic current account deficits, further reducing its ability to generate foreign exchange necessary for repaying debt.

While the export growth model is often prescribed to debtor patients for their debt-malaise, this medicine has had little more than a placebo effect on the economic health of Central America. Central America has historically sustained relative openness to international trade. For example, export earnings as a share of GDP amounted to 25 per cent in 1975, compared with only 10 per cent for all of Latin America during the same year. However, most countries depended on a few primary commodities, which increased their vulnerability to external shocks in the late 1970s and early 1980s.

In the past, economic recoveries were accompanied by strong commodity price rises, but the post-1982 recovery of the world economy experienced persistently depressed commodity prices. They fell by 5.3 per cent annually between 1981 and 1985. Coffee prices, a major source of foreign exchange to Central America wildly fluctuated and fell by 41 per cent between the first quarter of 1980 and the last quarter of 1987. With the collapse of the International Coffee Agreement in July 1989, prices would have to be expected to plummet further. Also, the substantial dollar devaluation in 1986 and 1987 caused the current dollar price of internationally traded goods to increase. However, commodity prices recovered less than those of manufactured goods. This 'scissors-effect' has caused ever deteriorating terms-of-trade for the commodity exporters of Central America during the 1980s.

High current accounts deficits throughout the 1980s and four years of net capital exports leave us with a region whose economies are in shambles. El Salvador, while having the most favorable lending conditions - 95 per cent of its outstanding and disbursed long-term debt is owed to official creditors - is in a precarious economic and political situation. In 1987, the United States provided $537 million to El Salvador's annual budget, while the government itself contributed only $551 million. El Salvador, with a population of only 5 million people, has become the fifth largest recipient of US assistance in the world. Despite this vigorous support, expenditures have consistently exceeded revenues since 1980. The infiltration of 1,500 guerrillas into the capital at the end of 1989 worsened an already critical situation. Nicaragua is in 'passive default'. Costa Rica has been unable to come to grips with its external indebtedness for more than ten years and is in arrears with commercial lenders.

Guatemala's debt increased by almost two and a half times since 1980, the second largest increase in Central America. It has also borrowed under the most unfavorable terms: the country's concessional element of loans decreased from 67.5 per cent in 1975 to a mere 19.8 per cent in 1985. This decreasing concessionality of lending coincided with an increasing use of variable interest rates. Only 3.2 per cent of Guatemala's public debt was charged with variable interest rates in 1975. In 1984, this figure stood at 38 per cent. Grace periods and maturities, which determine the repayment schedule also shortened substantially, especially during the first half of the 1980s. In essence, Guatemala borrowed money on much shorter terms and with higher interest rates.

Honduras's debt increased from $1.5 billion in 1980 to $3.3 billion in 1987. Even official credit has become scarce for Honduras and reduced the country to an exporter of capital even to official creditors in 1986 and 1987. By the end of 1989, Honduras had fallen into arrears with the IMF, the World Bank, the Inter-American Development Bank, the United States, Germany and Japan, and most official lenders had barred the country from new lending. With a per capita income of only $782, Honduras is the fourth poorest nation in the Western Hemisphere.

But the impact of the crisis is not only measured in dollars and cents. The combination of low per capita income and high per capita debt together with persistently low social indicators make Central America a special case. The so-called Physical Quality of Life Index or PQLI, a weighted average of life expectancy at birth, infant mortality and adult literacy was measured lower in all Central American countries except Costa Rica and Panama when compared with the average of all of Latin America during the 1970s. According to that index, only two countries in the Western Hemisphere, namely Bolivia and Haiti, scored lower than Honduras, Guatemala, and Nicaragua, and only one more, the Dominican Republic, measured lower than El Salvador. This situation appears to have worsened in the 1980s.

Studies on the impact of the debt crisis on social well-being are rare. However, in 1984, the Pan American Health Organization reported that 'many countries face sharp increases in the prevalence of malaria. Mortality due to infectious diseases and malnutrition is increasing.' In fact, in 1984, 188,851 blood samples taken in Central America (including Belize) proved positive for malaria. This number was twice as high as that a decade earlier and represented one fifth of all cases of malaria in Latin America.

Richard Webb came to some grim conclusions in a study on El Salvador. He identified three commonly cited trends:

1. Aggregate open and disguised unemployment and underemployment represent 30 per cent to 50 per cent of the labor force;
2. real median and average earnings have dropped by more than 50 per cent since 1978;
3. the informal sector, which is characterized by less stability and lower wages has grown steadily relative to the formal sector and now comprises a majority of the employed population . . . from 1979 to 1985, caloric and protein intake dropped to levels just under minimum daily requirements from levels well over those requirements. . . . Thus, on a national basis, dietary quality and quantity of nutrients available have probably decreased since 1979.

In December 1988, UNICEF reported that at least half a million young children had died during the previous twelve months because of deteriorating living conditions in developing countries, about one-third of them in Latin America. Among the countries of Central America, Costa Rica and Panama were affected.

While the causal relationship between social expenditure and performance of social indicators is difficult to measure, the significant social spending reduction in Central America during the 1980s is a concern. Shrinking government revenues in combination with fiscal austerity measures resulted in ever decreasing per capita social expenditures in Central America. In Costa Rica this figure has declined from $190 for 1977-9 to $160 for 1983-5. El Salvador registered a drop of per capita social spending from $68 for 1974-6 to $48 for 1983-5, and in Guatemala this figure decreased from $93 for 1980-2 to $37 for 1983-5.

Central America's deteriorating living standards have also caused significant emigration problems. It is estimated that from 1975 to 1985, 668,500 Salvadorians left their country; 500,000 of whom settled in the United States. This figure is alarming, especially since it is based on recorded departures only. While 250,000 Nicaraguans now live in Costa Rica, 150,000 are reported to have emigrated to the US.

The extent of Central America's economic and social decline during the 1980s, its extraordinary level of poverty in combination with the relatively small amounts of commercial debt in question make Central America the Sub-Saharan Africa of Latin America. A comprehensive approach to the Central American crisis should address the following agenda.

First, new lending is indispensable. In May 1988, the United Nations approved a Special Programme of Economic Assistance to Central America consisting of four categories:

1. emergency assistance (refugees, food aid, urgent energy needs),
2. immediate action (foreign debt, reactivation of CACM),
3. economic reactivation, and
4. social development.

The shortcoming of this plan is that the $4.4 billion of necessary financing were not actually committed with the approval of the program.

Second, available resources must be allocated with great efficiency. Careful targeting of such resources to the poor is of special importance. Often social expenditures are misdirected to reach the better-off and fail to benefit the poor.

Third, debt reduction mechanisms should be encouraged with special emphasis on debt buybacks. This instrument of debt reduction was successfully utilized by Bolivia who repurchased 40 per cent or $335 million of its commercial debt in 1988. Buybacks allow the debtor to grasp the full benefit of secondary market discounts on their debt papers. The foreign exchange necessary for such programs could be provided by official lenders through concessional loans, as it happened in the case of Bolivia, or by setting aside a certain percentage of export earnings for this purpose.

Fourth, in its efforts to adjust its economies, Central America should continue to place particular importance on a diversification of its exports, a policy which it has pursued with some success during the past few years, aided by such preferential trade agreements as the US Caribbean Basin Initiative.

Fifth, export promotion and diversification could be assisted by a revival of the Central American Common Market. For most of its existence, however, CACM has hardly been more than a free trade association. The Central American countries would need to enforce a common external tariff and to standardize their economic policies to reach the level of a common market.

Moreover, it has been the experience of the 1970s that integration will fail if focused on ISI and if its benefits are unequally distributed. Therefore, it would appear that an export oriented integrational model designed to protect the weaker countries might prove to be more successful.

During the 1980s, the European Community (EC) has become increasingly involved in the Central American integration process. In March 1989, the E.C. pledged a total of $1 billion for the 1989-91 period in direct economic assistance to the five member countries of CACM, as well as to CABEI, in an effort to revitalize integration.

The Caribbean: the curse of being small

The Caribbean is a heterogeneous region. The vast majority of countries are island nations with the exceptions of Guyana and Suriname, located on the South American continent. Most Caribbean countries are members of the British Commonwealth, others were once colonies of the French (Haiti), the Spanish (the Dominican Republic) and the Dutch (Suriname). Almost every ethnic group imaginable is represented, with Trinidad and Tobago and Suriname being particularly rich in ethnic diversity.

For purposes of this section, the Caribbean - unless otherwise indicated - will be defined as encompassing the Bahamas, Barbados, the Dominican Republic, Guyana, Haiti, Jamaica, Suriname, and Trinidad and Tobago. It does not include US, British or French overseas departments or dependencies, Cuba as well as the countries forming the Organization of Eastern Caribbean States (OECS), also known as the Windward and Leeward Islands. Especially with regard to the latter, it should be emphasized that their exclusion is not based on 'size', but rather on the inability to do justice to their individual cases within the limited confines of this chapter.

When referring to the Caribbean's diversity, it should be added that this diversity is also reflected in the level of development. The Bahamas and Barbados have the highest and third highest per capita incomes in Latin America, while Guyana and Haiti are the two poorest countries of the Western Hemisphere (see Table 3.2). Finally, there is a distinction of size among the countries of the Caribbean. Haiti and the Dominican Republic have populations of more than 6 million people and the Bahamas and Barbados have less than 300,000 inhabitants each.

Since 1980, Caribbean debt has more than doubled (see Table 3.3).

Table 3.3 Major indicators of Caribbean indebtedness

	1970	1975	1980	1981	1982	1983	1984	1985	1986	1987
Major flows (in US$ m)*										
Total external debt (EDT)	1,616	2,896	6,108	5,292	8,660	10,051	10,010	11,240	12,178	12,885
Total debt service (TDS)	307	481	833	832	816	1,007	804	1,030	1,196	1,192
Net transfers	−42	224	560	520	657	133	158	130	−668	−454
Current account	−426	−74	−827	−910	−1,865	−2,155	−1,269	−684	−783	−634
Principal debt ratios (in %)										
EDT/GNP	34.0	27.3	33.1	27.3	39.6	46.1	50.8	59.2	67.1	72.8
EDT/exports (XGS)	93.8	57.7	68.6	57.4	103.7	126.2	120.1	131.0	159.1	n.a.
TDS/XGS	4.1	4.0	8.0	8.0	9.0	10.5	8.9	11.5	14.8	n.a.

* Long-term debt only
Source: World Debt Tables, Washington, D.C., World Bank, 1988-9 (excludes Suriname, 1970 excludes Bahamas, 1986 TDS excludes Guyana)

While the total of $12.9 billion is roughly half of Central America's debt, it is worthwhile mentioning that the Caribbean's total debt service was almost as high in 1987 as that of Central America. Also, the economic decline during the 1980s resulted in a decrease of 10.5 per cent of income per capita in the Caribbean, only moderately below that of Central America, but twice as high as that of all of Latin America.

Barbados's debt has increased 3.7 times since 1980, the highest increase in all of Latin America. Barbados also has the second highest debt per capita in Latin America, which means that all three 'top-contenders' of this category are either from Central America or from the Caribbean underlining the urgency of the debt problem in these regions. A closer look at the debt structure of Barbados's debt reveals that 53 per cent of the public long-term debt came from private sources in 1987. Also, Barbados's average terms of new lending commitments were the least favorable in the entire Caribbean, including the Bahamas whose per capita income is almost three times that of Barbados.

Barbados's trade deficit of $307 million in 1987 was the second highest on that country's record. Since 1984, both imports and exports have declined, the former by 21.8 per cent, the latter by 60.2 per cent. Barbados's sluggish export performance appears to be a result of diminished competitiveness, both on the regional CARICOM market as well as outside that market. The manufacturing sector is particularly weak in Barbados and was further crippled by a contraction of the assembling electronics industries during 1985 and 1986. It is estimated that exports of manufactured goods were only at 40 per cent in 1987 of what they had been in 1986.

Despite these negative trends, Barbados has been an exemplary debtor. However, in view of increased, non-concessional borrowing during the mid-1980s, debt servicing could become a problem for Barbados if the competitiveness of the economy cannot be restored.

Jamaica's case demonstrates that an export-led expansion alone is no recipe for sustained economic and social development. After all, Jamaica's average annual growth of 5.9 per cent during the 1950s and 1960s was primarily based on rapidly increasing bauxite and alumina exports which accounted for 60.4 per cent of all Jamaican exports by 1969. The case of Jamaica also unwittingly states that foreign investment is not a magic wand whose touch will bring about prosperity. A whopping 32 per cent of total investment in Jamaica between 1953 and 1972 was foreign.

In spite of export-led growth and strong foreign investment, Jamaica's economy entered the 1970s with numerous imbalances: (1) chronic unemployment, (2) a weakening agricultural base, (3) increasing dependence on imports, especially food and consumer goods, and (4) an unequal and deteriorating distribution of income.

Redistribution of income by maintaining and improving real wages became a major policy objective in Jamaica during the 1970s. However, wage increases in 1974 and 1975 by far exceeded existing inflation rates. The government's wage policy in combination with an overvalued exchange rate discouraged Jamaican exports. Moreover, a production levy on bauxite, introduced in 1974, led to production cuts and divestment by the affected foreign bauxite companies. Supporters of the levy claim that foreign bauxite companies were already divesting in Jamaica before the levy was imposed, mainly for strategic reasons. They admit implementation problems, concede that the levy might have been too high, but defend the indispensability of this tax for purposes of revenue enhancement. The fact remains, however that bauxite and alumina export volume indices were depressed from 1975 onwards, and that record current account deficits were accrued in 1975 and 1976, while net capital inflows declined from 1975 to 1978 and finally turned negative in 1979. Between 1973 and 1980, the economy contracted by 23 per cent in eight years of consecutive negative growth, inflation averaged 23 per cent, and unemployment peaked at almost 27 per cent in 1980. In an effort to expand the state's role in the economy, another government objective in the 1970s, expenditure rose dramatically between 1972 and 1976, creating a gross budget deficit of 24 per cent of GDP by 1976.

By 1980, total external debt had reached $1.9 billion. Despite austerity measures, as well as large inflows of capital from official sources ($1.7 billion between 1980–85), and because of the continued poor performance of the vital bauxite sector, conditions remained bad. External debt, in fact, increased to $4.5 billion in 1987, more than twice the amount of 1980. That amount was equal to 263 per cent of the country's exports and 176 per cent of its GNP. By 1987, Jamaica had also become Latin America's fifth largest debtor per capita, and one of only three countries whose debt per capita exceeded its income per capita.

The prolonged period of economic decline on the poor has been of special concern. Per capita income has constantly declined between 1972 and 1984. Statistics show that a family of five with two wage earners earning minimum wages were able to purchase only 40 per cent of a least-cost minimum basket of goods in the mid 1980s. Simultaneously, government expenditure for social services has declined rapidly.

In order to contain this social decline, the government submitted a five-year Social Well-Being Program to Parliament in April 1988. This Program was intended to ameliorate the side-effects of diminished social services, removal of subsidies, partial cost recovery mechanisms and increasing utility rates without reversing the adjustment process. It recognized that adjustment could not be sustained, politically or economically, if accompanied by a further deterioration of social conditions. Jamaica's economy improved somewhat in 1988, but debt remained a problem.

Guyana's economic situation deteriorated since the late 1970s. Export prices for two of the country's three major export commodities, sugar and bauxite fell dramatically. The public sector deficit increased from 43 per cent of GDP in 1981 to 56 per cent in 1986. International reserves were depleted by the end of 1987, with arrears at $1 billion. By the same year, Guyana had a per capita debt almost twice as high as its per capita income; in fact, Guyana is the second poorest country in the Western Hemisphere. Total debt amounted to 519.4 per cent of the country's GNP in 1987, far above the Latin American average of 359.5 per cent.

Forceful action was required and, indeed, President Desmond Hoyte reversed many economic policies with roots in the 1960s and 1970s. In particular, he dismantled all restrictions to foreign investment in summer 1988. The new Investment Policy also provided that

> it is no part of government's policy to nationalise property. The objectives which led to nationalisations during the 1970s no longer exist. The era of nationalisations is therefore to be considered at an end.

Moreover, Guyana's currency has undergone serious devaluations since 1985. The government has also begun to rationalize the operations of public enterprises which are dominant in key sectors of the economy. In fact, in April 1988, legislation was passed to dissolve the state holding company GUYSTAC and President Hoyte announced that the sale of shares in public enterprises was being considered.

Guyana also agreed upon a wide range of additional economic reforms with the World Bank and the IMF. However, the reform program was still held up in early 1989 because Guyana was in arrears with the IMF, the World Bank and the CDB with over $165 million. While Guyana needed to mobilize bridge financing to cover these arrears, some creditor countries' legal parameters forbade such lending to a delinquent country, a vicious circle for Guyana. Meanwhile US government officials regarded the investment climate in Guyana as one of the most favorable ones in the Caribbean and rewarded that development by designating Guyana as a beneficiary of the Caribbean Basin Initiative in late 1988. In order to implement additional economic reforms, as previously agreed to, a mix of debt relief, debt forgiveness and increased domestic savings will be necessary.

Two Caribbean countries, Haiti and the Bahamas, are relatively debt-free for quite opposite reasons. Haiti is the poorest country of Latin America, while the Bahamas has by far the highest per capita income in the region. While Haiti's lending terms are extremely favorable, the Bahamas have very low debt ratios.

However, Haiti would appear to make a very good case for debt-for-nature swaps. Since the country is desperately concerned with its progressing soil-erosion, it might be attractive for environmentalist investors to attempt to acquire the outstanding private debt of $68 million on the secondary market in order to help Haiti halt this devastating ecological development. Such investment would lower Haiti's projected public debt service from between 27 per cent in 1989 and 16 per cent in 1993.

Suriname's economy has historically depended on Dutch foreign assistance. Because of political differences, Dutch assistance was suspended in 1982 causing some payment difficulties to that country. However, after Suriname's elections in 1987, relations between the Netherlands and its former colony improved, and the Dutch government has agreed, in principle, to resume aid.

The Dominican Republic is an excellent example for the blood, sweat and tears with which the path of development has been paved in the 1980s for so much of the developing world. Much of the social fabric of that nation has been torn apart. In April 1984, more than sixty people died in riots protesting at government austerity measures that had resulted in price increases of 200 per cent for all imported goods and varying increases of many basic foodstuffs. More violent clashes took place in February and June 1988 as a consequence of widespread discontent.

Meanwhile, total external debt has increased from $2 billion in 1980 to $3.7 billion in 1987. Debt ratios have continued to deteriorate during this decade. Reserves have been depleted and should have amounted to less than one months worth of imports in 1987. Finally, arrears accrued over 1986–88 were estimated at some $400 million.

Domestically, two major factors have restrained private investment and economic growth in the Dominican Republic during the 1980s. First, the country's ambiguity with regard to economic adjustment. A 1983 arrangement with the IMF was cancelled because of non-compliance. A 1985 IMF loan over SDR 79 million was fully disbursed by April 1986, but many of the agreed fiscal and monetary restraints were abandoned. Since then, no new agreement has been struck. Second, between 1985 and 1988, the government has changed its foreign exchange policies five times.

Externally, the economy of the Dominican Republic was particularly affected by the collapse of the world market price for sugar, its major foreign exchange supplier. In 1981, sugar accounted for almost half of the country's export earnings, when subsidized production of EC and US sugar led to a depression of the sugar price. While world market prices stood at $639.8 per megaton in 1980, they plummeted to $101.4 per megaton in 1985. With the reintroduction of quotas on sugar imports by the US in 1982, Dominican exports to the US were drastically reduced. In 1980, the Dominican Republic exported more than 550,000 short tons of sugar worth more than $250 million to the US. By 1987, volume and value of these exports had shrunk by some 70 per cent, with shipments of a mere 160,000 short tons of sugar worth less than $70 million. As a non-member of the EC Lomé Convention, the Dominican Republic is also not a party to the EC Sugar Protocol which provides import quotas at highly subsidized prices to its beneficiaries.

As a result of this combination of factors affecting sugar prices and export volumes, that commodity accounted for only 20 per cent of the Dominican export revenues in 1987. Meanwhile, tourism became the leading source of foreign exchange. Also, clothing cut and sewn from US cloth has become a major re-export of the Dominican Republic, since it enjoys exemption from custom duties under US Tariff Schedule, line 807 for the value of the US components. In 1986, over half of the Dominican Republic's manufactured exports to the US with a gross value of $330 fell under this provision.

This diversification of Dominican exports is certainly a positive development. Its effects could be further enhanced by a diversification of export markets. However, such diversification was hampered by the exclusion of the Dominican Republic from the EC Lomé Convention. Haiti, also excluded from Lomé, enjoys a comparative advantage over the Dominican Republic, since it is a beneficiary of the EC's preferential treatment to least developed countries. Thus, for many exportables the Dominican Republic lacks competitiveness compared to the other Caribbean countries, and the US continues to be its largest trading partner, buying 84 per cent of the country's exports in 1987. While it would appear desirable for the Dominican Republic to be included in the Lomé IV agreement under negotiation in 1989, such membership is still being opposed by the United Kingdom and the Netherlands. However, there is some optimism in the Dominican Republic with regard to its application. At the same time, it is unlikely that the

Dominican Republic would become a beneficiary of the EC Sugar Protocol even in case of its accession to Lomé IV.

Increasing and diversified exports supported by consistent foreign exchange policies, in combination with commercial and official debt reschedulings under the umbrella of an IMF agreement, might help the Dominican Republic to contain a remaining financing gap at manageable levels during the early 1990s.

Trinidad and Tobago is not regarded as heavily indebted, even though it has experienced some difficulties in raising adequate levels of external finance. Between 1980 and 1987 Trinidad's debt more than doubled, reaching $1.8 billion. More importantly, however, is the change of debt structure. While 50 per cent of all debt in 1970 was owed to official debtors, this percentage fell to only 27 per cent by 1987 since Trinidad is regarded as relatively 'rich'. Consequently, Trinidad's obligations became more costly and short-term oriented, and in the mid-1980s, the country was faced with a bunching of repayments and dwindling international reserves. In 1981, those reserves stood at $3.4 billion or 13.4 months of imports, in 1986 they had fallen to $495 million or 2.8 months of imports. By June 1988, they were a negligible $20 million. It is also of great significance that some 60 per cent of Trinidad's public debt in 1986 was denominated in Japanese yen and European currencies. With the US dollar's depreciation, the burden of that debt has risen, greatly affecting the country's repayment capacity.

Trinidad and Tobago represents the only oil-exporting country in the Caribbean (the Bahamas refines imported oil for exports). Like in the case of Mexico whose liquidity problems triggered the debt crisis in August of 1982, it must be asked why Trinidad is experiencing its current difficulties. After all, these two countries benefited from sharply increased oil revenues in the 1970s and should have 'taken-off', in development terms, at the beginning of this decade. This brings us back to those inherent, structural imbalances which were previously identified as the true culprits of the development crisis.

In the late 1950s, Trinidad and Tobago attempted to pursue Arthur Lewis's version of industrialization which focused on export promotion with an import-substitution component, often referred to as the Puerto Rican model. This was emphasized in the country's first development plan (1958–62). However, reality was different. There was no legislation to attract export-oriented industries. Consequently, Trinidad's industrialization model concentrated mainly on its import-substituting component. This policy thrust continued throughout the country's second development plan (1964–8). During the third development plan (1969–73), Trinidad and Tobago had reached, as many other countries, the limits of import-substituting industrialization and like others attempted to extend the benefits of that economic growth model by projecting it on a regional level. By mid-1973, however, the financial position of the country had become precarious. The energy crisis of 1973–4 and its oil price increases came to the rescue of the country and elevated it on to a new plane of industrialization. As for so many oil-exporting countries, Trinidad's oil resources would prove to be a blessing and a curse at the same time.

Total oil revenues increased from 6.8 per cent of GDP in 1973 to 28.3 per cent in 1978. Well aware of the scarcity of its oil reserves, Trinidad steered its economy towards energy-based industrialization focusing on the production of steel, fertilizers, petro-chemicals and liquified natural gas. Two decisions made by the government during the oil-boom were particularly important: First, to expand the role of the state in the economy. By 1987, the Ministry of Industry and Enterprise wholly or partially owned sixty-six state enterprises. Second, an ambitious welfare program to share and distribute the newly acquired wealth. Due to the oil-boom and because of high public investment, especially in construction, the economy grew at an average rate of 7 per cent per annum during 1976–82. So much for the blessing.

As of 1983, Trinidad and Tobago had to deal with the curse. With plummeting oil prices, the economy contracted in five consecutive years by a total of 35.5 per cent. Simultaneously, government expenditures did not decrease at the same rate creating a deteriorating fiscal situation. The country's current account as well as its overall balance-of-payments were negative every year between 1982 and 1987.

But it was not the plummeting oil price alone which diminished Trinidad's income. This was compounded by falling oil production from 230,000 barrels per day during the late 1970s to 155,000 barrels in 1987. Also, as a result of a reduction in public investment, the service and construction sectors contracted sharply. Thus, the country's unemployment rates increased drastically from 9.5 per cent in 1982 to 22.1 per cent in March 1987.

The Trinidadian government then took a number of actions in order to regain positive economic growth rates. In August 1988, a currency devaluation and budget cutting measures were announced. A Voluntary Termination of Employment Plan became effective on 1 November 1988, aimed at the retrenchment of 25,000 civil servants. In October, 20 per cent of the government's shares in the Trinidad Cement Company were offered to the public, 2 per cent to its employees. Efforts were made to reduce the 51.5 per cent state holding in the National Commercial Bank and plans were drawn up to divest up to 49 per cent of the state owned telephone company. Also a three-year Public Sector Investment Program was announced, directed at projects of productive activity as well as physical and social infrastructure.

The petroleum sector will continue to provide Trinidad with the largest share of its foreign exchange revenue. However, energy-based industries as well as the potential for tourism could increase significantly in their role as foreign exchange earners. The public investment program might provide the necessary financing to create growth in those sectors. Nevertheless, Trinidad and Tobago needs further debt rescheduling as well as new capital inflows exceeding $225 million per year over the next few years, in order to sustain the recovery as well as to meet the country's debt service payments and build up reserves. A first step in that direction was taken in February 1989, when the IMF approved a $128 million standby loan and private banks agreed, in principle, to refinance $450 million due between September 1988 and 1992.

In order to answer the question: 'Is there life after debt in the Caribbean?' as Scott MacDonald phrased it in his article on the subject, two distinguishing features of Caribbean economies should be stressed:

1. the nature of most Caribbean countries as small developing countries, and
2. their export performance to earn the necessary foreign exchange in order to repay debt.

It is widely recognized that economic planning in small developing countries faces particular constraints and limitations. Some of these constraints are: narrowness of resource base (land, manpower, capital), high dependence on foreign capital, limited domestic markets, high unit costs of production for domestic markets, limited bargaining power, and high over-head costs of government services and administration. As a result of these and other constraints, economic growth in small countries depends largely on the rate of the growth of exports. Moreover, such open, export-oriented economies of small states tend to be less diversified than those of larger countries. The scarcity of manpower and capital demand careful targeting of investments. Finally, limited domestic markets also result in less capacity for import-substituting industrialization. Hence, the economies of small countries are disproportionately exposed to external shocks which increase their import costs or depress export prices for their primary commodities.

Therefore, many industrialized countries have granted preferential treatment to these countries through a variety of trade regimes (EC Lomé Convention, US CBI, CARIBCAN). In spite of these preferences, Caribbean exports grew less dynamically from 1980–86 than either world or developing country averages. In fact, non-fuel exports of all developing countries to the EC/US/Canada grew at an average rate of 6 per cent during that period, while non-fuel exports of the countries of the Caribbean Group for Cooperation in Economic Development (CGCED) grew by only 1.5 per cent annually, thus losing approximately 20 per cent of their market share and forfeiting $1.7 billion in additional export earnings.

There are, above all, two reasons for this somewhat disappointing performance. First, the Caribbean countries still depend on very few primary commodity exports, which have suffered declines in volume and value in this decade. Second, most currencies of the Caribbean countries are pegged to the US dollar. Since the dollar appreciated strongly until 1986 relative to European currencies, Caribbean exports to Europe were less competitive than those of other developing countries. At the same time, the Caribbean countries were confronted with strong competition on the US market from countries whose real exchange rates had not appreciated as rapidly as those of the Caribbean.

Still, there has been progress with regard to the region's manufactured exports whose growth rates compared well with those of other developing countries. This performance might be strengthened through a variety of actions. The industrialized countries, for example, might wish to expand their trade regimes. The US Congress considered legislation during 1989 to extend duty-free treatment under the Caribbean Basin Initiative also to such goods as leather products, watches, canned tuna, and apparel made from US fabric, which are currently excluded. The new CBI was also to extend the expiration date of the agreement. However, a final decision was not made during 1989 and the latest legislative proposals have been robbed of much of the substantive improvements.

The European Community is currently negotiating Lomé IV and it would help Caribbean integration, if Haiti and the Dominican Republic could also become beneficiaries. It seems unfortunate that the goodwill of the EC to encourage Caribbean diversification of exports is sometimes offset by antidumping actions taken by the Communities. Thus, in 1980 a Dominican Republic exporter was accused of dumping furfural. In 1983, a case was filed against Surinamese aluminum exports. In 1985, exclusion orders against steel rods and in 1986 against urea exports from Trinidad and Tobago were lodged. It would appear most effective if the US and the EC could reduce their protectionist policies, especially with regard to sugar. This action alone would create significant foreign exchange earnings in the Caribbean and enable many countries to improve their repayment capacity.

Finally, intra-regional trade must be revived. It is widely accepted that the need for integration is especially urgent for small states. As William G. Demas noted there are three major reasons: to create a larger regional market; to combine all natural resources; to pool Caribbean sovereignty in order to increase their collective bargaining power.

Some progress has been made in that regard. In 1987, intra-regional trade grew by 8 per cent and during the first three quarters of 1988, the value of trade grew by 9 per cent over the same period in 1987. Also, in October 1988, CARICOM decided to dismantle all barriers to trade within the community, while allowing a list of products produced in the smallest countries to enjoy some protection for the next three years. Of course, CARICOM is not truly integrational as long as Haiti and the Dominican Republic are not included.

While there has been much talk recently about alleged animosities between the World Bank and the International Monetary Fund (IMF) on the debt issue, these two organizations as well as other donors and Caribbean recipients have set an example of how to coordinate their activities by forming the Caribbean Group for Cooperation in Economic Development (CGCED) in 1978. This group gathers every eighteen months under the chairmanship of the World Bank. Their discussions cover a broad range of economic policy issues affecting the region as a whole as well as individual countries. They discuss country-specific economic programs and external financing requirements. CGCED has proven to be an excellent forum of coordination. It has helped the region to cope with the debt crisis and has broadened the horizon of both donor and recipient community alike.

Every cloud has a silver lining

There are no easy solutions to the debt crisis. Between January 1980 and September 1988, Central America and the Caribbean negotiated twenty-five separate multilateral debt relief agreements with commercial banks and seven such agreements with official creditors. This underlines the complexities of the crisis.

It was the purpose of this chapter to unmask some of these complexities. No two debtors are alike. Private and official lenders have different agendas. Sometimes there are rivalries even within a given group of creditors, such as between commercial banks and private bondholders. The export growth model, often prescribed to increase foreign exchange earnings of debtor countries, should not be expected to resolve inherent economic or societal imbalances in those countries. Finally, while economic adjustment is necessary to revitalize the economies of Central America and the Caribbean, it is not sufficient. Economics is not an exact science.

However painful the past seven years might have been, and however disillusioned debtors and creditors might have become since 1982, they have come a long way. When the crisis first broke in August 1982, it was widely regarded as a liquidity crisis, quickly to be fixed with IMF Stabilization Programs. It became obvious that it was not just a matter of balance-of-payments difficulties and the more medium-term oriented structural adjustment lending was increased. The Baker plan of 1985 was designed to create growth during the adjustment process. In 1987, deteriorating standards of living in many debtor countries triggered increased consideration of poverty alleviation. Still, the poorest countries were apparently unable to service their debt. Hence, 1988 brought about far-reaching debt forgiveness of official debt to the countries of Sub-Saharan Africa. In 1989, it was learnt that middle-income countries, too, have increasing difficulties to repay their debt and debt reduction as well as debt forgiveness dominated international deliberations. It should be remembered that debt forgiveness was a taboo in 1982.

This evolution of debt resolution strategies, was reflected in a progressive change in the World Bank's approach towards this nagging problem. At first, the Bank tried to provide the basis for most debtors to outgrow their financial difficulties, by encouraging broad, macroeconomic policy changes supported by so-called structural adjustment lending. Then, in order to target specific segments, i.e. sectors of the economies of the debtor countries, the World Bank began to prefer sectoral adjustment loans. Finally, it became apparent that domestic and foreign investment, the key to future growth, was declining throughout the developing world. Therefore, the World Bank created a mix of policy-oriented and investment-specific lending, named hybrid loans. Today, it is widely acknowledged that adjustment is a slow process and must be pursued with great patience.

Looking into the future, the prime objective is to reverse the trend of negative net transfers to Central America and the Caribbean, and to increase domestic and foreign investment. For this purpose, the governments of Central America and the Caribbean must continue their efforts 'to adopt the often difficult and politically unpopular economic and financial measures necessary to create a favorable environment for development', as the World Bank has stated many years ago in its Fourth Annual Report in 1949. Those countries which have not yet joined this process might benefit from a World Bank study published in 1988, which established that, on average, countries without viable adjustment programs were worse off in the late 1980s than those who had previously participated.

Debt reduction mechanisms, such as debt-equity, debt-nature and debt-development swaps as well as debt buybacks can help to loosen the grip on the economic growth potential of the countries. Their limitations must be understood, however, with regard to size as well as potential side-effects. While debt buybacks avert some of the side-effects, debt-equity swaps, if designed carefully, can increase additionality and channel investments into priority areas.

Interest capitalization could also help the payment capacity of Central America and the Caribbean. While it does not reduce debt, it reduces debt service and is, in a way, an automatic form of rescheduling. There are certain tax and regulatory restrictions in some creditor countries, as a result of which the commercial banks have shown little enthusiasm for this feature in the past.

But there should also be some straightforward debt-forgiveness, particularly, but not exclusively, to the poorest countries and mainly, but not only by official creditors.

Increased exports will also enhance foreign exchange earnings in Central America and the Caribbean and enable those countries to better service their debt. But, as US Secretary of the Treasury, Nicholas F. Brady, remarked on 10 March 1989 'we cannot reasonably expect the debtor nations to increase their exports and strengthen their economies without access to industrial country markets.'

Last, but certainly not least, an injection of new money into Central America and the Caribbean is crucial. There are many investment opportunities in these two subregions and their growth potential is significant.

As pointed out in the first section of this chapter, there is enough blame to go round for everybody. As a result of past mistakes, we arrived at the 1980s with the developing countries overextended, the commercial banks overexposed and the governments of the industrialized countries overwhelmed. Desperately seeking the least-cost solution many proposals made over the years were mutually exclusive. There is a price tag attached to this dilemma and procrastination will only inflate this price.

References

Ambursley, Fitzroy, 'Jamaica: from Michael Manley to Edward Seaga', in Fitzroy Ambursley and Robin Cohen (ed.), *Crisis in The Caribbean.* New York: Monthly Review Press, 1983.

Axline, W. Andrew, *Agricultural Policy and Collective Self-Reliance in the Caribbean.* London: Westview Press, 1986.

Barsotti, Frank , 'Industrialization in a Small Open Economy: The Case of Trinidad and Tobago, 1945-1987', *Caribbean Affairs*, April-June 1988.

Boyd, Derick A.C., *Economic Management, Income Distribution, and Poverty in Jamaica.* New York: Praeger, 1988.

Boyd, Derick, 'The Impact of Adjustment Policies on Vulnerable Groups: The Case of Jamaica, 1973-1985', in Giovanni Andrea Cornia, Richard Jolly, and Frances Steward (ed.), *Adjustment with a Human Face.* Oxford: Clarendon Press, 1988.

Carnoy, Martin, *Industrialization in a Latin American Common Market*, Washington, D.C.: The Brookings Institution, 1971.

'Costa Rica: A Case History' in *Default and Rescheduling.* Washington, D.C.: Euromoney Publications, 1984.

Demas, William G., 'Economic Independence: Conceptual and Policy Issues in the Commonwealth Caribbean', in Percy Selwyn (ed.), *Development Policy in Small Countries.* London, University of Sussex, 1975.

The Economist Intelligence Unit, *Country Profile*: Barbados, 1988-89.

The Economist Intelligence Unit, *Country Report*: Costa Rica, April 88.

The Economist Intelligence Unit, *Country Profile*: Dominican Republic, 1988-89.

The Economist Intelligence Unit, *Country Profile*: Guyana, 1988-89.

The Economist Intelligence Unit, *Country Report*: Trinidad and Tobago, April 88.

Greene, Duty D. and Terry L. Roe, *Trade, Exchange Rate and Agricultural Pricing Policies in the Dominican Republic.* Washington, D.C.: World Bank, 1989, volume 1.

Grunwald, Joseph, Miguel S Wionczek, Martin Carnoy, *Latin American Economic Integration and U.S. Policy.* Washington, D.C.: The Brookings Institution, 1972.

Inter-American Development Bank, *Annual Report.* Washington, D.C.: Inter-American Development Bank, 1986.

Inter-American Development Bank, *Annual Report.* Washington, D.C.: Inter-American Development Bank, 1987.

Inter-American Development Bank, *Economic and Social Progress Report.* Washington, D.C.: Inter-American Development Bank, 1988.

MacDonald, Scott, 'Economic Development of the Caribbean in the 1980s: Is there Life After Debt?', in W. Marvin Will and Richard Millett (ed.), *Crescents of Conflict.* New York: Praeger, 1990.

McClelland, Donald, 'The Common Market's Contribution to Central American Integration - a First Approximation', in Ronald Hilton (ed.), *The Movement Toward Latin American Unity.* New York: Praeger, 1969.

Masor, Edward S. and Robert E. Asher, *The World since Bretton Woods.* Washington, D.C.: The Brookings Institution, 1973.

Pan American Health Organization, *Priority Health Needs in Central America and Panama.* Washington, D.C., 1984.

Prebisch, Raul, 'Five Stages in My Thinking on Development' in Gerald M. Meier and Dudley Seers (ed.), *Pioneers in Development.* New York: Oxford University Press, 1984.

Sandoval, José Miguel, 'State Capitalism in a Petroleum-Based Economy', in Fitzroy Ambursley and Robin Cohen (ed.), *Crisis in the Caribbean.* New York: Monthly Review Press, 1983.

Seiber, Marilyn J., *International Borrowing by Developing Countries.* New York: Pergamon Press, 1982.

Ward, Michael, 'Dependent Development Problems of Economic Planning in Small Developing Countries', in Percy Selwyn (ed.), *Development Policy in Small Countries.* London: University of Sussex, 1975.

Webb, Richard, Alain Thery, Ernesto Kritz, Eliane Karp, *El Salvador: Income, Employment, and Social Indicators Changes over the Decade 1975-1985*, prepared for Agency for International Development, International Science and Technology Institute, Inc., January.

Weeks, John, *The Economies of Central America.* New York: Holmes and Meier, 1985.

World Bank, *World Debt Tables 1988–89.* Washington, D.C.: World Bank, 1989, vol I, p. xxiii.

World Bank, Country Economics Department, *Adjustment Lending, an Evaluation of Ten Years of Experience.* Washington, D.C.: World Bank, 1988.

World Bank, *The Caribbean, Export Preferences and Performance.* Washington, D.C.: World Bank, 1988.

World Bank, *Trinidad and Tobago, A Program for Policy Reform and Renewed Growth.* Washington D.C.: World Bank, 1988.

Chapter 4

North Africa and the Middle East

*John Roberts and Scott B. MacDonald**

Introduction

There has been little discussion about the global debt crisis in the Middle East and North Africa. Yet in the region that extends from Morocco on the Atlantic Ocean to Afghanistan and Pakistan the debt question has been a point of concern. The parade of countries through rescheduling meetings in London, New York and Paris has included a number of Middle Eastern and North African nations: Egypt, Iraq, Morocco and Pakistan have been involved in this process in the 1980s. Algeria in 1988 was racked by violent riots linked to debt-inspired austerity measures. Syria has perennial debt problems and Jordan in 1989 was forced to reschedule. Of all the region's non-oil producing countries, only Afghanistan and Lebanon, beset by problems of quite another kind, remained relatively free of international debt. Although external debt is not a primary policy issue for most of the region's (hereafter the 'Middle East') main oil producers, two of its largest countries, Iran and Iraq, must reconstruct war-damaged economies. This will take considerable outside capital, raising concerns about access to international capital markets, politics within the OPEC (Organization of Petroleum Exporting Countries) and relations with the West. This chapter examines the place of the Middle East in the global debt crisis.

A diverse region

The Middle East is a remarkably diverse region. Three of the world's major religions, Islam, Judaism and Christianity have their roots here, whilst the Tigris-Euphrates basin and the Indus and Nile valleys were amongst the earliest cradles of civilization. There is a rich history of empire, from the Egyptian, Babylonian, Persian, Macedonian and Roman empires of antiquity, to the great medieval Ommayyad and Abbasid caliphates and to the more recent Ottoman, French and British empires. This historical legacy has left behind a mixture of peoples, including Arabs, Persians, Berbers, Kurds, and

---

* Mr. MacDonald is an official of the Office of the Comptroller of the Currency. The views expressed in this chapter, however, are solely his views and do not purport to represent the policies of the Office of the Comptroller of the Currency.

the multifarious peoples of Afghanistan and Pakistan.

Culture, politics and religion have all left their mark on the region. Some twenty-one states, as well as the embryo Palestinian state declared by the Palestine National Council in November 1988, define themselves as 'Arab', at least to the extent that they are members of the Arab League. Seventeen of these fall within the area regarded as 'the Middle East' for our purposes. This grouping includes all the North African countries (Morocco, Algeria, Tunisia, Libya and Egypt); all the countries on the western or southern shores of the Persian Gulf (Bahrain, Iraq, Kuwait, Saudi Arabia, the United Arab Emirates, Qatar and Oman); three countries abutting the Red Sea (Jordan, North Yemen and South Yemen) and two with coastlines along the Eastern Mediterranean (Syria and Lebanon).

Non-Arab states in the region include Iran, where Persians and the Persian language give the country much of its identity, Israel, Afghanistan and Pakistan. Although Turkey is often considered a Middle Eastern country, its people are not Arabs and, by virtue of its ties to Europe and membership of the Organization for Economic Cooperation and Development (OECD), its conventional debt situation is considered elsewhere in this volume (Chapter Eight, Southern Europe). The debt problems of four Arab League members - Sudan, Djibouti, Somalia and Mauritania - are also considered elsewhere (Chapter Five, Sub-Saharan Africa).

The Middle East is politically diverse and economically disparate. Six of the more conservative and traditional Arab countries - and all of them monarchies - in 1980 formed the most effective of the regional economic groupings, the Gulf Cooperation Council. In early 1989, two more Arab groupings were established: one linking North Africa from revolutionary Libya to monarchical Morocco and the other grouping of four countries for what appear to be mainly political reasons, since economic union between such disparate and geographically separated states as North Yemen, Egypt, Jordan and Iraq seems only a very dim prospect.

The radicalism and conservatism of the various countries is not necessarily reflected in their constitutional structures. Republican Egypt and monarchical Jordan are both fairly conservative societies. Algeria, founded in bitter revolution against French colonial rule, has ceased to proclaim socialism as the answer to its problems. Iraq's war with Iran prompted it to drop its revolutionary rhetoric and to proclaim its adherence to more traditional Arab nationalist ideals and aspirations as it sought economic and military assistance from other Arab nations. And while the Gulf Cooperation Council is generally conservative, monarchical Kuwait is, in many social, diplomatic and economic fields, a radical. Only one Arab state, South Yemen, is avowedly Marxist, and whilst socialist principles were long asserted by the ruling parties in Algeria, Iraq, Syria and Egypt, only Syria, the original home of a peculiarly Arab variant of socialism known as Baathism, seems slow to modify its socialist ideals.

Table 4.1 Selected basic indicators for Middle East countries

Country	Population (millions) mid-1986	GNP per capita 1986 dollars	Life expectancy at birth (years 1986)
Afghanistan	19.5 (1980)	$110 (1979)	40 (1979)
Algeria	22.4	2,590	62
Bahrain	.431	8,510	70
Egypt	49.7	760	61
Iran	45.6	. . .	59
Iraq	16.5	3,020 (1980)	63
Israel	4.3	6,210	75
Jordan	3.6	1,540	65
Kuwait	1.8	13,890	73
Lebanon	. . .	. . .	. . .
Libya	3.9	8,640 (1980)	61
Morocco	22.5	590	60
Pakistan	99.2	350	52
Oman	1.3	4,980	54
Qatar	.317	13,200	69
Saudi Arabia	12.0	6,950	63
Syria	10.8	1,570	64
Tunisia	7.3	1,140	63
United Arab Emirates	1.4	14,680	69
Yemen, Arab Rep.	8.2	550	46
Yemen, Peoples Rep.	2.2	470	50

Source: World Bank Development Report, 1988, pp. 222–3

Parliamentary democracy remains a fragile bloom in most of these countries. It does not exist in Gulf states (Kuwait has had a vocal parliament, but it currently stands dissolved) and in most countries it has been traditionally little more than a rubber stamp. But Pakistan in 1988 and 1989 returned to parliamentary government, whilst there are signs in a number of countries, including Egypt, Tunisia and Algeria, that parliament might be becoming a more genuinely democratic forum and chamber for debate as more open political systems evolve. Israeli parliamentary politics remain lively, as do those of revolutionary Iran, where they reflect the intense debates and arguments within a country often considered to be an Islamic theocracy. Afghanistan and Lebanon exist as violently polarized and byzantine societies, in which political, sectarian and tribal groups compete for power on a local or national scale – often with the help of outside allies – in seemingly-endless civil wars.

Considering the political diversity of the Middle East, the levels of economic development vary as well. This is one of the important factors in the region's response in the global debt crisis. Table 4.1 mirrors the wide range between the most wealthy, the United Arab Emirates, and the poorest, Afghanistan.

Although the indicators are not all inclusive, they provide a rough idea of the break down between the countries that constitute the Middle East. Bahrain, Kuwait, Qatar, Libya, Saudi Arabia and the United Arab Emirates (UAE) clearly lead the way in terms of a higher standard of living and their wealth is directly related to oil. The spectacular rise in oil prices in the 1970s, especially after OPEC I in 1973/4, brought a considerable inflow of capital and wealth. Furthermore, the new found oil wealth turned some of the larger countries, Iran, Iraq and Saudi Arabia, into regional powers. To a lesser extent, Algeria and Libya emerged as regional actors. The latter in particular, led by Colonel Muammar Gaddafi sought to create an inner African empire that included Chad, parts of Niger and Burkina Faso (formerly Upper Volta) and had linkages to Benin, the Sudan, and Idi Amin's Uganda.

The 'high-income oil exporters' - Saudi Arabia, Kuwait, UAE and Libya - embarked upon large-scale development projects. These included establishing aluminum smelting plants in the UAE, the tapping of underground lakes deep in Libya's Sahara to make man-made rivers, and the distribution of national wealth in the form of widespread health programs and free education. The purchasing spree that accompanied this ranged from commercial and military aircraft to consumer goods. Saudi merchandise imports steadily rose from $1.85 billion in 1973 to a peak of $34.4 billion in 1982.

While the high-income oil exporters enjoyed their newly-discovered wealth in the mid-1970s, there existed a number of other Middle Eastern countries not blessed with such an abundance of oil. Many contained no reserves and even though some others had oil, its largess was dwarfed by the needs of their larger populations as in the cases of Algeria, Iran and Iraq (and later Egypt). However, two factors helped the rest of the Middle East in the mid-1970s to the early 1980s. The most evident was that the strong economic growth in the oil states functioned like a locomotive, dragging the other regional economies along. This often came in the form of direct assistance in the forms of grants and cheap loans from the wealthy oil states, as in the case of Jordan and its assistance from Saudi Arabia and Kuwait. The second factor was the rise in other commodity prices over the same period.

Saudi Arabia, Libya and the Gulf states of Kuwait, Bahrain, the United Arab Emirates and Qatar had relatively small populations and lacked expertise in many fields. Consequently, foreign expertise was imported. This was an economic boon for countries like Egypt, Jordan and Pakistan which possessed large pools of educated labor (including the politically restive Palestinians) that faced high unemployment levels at home. Once employed in one of the Gulf states, Saudi Arabia or Libya this emigrant work force became a source of capital inflow for the workers' homeland through remittances of earnings to their families. Additionally, workers from other Islamic states usually posed fewer problems than other nationalities because of religious similarity, most being one form of Muslim. Even in cases where there were differences between Sunnis and Shiites, the differences were of a different magnitude from those of Christians and Hindus.

The other Middle Eastern countries also benefited from new trading activities and financial assistance. Both of these became important policy tools for the competing forces in the region, such as the radical bloc of Arab countries (Libya, Syria, Iraq and Egypt under Nasser) and the more conservative bloc led by Saudi Arabia and Kuwait (Jordan, Oman, and Egypt under Sadat and Mubarak). Financial assistance was also used for the 'front line states' around Israel, Jordan, Syria and Egypt and in some cases, for the support of terrorist groups. The Saudis, in particular, have been willing to support a wide-ranging sweep of forces abroad that included Afghan rebels, Islamic groups in the Sudan, and the Eritreans in the Ethiopian civil war. For a number of non-oil states, such as Jordan, this inflow of financial assistance meant the difference between bankruptcy and harsh economic reforms and operating in the black.

Table 4.2 shows the amount of official development assistance that was provided by the major Middle Eastern donors.

Table 4.2 Official development assistance of major Middle Eastern donors

	Amount ($US dollars)					
Country	1976	1978	1979	1980	1981	1982
Saudi Arabia	2,791	5,250	3,941	5,682	5,514	3,854
Kuwait	706	1,001	971	1,140	1,163	1,161
U.A.E.	1,028	889	968	1,118	805	406
Libya	98	132	145	376	257	44
Qatar	180	95	282	277	246	139

Source: World Bank Development Report 1988

The rise in non-oil prices brought higher growth rates throughout the Middle East. Phosphates, a major export for Jordan, Morocco and Tunisia rose from 29.4 cents per metric ton in 1973 to 113 cents in 1974. Because of this Tunisia ran one of its few current account balance of payments surpluses in 1974. The price upswing enhanced Tunisia's credit ratings and in the international atmosphere of commodity 'cartel-phobia', there was some doubt that prices would swing downwards in the medium term. Consequently, Tunisia was able to tap international markets for funds which were badly needed for development programs. The North African country's public and publicly guaranteed debt rose from $695 million to a little over $1 billion in 1975.

Commodity prices, however were not destined to remain at what were in some cases historic highs. Phosphates rose to a peak of 145.6 cents per metric ton in 1975 and fell precipitously by over half to 76.7 cents in 1976. With oil import prices still high, exports falling, and many development projects in mid-stream, the 'least-bad' option for a number of countries was to borrow. Tunisia still had oil exports to blunt the downturn in phosphates, but a number of other countries, like Jordan and Morocco did not and were actually oil importers. The following table provides some insight into the steady rise in external borrowing on the part of a number of Middle Eastern countries in the 1970s.

Table 4.3 The debt run-up in the 1970s

	(Debt outstanding including undisbursed in $US billions)					
Country	1970	1972	1973	1974	1976	1979
Egypt	2.3	2.9	3.0	4.5	9.0	16.75
Israel	2.6	4.1	4.9	5.6	7.8	12.3
Jordan	.186	.246	.367	.476	.689	1.94
Morocco	.953	1.2	1.3	1.8	3.2	9.9
Pakistan	4.6	4.8	5.4	6.75	7.9	10.65
Syria	.342	.526	.663	1.3	2.8	3.98
Tunisia	.861	1.1	1.3	1.5	2.3	4.9
Total	$11.842	14.872	16.93	21.926	33.689	60.42

Source: World Bank, *World Debt Tables*

By the early 1980s the debt crisis was emerging as a problem in other regions of the developing world. Latin America, in particular, was beginning to creep into the consciousness of policy-makers as a potential trouble area. The Middle East in contrast did not attract this early attention. Even in 1982, when Mexico and a number of large developing countries moved to reschedule, the Middle East was not regarded as a significant problem in the field of international finance. Concerns about the Middle East had other political focuses: the on-going Arab-Israeli dispute, the Gulf War between Iran and Iraq, the destabilizing and rising tide of Islamic fundamentalism, terrorism, warfare between Morocco and the Western Sahara's Polisario independence movement, and the containment of Libya's African adventures. Concern about Middle Eastern economies, however, would belatedly emerge as oil prices fell gradually after 1982 and more dramatically in late 1985 and 1986.

The great slowdown, 1982–8

This section covers the 'great slowdown' in Middle East economies linked to the fall in oil prices. Following a general discussion, a menu of some of the region's largest debtors follows. Petroleum prices reached their peak in 1981 and 1982 and then declined, especially in late 1985 and 1986. Oil prices have not yet recovered to the previous levels, hovering in the $13–18 level in the 1987-9 period. The rise and

Table 4.4 Average yearly oil prices (1981-8)

	(US$/barrel) 1/1/1981	1/1/1986	1/1/1987	1/1/1988	25/11/1988
OPEC	$34.82	27.81	16.10	16.77	11.53
Non-OPEC	38.54	26.14	16.44	16.21	12.40
World av.	35.49	27.10	16.34	16.57	11.83

Source: Petroleum Economist, January 1989, p. 41

fall of prices provides some background to how a number of Middle Eastern countries, especially those that had accumulated large external debts, were effected. Table 4.4 demonstrates the decline in petroleum prices on a yearly average basis.

The slowdown in the oil-based economies had a multitude of ripple effects which took several years to be felt. Some of the countries not dependent on oil or oil-generated financial assistance also found the 1982–8 period a time of adjustment and economic hardship. With reductions for financial assistance from the Gulf states, a decline in workers' remittances and a fall in trade, belt-tightening became the order of the day for countries such as Jordan and Egypt. Additionally, a number of Middle Eastern countries were confronted with similar problems of growing debt burdens and negative trends in the external accounts. The Table 4.5 provides data on the size of the total external debt of the most-heavily indebted Middle Eastern countries and the following part of this chapter highlights the cases of the largest debtors.

Table 4.5 Total external debt for most heavily indebted Middle Eastern countries, 1983–8

	(US$ billions) 1983	1985	1986	1987	1988
Algeria	15.1	16.5	19.9	23.4	21.4
Egypt	21.8	27.1	28.6	34.4	35.0
Iran	7.6	5.5	4.1	3.9	4.1
Iraq**	26.4	65.0	75.0	80.0	NA
Israel	22.8	24.1	25.1	26.4	25.9
Jordan*	1.94	2.50	2.7	2.75	3.57
Libya*	2.7	3.2	3.5	NA	NA
Morocco	10.3	12.8	14.6	18.5	21.1
Pakistan***	9.3	9.7	11.1	12.0	12.4

* Public external debt only
**These are estimated figures and they also allow for debts to Arab states, in terms of direct loans and counter oil sales. Western creditors account for around $15 billion and Iraq owes Turkey $2.1 billion in trade finance.
***World Bank, *World Debt Tables*.
Source: Economist Intelligence Unit, 1989

Debt issues remain a particular problem in Algeria, Egypt, Morocco, Tunisia and Pakistan and also in some of the smaller countries of the region, notably Jordan. These countries look as much to the World Bank as to the International Monetary Fund for assistance and, significantly, they believe they get a more sympathetic hearing from the World Bank. The World Bank's Enhanced Structural Adjustment Facility, on which such countries as Pakistan and the two Yemens can draw, provides some assurance of new financing to ensure these countries are able to pursue economic growth as well as debt repayment. However, fresh financing has remained hard to come by in large part because of the retreat of commercial banks in lending to developing countries in general.

While the region contains some of the world's most problematic debtor nations, it should also be noted that it holds creditor institutions as well. According to Ziad Abdelnour some twenty Arab banks participated in loan syndications amounting to $45 billion between 1978 and 1985. The major Bahrain-based banks eased their situation in early 1988 when they decided to dispose of their Latin American debt problems by boosting their reserves.

Specific countries

Egypt is perhaps the classic example of the argument that in many cases the problem of debt is more political and social than it is financial. The country's debt problems dwarf those of any other country in the Middle East. It is not merely their magnitude - accumulated external debt probably exceeded $50 billion by early 1989 if military loans are included - but the bitter emotions that the very mention of loans and debts conjures up for both debtor and creditor. For Egypt is a troubled country, with some 53 million people, an obstinately high birth rate, a grossly inefficient overt economy and a mass of political, diplomatic, economic, social and religious problems. It has varied sources of regular foreign exchange, most notably remittances, tourism, the Suez canal, US aid, and oil and gas revenues. But these are not enough to raise Egypt from poverty and meet its debt obligations.

For most Egyptians, Egypt is still the gift of the Nile; agriculture continues to be vital and one of the most depressing considerations remains the country's persistent need to import even basic foodstuffs. Yet millennia of centralized government have accustomed Egyptians to manage their other economies, subsistence farming and the substantial black market, with sufficient success that total economic collapse has been staved off time and again. There may be food in the countryside, but getting it to the cities - and Cairo is now one of the biggest urban centers in the world with a population approaching 15 million - is another question altogether. These economies constitute one major factor in the Egyptian economic equation; another is the reluctance of the United States and its fellow Western creditors to risk losing through economic failure what the West appears to have gained politically since the late 1970s.

By Western standards, the Egyptian economy looks permanently on the verge of collapse. Accurate statistics are difficult to come by. In the mid-1980s, there were rival GNP statistics showing on one hand that the country was achieving modest economic growth of some 2 per cent above its estimated increase in population, and on the other hand that it was shrinking by a similar amount in real per capita terms. What was clear was that it was not only the Egyptian government that considered the price of debt to be too high to pay, but that some officials in major international institutions, such as the World Bank, shared that view.

Since 1982, the Egyptian government has moved to reduce the massive role that subsidies have played in ordinary life as part of its efforts to restructure the economy in accordance with the wishes of the International Monetary Fund. The Fund and the World Bank provided substantial loans for both development and balance of payments support, whilst the United States pumped billions of dollars in fresh economic and military assistance. In the late 1980s, annual US aid to Egypt settled at $1.3 billion in military assistance, $815 million in economic aid and around $160–190 million in food aid. After 1985, all US aid was on a grant basis, but unlike Israel, which received all of its annual $1.2 billion economic assistance in cash, only $115 million took the form of cash transfers.

The proportion of short-term external debt to total debt fell in the late 1980s. However, by 1986 Egypt was substantially in arrears to a variety of debtors. The International Monetary Fund reported that by mid-1986 Egypt was no less than $4.3 billion behind in its payments, four-fifths of which was due in interest payments. At one stage Egypt was at least $590 million behind in its military repayments to the United States, and only some deft footwork averted what should have been a Congressionally-mandated cut-off of further US military aid. As the country's foreign exchange earnings plunged in the wake of both the oil price crash of January 1986 and the massive slump in tourism, which followed the seizure of the Achille Lauro cruise ship in the Eastern Mediterranean in October 1985, the government began a desperate search for additional finance. By then, the International Monetary Fund was already bitterly at odds with the Egyptian government over its handling of the economy. Despite that President Hosni Mubarak asked the Fund for a $1 billion standby credit.

Relief for Egypt came in 1987 when the Paris Club of creditor nations agreed to reschedule $12 billion in debt over a ten year period, with a five-year grace period. In effect, Egypt gained about two years of breathing space before a further feeling of impending doom set in during early 1989, as once again Cairo began looking to Washington, and to the Fund in particular for debt relief. The Fund remained insistent that Egypt's subsidy levels had to be drastically reduced. Egypt, conscious of the impact of the food riots of 1977, was only prepared to reduce subsidy levels very gradually. When President Mubarak visited Washington in April 1989, Egyptian emphasis on the country's political and diplomatic importance to the West and its role as the leader of an emerging block of moderate Arab states, were stressed. The point was obvious: the West, especially the United States, risked losing all it had gained from the decisions taken by President Anwar Sadat to re-orient Egypt away from Moscow and towards Washington if it did not understand that Egypt really could not run the risk of another round of food riots.

Another of the Middle East's largest debtors in Morocco, which was the only Middle East country to be considered in the World Bank debt tables as a Heavily Indebted Country (HIC). The debt trap that Morocco fell into during the early 1980s has many parallels in other parts of the developing world. Because of these two factors, we will examine Morocco's debt crisis more closely.

Morocco's economic development since independence in 1956 was a case of delicate forward momentum guided by the philosophy of import substitution. The economy was based on agricultural performance and the export of phosphates, stimulated by public sector expansion and the need to maintain growth above the expansion of the population, which averaged 2.5 per cent from 1965-80. The significance of high population growth has been both negative and positive. On one hand the rapid population growth has posed ongoing problems in terms of education, training and employment and on the other hand, the country's abundant supply of unskilled labor has kept wages low and has given its exports a comparative advantage in international markets. Moreover, Moroccan emigrant workers in Europe and elsewhere in the Middle East have become an important capital source in terms of remittances sent back home.

It was the temporary surge in phosphate prices (1974-5) that launched Morocco down the path to numerous reschedulings. The earlier period of rapid economic expansion in the late 1960s had been accompanied by conservative fiscal policies, which helped maintain a balanced external position as well as domestic equilibrium. However, the mid-1970s were different: feeling flush with the inrush of capital in 1974-5, the government embarked upon a rapid increase in public spending. The rise in public spending was partly financed with increased export revenues. It was, however, not enough for the scale of development the King's government envisaged. Consequently, the Moroccan government turned to commercial banks in the United States, Europe and Japan for loans. Morocco appeared to be a good risk and its future source of repayment, phosphate revenues, secure. Moreover, concern about the inflationary impact on petro-dollars from the oil-producers in the industrialized countries helped move the process along.

The government of King Hassan II, able to tap international markets, launched a massive investment program across all sectors of the economy. At the same time, the government began procuring a considerable amount of military hardware, which pleased elements of the armed forces and gave Morocco more strength vis-à-vis what were then perceived as more radical states in Algeria and Libya as well as potential radical anti-monarchy forces within the country.

The desire to make advances by enlarging the state's economic role, coupled by an arms build up, stimulated the growth of Morocco's external debt. The arms build up was caused by the Saharan war with the Polisario Liberation Front, which began after Morocco's annexation of former Spanish Sahara in 1975. In 1970 Morocco's public and publicly guaranteed long-term debt (including undisbursed debt) was $953 million, which was equal to 24 per cent of the country's gross national product (GNP). The country's total debt service was $61 million, equal to 8 per cent of goods and services exports. By 1979, Morocco's external debt stood at $9.9 billion, 64 per cent of GNP. Total debt service had risen as well: in the same year it was $853 million, equal to 23 per cent of goods and services exports. Morocco's structure of debt had also changed. Private creditors in 1970 accounted for $150 million or 16 per cent of total debt. The amount rose to $4 billion in 1979, which was 41 per cent of the total. The increasingly heavy reliance on private creditors as opposed to multilateral lenders, like the World Bank, meant higher costs in terms of interest rates.

What greatly complicated matters for Morocco and its international creditors was the faulty assumption that phosphate prices would remain high. This led the government to plan for far greater expenditures in the public and semi-public sector than revenues. Despite the drop in earnings in 1976, the new investment targets were maintained despite the sharp rise in Treasury deficits (from 5 per cent of GDP in 1974 to 18 per cent in 1976 and 1977). Additionally, new public sector companies were created and state participation in industrial development increased.

While the government actively poured money into the economy, especially in construction, government services and capital-intensive industries (sugar, fertilizer, pulp and paper, and petroleum refining), there was a failure in increasing exports in sufficient amounts to offset the rise in imports and adjust the external account. Imports continued to outstrip exports through the 1970s and into the early 1980s. The growing burden of interest payments on external debt also was a negative trend contributing to large current account deficits of over $1 billion annually from 1976–9.

The government responded to the situation by implementing a number of austerity measures in the 1978–80 period. Despite public expenditure reduction, oil prices remained high and in 1979–80 increased substantially, further adding pressure on the budget deficits and external accounts: 1980's and 1981's current account deficits were well over $1 billion each. Economic expansion of 5.6 per cent in 1982 belied the growing plethora of problems confronting the government. The trade balance and current account deficits continued to widen (the latter to $1.88 billion), and the country struggled to pay its $1.8 billion debt service. What was increasingly alarming was the drop in international reserves (minus gold) from a peak in 1978 of $618 million to $218 million at the end of 1982.

Disaster came home in 1983 as the economy slowed considerably. Morocco was confronted by the imbalance between production and consumption. This was mirrored, according to Rhazaoui,

> by a 2.1 per cent increase in GDP (versus a 3.2 per cent annual population growth rate); only 1 per cent growth from 1981 to 1984 in industrial production, commerce and services, public works, and construction; wage freeze and elimination of 8,600 government posts in 1983; an unemployment rate of 29.6 per cent (percentage of active population without work over total population); and 45 per cent of the total population living below the poverty threshold of $238 per capita (according to the World Bank).

The political component of Morocco's debt crisis was evident by the violence of the 1981 demonstrations over increases in food prices. In 1983 Morocco was forced to negotiate with its creditors to reschedule its debt, which eventually led to further demonstrations in 1984 over austerity measures, especially cuts in food subsidies. It also meant that there was recognition that past policies based on import substitution had failed to make Morocco more self-sufficient. If anything, Morocco suddenly found itself more dependent on the outside world.

Morocco's shift from its import substitution program to an export-growth model led to a comprehensive structural adjustment program. Morocco's economic performance since 1983 was one of steady improvements despite weak global phosphate prices, periodic drought, and the cost of the war in the former Spanish Sahara. Although the economy slowed to 1.0 per cent growth in 1987, it rebounded to 6.0 per cent in 1988 and prospects for 1989 were good. Moreover, the external accounts demonstrated a gradual improvement: the merchandise trade deficit almost consistently shrank from 1982's peak of $1.77 billion to an estimated $850 million in 1988. The current account balance also reflected a positive trend, shifting from large deficits in the early part of the 1980s to a positive $50 million in 1988.

Morocco's reforms have included the adoption of a more flexible exchange rate policy, the opening up of its markets to foreign countries, lowering customs duties and reducing bottlenecks which had prevented the effective distribution of goods. Even the once substantial tariff barriers have been reduced. Additional steps to opening trade and reducing state control have included the elimination of licensing requirements or taxes for private exporters and allowing them to use a percentage of foreign exchange profits to import necessary inputs. Furthermore, the government dismantled the state-run Office de Commercialisation et d'Exportation, which had a monopoly on farm produce and processed foodstuff exports. Other areas of reform included the removal of limits on foreign investment, implementation of stronger tax and export incentives, guarantees for repatriation of capital, and restraints on remittances of dividends, all meant to enhance Morocco's attractiveness to foreign investors.

The Moroccan government has also sought to diversify its exports away from its dependence on phosphates by promoting other sectors of the economy. The phosphate industry, including phosphates and phosphoric acid, accounted for 41 per cent of exports in 1982. The expansion of other export industries, notably manufacturing, citrus and leather goods, helped reduce phosphate's share of exports to around 30 per cent in 1988, a significant decline. Manufacturing now accounts for 55 per cent of merchandise exports, compared to 36 per cent in 1980. The diversification process has also developed the country's tourist sector, which netted Morocco $1 billion in 1988.

There has also been progress in managing the external debt. Morocco's total medium- and long-term debt, according to the World Bank, totalled $19.9 billion in 1988. Other sources, such as the Banque Nationale de Paris, indicate that total external debt, including short-term debt, was a little over $21 billion in 1988. This would make Morocco's external debt slightly greater than its total gross domestic product. However, repayments have been relatively well-managed because of successive reschedulings. These have stretched payments out over a longer period of time and greatly reduced the amount of new loans, especially those from commercial banks. In October 1988, the Paris Club rescheduled principal and interest payments totalling $936 million from June 1988 to December 1989.

In return for a breathing space in the form of stretched out debt payments, Morocco has made considerable changes in its economy and increasingly turned to the World Bank for new financing. An example of this was in August 1988 the IMF arranged a $271 million stand-by credit for sixteen months, which was followed in December by a World Bank Structural Adjustment Loan of $200 million. Although there remains room for improvement in the structure of the economy and the potential for slippage continues to exist, World Bank loans and the Moroccan government's reforms have gone a long way to change the economy.

Morocco, like a majority of Middle Eastern nations, continues to face the pressure of rapid population growth. According to the World Bank, Morocco's population will increase by 73.3 per cent by the year 2000, reaching 30 million. While continued population pressure will weigh heavily on the country, there will also be concern about the threat of protectionism on the part of the European Community, which is Morocco's largest market.

In the 1990s, protectionism in European markets could jeopardize Morocco's export growth model and make much of the structural adjustment meaningless. Morocco and other countries will thus be forced to look beyond national frontiers in developing economic policies, especially if they are heavily indebted. The possibility that the US Brady Plan (official debt policy) will be successfully extended to Morocco carried with it great significance not only for that country, but also for non-Latin American debtors in the developing world. In early 1990, Morroco was voicing cautious optimism that it would be able to secure a satisfactory degree of debt reduction under the Brady Plan for its $4.1 billion in commercial bank debt, and an agreement was concluded in April.

For Iran and Iraq the Gulf War, which began in 1980, was an additional factor that ravaged their respective economies. A few brief comments about Iran and Iraq are merited because of their size as two of the region's largest countries and significant military power. In the great slowdown of oil prices, Iran and Iraq ran an exceedingly costly war: according to Vahan Zanoyan, a director of The Petroleum Finance Company, the war cost Iraq up to $90 billion in lost oil and non-oil revenues and Iran around $30 billion of earnings. Zanoyan estimated the total cost of the war itself close to $150 billion for Iraq and nearly $70 billion for Iran.

The London-based Economist Intelligence Unit estimated Iraq's total external debt at around $80 billion in 1987, a daunting amount of money despite much of it being at concessionary terms. Iraq's emergence as a significant debtor nation was the result of two factors: its decision to launch a full-scale war with Iran in September 1980 and its subsequent decision that despite the enormous costs of the war, it would continue to maintain comparatively high standards of living for its people. As a result, the eight years of fighting watched Iraq run up some substantial commercial debts as well as major military debts owed to such arms suppliers as French and the Soviet Union. In 1983, it began rescheduling its Western commercial debt, and further reschedulings were carried out regularly thereafter. At various stages, Iraq was in real or technical default on loans guaranteed by most of the major Western export credit agencies. In the case of Iraq, the World Bank may begin looking at the resumption of programs, particularly in the fields of water supply and irrigation, senior officials said in late 1988. The World Bank, however, has waited to see if the country is truly at peace and if its staff can secure the financial information required to draw up loan agreements. As of mid-1989, the Iraqis have been highly reluctant to disclose accurate information concerning the true state of the country's finances.

One last figure to consider in the cases of Iraq and Iran is how much money will be required to rebuild both economies; probably over $100 billion. Considering the relatively low prices for oil, both countries will be forced to seek new capital. Iran remains in better shape because its external debt is under $10 billion, but the constitution, with its interpretation of Islam's ban on usury, hinders borrowing. The combination of war and lower oil prices has left two of the Middle East's largest powers in dire need of new funds for reconstruction and Iraq with an onerous debt burden. Iran, with its considerably lower debt and prompt record of payments, is likely to become increasingly attractive to lenders despite its decidedly anti-Western rhetoric and policies.

Libya with $3.5 billion in external debt (1986) has also been affected by a combination of factors, that include lower oil prices, gross economic mismanagement of oil wealth and hostility from the United States. The last led to the evacuation of US nationals working in the North African country and the bombing of Tripoli in 1986. This combination of factors and US-inspired economic pressures were reflected in the external accounts. In 1980, Libya's current account was in a substantial $8.2 billion surplus; in 1981 due in part to US pressure the current account had swung into a $3.9 billion deficit. Exports had fallen from $21.9 billion to $14.7 billion, while imports had increased from $10.4 billion to $14.6 billion.

Libya's days of oil wealth were over and the government was forced to take austerity measures. These included import compression: imports fell from 1981's $14.6 billion to $5.7 billion in 1985. It also meant the suspension of 300 'non-essential' foreign contracts in February 1985 that had been placed with European companies. Cash shortages resulted in the military being paid two or three months late, while shortages of consumer goods and certain foods meant lengthy queues. In August 1985 the Libyan government took the further step of expelling 38,000 foreign workers, including 25,000 Tunisians and 6,000 Egyptians. The Libyan economy was deeply troubled and political complications, ranging from ongoing tensions with the United States and a protracted war in neighboring Chad, greatly limited the regime's ability to tap international credit markets or increase oil exports.

One of the most recent and dramatic examples of the debt crisis afflicting a Middle Eastern country is Algeria in the late 1980s. Algeria was amongst the Middle Eastern countries most grievously hit by the oil price crash of 1986. Whereas the rest of its Arab colleagues in OPEC have considerably smaller populations - and vastly higher potential per capita hydrocarbons income - Algeria has a large population and, in OPEC terms, a relatively low level of oil and gas revenues. The Algerians were more prudent than many OPEC countries and ceased to take on substantial fresh borrowing from 1980-81 onwards. Between 1982 and 1985, Algeria managed to keep its total foreign debt at around $16-17 billion. But fresh borrowing was needed to offset at least some of the virtual halving of oil revenues from 1985 to 1986. By the end of 1988, Algerian external debt was approaching the $24 billion mark, although considerable progress had been made on reducing the budget deficit, so that it was only 2.1 per cent of GDP, compared with 3.8 per cent in 1988. But there were riots over planned austerity measures in early October 1988 in Algeria's major cities, including the capital, Algiers, and the second largest city of Oran. Although there were austerity-related riots in 1986, the October riots were the most violent demonstrations seen in the country in two decades. Extensive damage was caused to government buildings, shops and cars, over 200 people died, and a state of siege was imposed.

Algeria's October 1988 riots illustrated the limits to which debtor countries could go to meet the austerity demanded of them by international lenders. The substantial economic restructuring undertaken by President Chadli Ben Jedid in the late 1980s, which in 1988 was coupled with significant liberalization of the political process, should make it easier for Algeria to generate the wealth needed to meet its debt obligations. But such liberal, free-market economic restructurings usually take time to work, and while they are being implemented, such measures often make it difficult for the poorer people to get the cash they need for basic goods. The October riots were thus a reminder to both Ben Jedid and his country's creditors that successful economic liberalization can be jeopardized if it is not accompanied by effective debt relief.

Algeria's problems however, are deeper than falling oil prices and the need for debt relief. With a population growth rate of 3 per cent there has been concern about the heavy pressure on education and employment opportunities. More than three-quarters of the country's 23 million inhabitants are under thirty years of age and in Algiers unemployment is estimated (unofficially) at around 40 per cent of the work force. The government has sought to deal with the situation by economic diversification with both export-expansion and job creation. The government, which dominates the economy, was burdened by a number of inefficient state industries and caught between sharply falling foreign income (down from $13 billion in 1985 to $8 billion in 1988) and the difficult task of diversifying exports quick enough to make a difference. Another element in the Algerian calculus is political: in the late 1980s the differences between the majority of the population and the nomenclatura, which includes the party, bureaucracy and military, are more evident. For Algeria, the debt crisis continues to loom over the political and economic landscape, casting a long shadow over the future development of the country and the government's ability to implement reforms and make a durable and meaningful political opening.

Another large Middle Eastern debtor is Israel. The longstanding nature of confrontation with the Arab world has greatly complicated Israel's economic situation: the society remains at a high state of military preparedness which has put a considerable drain on expenditures. Israel's total external debt of $26 billion is substantial and if the country could not count on the largesse of the United States it would have already undergone numerous reschedulings. The annual amount of US financial aid, at $1.2 billion (given as a cash grant), has been a tremendous help in keeping the economy going. Moreover, generous military aid of $1.8 billion is also provided and between 1987 and 1989 Israel was able to convert a substantial portion of its $25 billion military debt to the US from loans bearing interest of up to 15 per cent to loans of between 9.0 and 9.5 per cent. All US aid to Israel since the mid-1980s has been effectively been on a grant basis.

In the early 1980s Israel was plagued by out-of-control inflation that reached 445 per cent in 1984. The 1985 Economic Stabilization Program, managed with substantial US aid, succeeded in reducing inflation down to around 20 per cent in 1986. However, progress in 1987 (such as a 5.2 per cent growth rate) was neutralized in 1988 by increased military and police expenditures, a slump in tourism, and boycotts in the West Bank and Gaza Strip, all related to the Palestinian uprising. The work slowdowns and strikes have hurt the construction sector and the Israeli economy continues to be highly dependent on the United States for its economic survival. Although the economy is in need of structural change, the ongoing nature of the Arab-Israeli struggle and the difficulty in arriving at a political consensus continue to guarantee that economic reforms will not make any lasting transformations.

Four other countries that deserve brief mention are North Yemen, Jordan, Syria and Tunisia. For the first, the discovery of oil and the startup in oil exports have so far played a largely compensatory role for other lost revenue sources in North Yemeni financial affairs. The oil came on stream just as oil prices were falling in late 1985, prompting a shakeout in the major Gulf states, notably Saudi Arabia, that employ Yemenis. Consequently, although remittances fell, the newly tapped oil exports compensated and the overall financial situation remained relatively unchanged. The World Bank noted in 1988 that the resumption of strong economic growth would require both external assistance and the urgent reform of the economy to diversify production, promote exports, restrain public expenditure and exploit the country's mineral resources.

Jordan continued to feel the reduction of foreign aid throughout the slowdown of the 1980s. Growth was limited to an average of 2 per cent and unemployment rose to 8 per cent. Reduced prices for imports and a better-than-expected flow of remittances helped the country avoid further strain on its balance of payments. Although Jordan's debt service, according to the World Bank, in 1988 remains at a modest 13 per cent of exports, the total external debt burden of around $5.5 billion has heavily leveraged the country's future and forced it into a rescheduling in 1989. Jordan's financial straits resulted in serious rioting in the southern town of Maan in April 1989, which, together with widespread middle-class unrest, prompted King Hussein to call for the country's first parliamentary general elections since the loss of the West Bank in 1967. In the short run, the liberalisation of the system alleviated political and economic pressures, but the considerable success of Islamic candidates in the November elections meant Jordan entered 1990 with unresolved tensions between the King and new democratic forces.

Jordan also benefited from prompt World Bank, Arab and US assistance in mid-1989. This encompassed food aid and short-term finance, which gave King Hussein room for manoeuvre in the run up to rescheduling. However, the Kingdom's underlying financial weaknesses were demonstrated by problems concerning Petra Bank, which was once the country's largest private bank. That institution effectively came under government control in 1989. The Petra Bank crisis severely undermined Jordan's reputation for sound financial management. As it entered the 1990s, the government was clearly seeking to show its ability to manage a sound economy in straitened circumstances. It remained hampered by lingering political and economic concerns. The Kingdom's viability was ultimately dependent on two main factors: a peaceful resolution to the Israel-Palestinian dispute involving its former West Bank territories and the continued health of the King himself.

The World Bank has a tactful phrase to describe Syria's financial plight. It is, the World Bank has declared in recent years, 'not currently in a position to make use of the Bank's resources.' World Bank officials remain extremely concerned at Syrian finances, commenting in private that increased Syrian oil revenues will be of little use unless the economic direction of the country is drastically overhauled. In comparison with many other countries, Syria's external non-military debt of $4.9 (1988) billion is not large. However, the wide range of structural problems with the Syrian economy, shows the country will have substantial repayment dilemmas in the 1990s. One estimate indicated that there were severe cuts in the personal incomes of two main pillars of the regime between 1983 and 1988. Ordinary civil servants suffered substantial declines in incomes, while soldiers' real incomes may have fallen by as much as two-thirds.

The outlook for the 1990s is affected by two contradictory factors. First, new oil fields, bearing high quality light crude suitable for export, began coming on stream in 1988 and 1989 and will provide badly needed foreign exchange. Second, Syria's dismal record in using previous foreign assistance, raises serious questions about its ability to capitalise on its new found resources. Moreover, it will have problems attracting badly needed expertise for developing non-oil sectors of the economy. This problem is compounded by increased Soviet caution on provided aid to Syria. As Syria entered the 1990s, there were strong indications of a changed international outlook, epitomised by improved relations with Egypt, but it was difficult to imagine that the institutional framework could accommodate a significant economic liberalisation internally. Considering the rigid ruling power structure of President Assad and the regime's dependence on the armed forces, significant change within the regime will be slow. In addition, Syria enters the 1990s with a new and very real problem affecting both its economy and its foreign policy. Heightened tensions with Turkey, over Syrian support for Kurdish nationalist gunmen, prompted Ankara to threaten to reduce water supplies to Syria in late 1989. Syria is very heavily dependent on the Euphrates and its tributaries for both irrigation and hydropower. By September 1989, however, its massive Soviet-built Euphrates Dam was generating only one-tenth of its potential hydropower, while Turkey was announcing the start of a massive programme to fill up the lake behind its own Ataturk Dam. Tensions over water resources could well lead potential investors to take a highly sceptical look at Syrian prospects in the 1990s.

Tunisia's emergence from the fading bureaucratic and increasingly autocratic guidance of founder-President Habib Bourguiba, into the more liberal era of President Zine al-Abidine Ben Ali has significantly improved the prospects for renewed US and international assistance to ease its debt burden. Even in Bourguiba's waning years, Tunisia was considered a real prospect for essentially non-oil generated economic development. Like Jordan, it was considered to have conducted its financial and economic affairs with some prudence and, like Jordan, this was probably an exaggeration. But Tunisia's reputation did enable it to put together a significant relief package in late 1986, when its finances were severely strained by the need for debt repayments at a time of weaker than expected economic growth. Tunisia managed to secure an eighteen-month standby credit from the IMF worth $110.3 million; it also garnered $139 million under the Fund's compensatory finance facility, and $150 million from the World Bank to curb its agricultural deficit, together with lesser loans to boost international exports. The agricultural loan was the largest single loan ever to have been granted to Tunisia and was equivalent to around the total sum of World Bank funds that the country usually receives in a full year. Tunisia's total external debt at the end of 1988 was $6.7 billion.

Military debt

For the Middle East in particular, there is another aspect of external debt to be considered: military debt. The region contains five of the world's biggest military debtors - Egypt, Iraq, Israel, Syria and Pakistan. The number rises if Turkey is also considered to be a Middle Eastern country. As of early 1989, Egypt still owed some $4.5 billion in principal on military loans supplied by the United States before 1985, when US military aid was effectively placed on a grant basis. This aid carried interest totalling around $9.8 billion according to 1986 estimates by the US General Accounting Office.

Moreover, Egypt was believed to owe other countries at least $4 billion in military debt. In March 1987, an agreement was concluded with the Soviet Union to repay an estimated $43 million in military debts over a twenty-five-year period. The size of this debt appeared to have been substantially scaled down from the estimated $7–8.5 billion believed outstanding in the mid-1970s. There have been suggestions that Moscow acquiesced in a recalculation of the debt, to reflect exchange rate revisions, simply in order to tidy up an outstanding diplomatic problem at a time when it wished to improve relations with Egypt.

In the case of Syria, however, the Soviet Union was showing signs in early 1989 of taking a tougher approach. Total Soviet military debt to Moscow was estimated by some US sources at that time as being around $15 billion - although even this could prove to be an underestimate. Syria's impoverishment, however, meant there was little prospect of getting its cash back, unless it was prepared to use major pressure to ensure that some of Syria's anticipated oil-generated wealth in the 1990s flowed in Moscow's direction.

When the United States moved in the mid-1980s to place all its $3 billion a year military and economic assistance to Israel on a grant basis, Israel was already in the uncomfortable position of being Washington's largest single military debtor. According to the General Accounting Office of the US Congress, Israel received no less than $19.7 billion in US military sales loans between 1950 and 1985. The overwhelming majority of this was run up in the years 1974–84, and although some $8.4 billion was at various stages forgiven, by 1986 Israel was still accounted to owe the United States no less than $25.5 billion in principal and interest due on military loans.

Israel's plight prompted a sympathetic US government and Congress to attempt to find ways of easing this burden. Concern also prompted by the fact that loans taken out by Israel - and by Egypt - in the years following the Camp David Accords of 1978 were at very high rates of interest, commonly amounting to 13 or 14 per cent, and sometimes even more. By autumn 1988, Israel was able to take advantage of a new US scheme under which the US government would guarantee 90 per cent of replacement loans, if the debtor country could find commercial banks willing to provide the remaining 10 per cent. Israel was able to raise $4.5 billion in this way - with interest rates averaging around 9.3 per cent - and in early 1989 was contemplating a further replacement in this fashion of some more of its earlier US military debt.

Jordan was also understood to be actively interested in reducing the amount of its military debt repayments in this manner. But there were few signs that Egypt, expected to be one of the main beneficiaries of the scheme, was likewise seeking to follow suit. Indeed there was some concern in US financial circles that Egypt's lack of interest in the scheme shows that Cairo was seeking a far more ambitious approach to debt reduction, namely outright forgiveness of part or all of its military debt burden.

With Iraq, a very basic question has to be asked: when is debt no longer to be reckoned as debt? Iraq borrowed at least $30 billion from Saudi Arabia, and perhaps a further $10 billion from other Arab Gulf countries, to help finance its twin policies of guns and butter during the eight years of open warfare with Iran from 1980–88. These sums represent a considerable proportion of the country's total debt. According to the testimony given to Congress by the US military, Iraq's total debts as of early 1989 totalled as much as $85 billion. Financial sources more usually estimate it around $50–60 billion - including the Saudi and Gulf loans. However, there is little expectation amongst either Western banking circles or specialist analysts of the Middle East that Saudi Arabia and its colleagues in the Gulf Cooperation Council will ever get their money back.

Whether Saudi Arabia will even attempt to reach a face-saving formula over these enormous subventions remains a key issue. If it does not, then a precedent will have been established for Egypt and Morocco to withhold payments on their debts to Saudi Arabia. Although figures remain imprecise, it is generally believed that Saudi Arabia has provided as much as $5 billion in total to these countries - the bulk of this going to Cairo. As Egypt's reintegration into the Arab mainstream continued in 1989, there was talk of fresh Saudi loans, perhaps geared to the revitalization the Egyptian munitions industry.

Conclusion

The debt crisis in the Middle East has not been a widespread problem in the 1980s as it has been elsewhere in the developing world. Although a small number of states were forced to reschedule, the majority have not. However, the fall in oil prices in the mid-1980s caused the region to undergo an economic slowdown. This prompted wild fluctuations in the revenues of the principal oil exporting countries to the extent that between late 1985 and early 1989 they were denied any ability to prepare realistic annual budgets.

As the Middle East entered the 1990s, the most important single factor affecting the region's finances was the prospect of renewed oil price stability. Power within OPEC was clearly moving towards a small cluster of Gulf states - Saudi Arabia, Iraq, Kuwait and the United Arab Emirates - able to increase capacity in the early 1990s to meet anticipated demand increases, mainly from Asian NICs. The question, however, was whether the cost of expanding capacity to meet a hypothetical need for increased sustained production would exceed the value gained from higher export revenues. Significantly, Iran was not one of these core nations and, lacking the capital for rapid capacity expansion, its influence on oil matters seemed likely to be limited for a few years.

The return of reasonably stable oil prices, together with modest prospects for a slow but steady improvement in the 1990s, will ease the position not only for the oil-exporters, but also for countries closely linked to them. Jordan, Syria and the Yemens stand to benefit, but prospects for Egypt are not as positive, since Baghdad has made it clear it no longer favours the presence of a massive Egyptian workforce in Iraq. The 1990s are likely to witness ongoing problems in debt management in Egypt and Iraq. With their substantial foreign indebtedness, they remain in need of new capital to repay old commitments and to implement development programs. Egypt has the greatest potential for explosive political turmoil: the needs of its population is beyond the state's capacity. Without outside largesse, circumstances would be bleak.

Throughout the region, all countries will be forced to contend with the need to maintain higher economic growth to keep pace or ahead of population expansion. In large part, this will entail structural adjustment in regional economies as most are inward-looking or dependent on one or two export commodities. As a group the Middle Eastern states will require both economic reform and new infusions of capital to maintain and upgrade industrial and agricultural infrastructures and to expand into new areas.

The Middle East's ongoing political tensions on a number of fronts - Arab-Israeli, Syrian-Turkish, Iran-Iraq, will also mean continued heavy expenditure on military equipment. It is the last that could help push up external debts in a number of countries, many poorly suited to bear the costs as in the cases of Egypt and Jordan. In the 1990s, the Middle East's problems with debt could be more political than economic and economic reforms will always operate under such a cloud.

References

Abdelnour, Ziad, 'Arab Banks and the LDC Debt Crisis', *Arab American Affairs*, Issue No. 27, Winter 1988-1989, Washington.

The Economist, 'Out of the Gulf's rubble', 20 August, 1988.

The Economist Intelligence Unit, *World Outlook 1989*. London: The Economist Intelligence Unit, January 1989.

International Monetary Fund, *International Financial Statistics Year Book 1987* Washington, D.C.: International Monetary Fund, 1987.

Keesings' Contemporary Archives, vol. XXXII, 1986.

Rhazaoui, Ahmed, 'Recent Economic Trends: Managing the Indebtedness', in I. William Zartman (ed.), *The Political Economy of Morocco* New York: Praeger, 1987.

World Bank, *World Debt Tables: External Debt of Developing Countries, Vol. III. Country Tables, 1970–1979*. Washington, D.C.: World Bank, 1989.

World Bank, *World Development Report 1988*. Washington, D.C.: Oxford University Press, 1989.

Chapter 5

Sub-Saharan Africa

David L. Crum

The African continent is often overlooked when the international debt crisis is examined. Although certain countries such as Nigeria or Zaire occasionally get attention, the focus is usually on the Philippines, Latin America and Eastern Europe. This emphasis is reasonable from the perspective of those in the creditor countries, because it is in the Brazils, Mexicos and Polands where the heaviest concentrations of debt dollars lie.

From the opposite side of the coin, the perspective of the debtor countries, greater emphasis on Africa is merited. The absolute amounts owed by the African nations are usually less than those found elsewhere, but the relative weight of that debt on their economies is at least as great as that on Latin America. Nor are the effects of the debt service burden and the reduction of new disbursements on the development process any less devastating. Between the man-made and natural crises of the debt squeeze and the drought that plagued much of the continent for several years, many observers view the 1980s as a lost decade for Africa with living standards slipping back to the levels of the 1960s.

This chapter does look at the international debt crisis in Sub-Saharan Africa or Black Africa ('Africa') from the flip side of that coin. It reviews some of the political, economic and financial elements of the African countries which have a bearing on this issue. It describes the present state of foreign debt in terms of its magnitude, creditor composition and orientation. Additionally, it discusses the recent historical process which brought Africa to its current state. Several countries will be examined to highlight some of the key issues facing the African nations. A final point for consideration will be the interrelated issues of the prospects and the strategy options for dealing with Africa's own version of the international debt crisis.

This region contains a large number of political states, many of them inheriting boundaries and infrastructures that reflect more the imperial needs of their erstwhile colonial powers than those of the newly independent countries. The area being considered in this chapter contains some forty-five mainland and island countries from the Saharan desert south to the border of the Republic of South Africa.

Because of the number and diversity of the states involved, it will not be possible to review each one or even each one with a significant debt burden. Rather common variables and prospects will be examined with individual examples drawn upon as proves useful. Four countries will be considered briefly to illustrate issues important to all of Africa: Sudan highlights the chronic debt difficulties of a number of the poorest nations. Nigeria reveals the impact that poor internal political choices have on the debt picture. The Côte d'Ivoire illustrates how external factors can contribute to financial problems despite adherence to the structural adjustment regimen prescribed by the international development and monetary agencies. Kenya has been able to manage its external debt without rescheduling, but portrays the difficulties of attracting alternative sources of capital for development. South Africa's level of development, integration with western economies, and its apartheid system of white minority rule set it apart from the rest of Africa and outside the scope of this chapter. (South Africa is discussed in Chapter 6.)

Social, economic, and political characteristics

Several of Africa's social, economic and political characteristics set the stage for a discussion of the current debt picture. The first is the depth and breadth of poverty throughout the continent. The second is the dominance of subsistence, agricultural and commodity production and the weakness of the industrial base. And the third is the importance of financial support from the industrial nations.

The prevalence of poverty is impossible to ignore in a discussion about Africa. According to the World Bank, almost two-thirds of the countries included in its poorest 'low-income economies' bracket are African. In contrast, Africa accounts for one-fifth of the 'lower-middle-income economies' in the next earnings level, only one of the eighteen 'upper-middle-income economies', and none of the 'high-income economies'. Africa has an average per capita income of $330 compared with $700 for the entire developing world[1].

Unfortunately the average African's income has been growing at a snail's pace, and has even been negative in a number of countries, giving credence to the notion of a lost African decade. The region's real economic growth per capita was only 0.6 per cent during the years from 1965 to 1987. And thirteen African states with a population of 153.0 million actually showed a negative per capita figure over that twenty-two-year span.

Of course, poverty is not just a financial phenomenon. Social and health statistics help provide an indication of its broad scope. On a world scale, low-income nations had one physician for each 5,772 people in 1980, but low-income Africa had less than one-quarter of that number with a ratio of one to 27,607. Apparently the need for doctors is being met in many cases by nursing personnel which are more prevalent in low-income Africa where they numbered one for every 3,404 people compared with one to 4,841 worldwide. While the ratio of both physicians and nurses has improved 100 per cent in Africa between 1960 and 1980, their numbers still pale compared to the industrial world where the respective ratios are one to 554 and one to 180.

These medical professionals are desperately needed to serve the fastest growing and youngest population in the world, one that is expanding at a 3.2 per cent annual rate and will increase from 443 million in 1987 to 659 million by the turn of the century. In 1981, the African diet provided just 90 per cent of the daily caloric requirement compared with the 97 per cent for all low-income countries. The mortality rate for African children between the ages of one and four has been cut almost in half in the twenty-two years to 1982, but was still 23 per 1,000 about double the rest of the developing world. Nor are these children receiving a comparable level of education to develop the human capital required for development. Just 69 per cent of the eligible children were enrolled in primary school in low-income Africa in 1980 compared to 94 per cent in the low-income world.

The African economy is dominated by subsistence agriculture and commodity production. The region has lacked the industrial base required to provide much value-added to its raw materials. This reality reflects in large part the place of the African colonies in the imperial system. They were the providers of the energy and raw materials to fuel the industrial economies of Europe. This lack of industrial capability and concomitant reliance on commodity production may not have appeared too insidious in the period of run-up of resource prices which culminated in the twin OPEC prices shocks of 1973 and 1980–81. However since that latter date, the weakness in commodity prices, accelerating desertification, and several years of severe drought has compounded the disadvantages inherent in a reliance on primary commodities.

Agriculture accounts for fully 33 per cent of African gross domestic product (GDP) in 1987 compared with 28 per cent for industry. No other region shares this dominance of agriculture and outside the region only Bangladesh, Bhutan, Nepal and Papua New Guinea exceed the African average. The importance of food and resource production also is striking in the structure of merchandise exports. In 1987, fuels, minerals, metals, agricultural goods and other primary commodities accounted for 88 per cent of these exports, only a four percentage point drop from 1965. On the other hand, 74 per cent of imports were of machinery, transport equipment and other manufactures.

Because of the low income level through the continent, Africa needs and receives a high level of foreign aid both in the form of grants and concessional loans. These ‘soft’ credits typically carry below-market (or even negative inflation-adjusted) interest rates, long repayment terms, and extended ‘grace’ periods when no principal repayment is due. According to the World Bank, net disbursements of official development assistance accounted for fully 8.3 per cent of African GNP in 1987.

There are political considerations for the donors themselves which increase Africa's attractiveness as an aid recipient beyond its evident need for such assistance. One is that as Africa is the most recent continent to gain independence from European colonial powers, many countries maintain and sometime have broadened their extensive ties with their former rulers. This is particularly evident in regard to France which continues to supply military aid, budgetary assistance and currency support to most of its former West and Central African empire. These ties can provide the donor country with an unique foreign policy role independent of its place in the post-Second World War alliance structure. Improving African incomes helps restrict immigration of former colonial subjects into donor countries where sluggish job creation is already a problem. At a time when international trade flows appear to be characterized increasingly by regional trading blocs and restrictions on manufactured goods, these ties often help maintain markets for Europe's industrial products. Another attraction is that many recent African military conflicts have been perceived as part of the surrogate war between East and West. Nonetheless, it can be argued that in most cases superpower rivalries have been superimposed on what are truly local conflicts. The case of warring Ethiopia and Somalia - who actually swapped superpower mentors - gives pause in assessing the depth of many nations' true commitment to either the US vision of capitalism or the Soviet model of communism. In any event, the combatants have attracted large sums of military and civilian assistance.

Many political characteristics also weave a common thread among African countries. First, these states are among the newest independent nations in the world and have the most recent memories of colonial status. While there are some exceptions - such as Ethiopia, Liberia and South Africa which were already at least nominally independent - almost all African nations gained independence from European rule in the last three decades. This process began with the British colony of Gold Coast when it became the independent nation of Ghana in 1957 and continued most recently with the end of Portuguese rule in Angola, Mozambique and Guinea-Bissau in the 1970s. Most Asian and North African nations gained independence from western rule by the close of the 1950s. And the majority of Latin American countries broke away from Spain and Portugal in the first half of the nineteenth century.

While nations such as France and Britain brought indigenous African leaders into the process of colonial government to some degree, few of these new countries possessed an adequate depth and breadth of political leadership at independence. The impact of this inexperience was exacerbated by the problems which most of these fledgling nations faced: border disputes brought about by boundaries that often did not reflect tribal, religious, linguistic or geographic realities (even when the maps were well defined); infrastructures (in cases where they were not deliberately destroyed such as by the Portuguese in Angola) which reflected colonial rather than national structures; and a low level of economic development and welfare.

This lack of experience in self-governance by the population and their would-be leaders goes a long way towards explaining the general lack of true western-style democratic government in the continent. Even though the major colonial powers of Britain and France had long-established multi-party parliamentary traditions, most African nations chose a more autocratic form of government. Often this was imposed via a dictatorship (supported by the military, often the sector with the most organisational training and experience), but when the franchise was extended there usually was only one viable political party; thus compromises are made within cliques or parties rather than by popular decision. These political systems increase the opportunities for corruption and cronyism (that goes beyond tribal loyalties) which have become endemic in several countries.

This pattern of government has implications for management of the debt crisis. Because constituents usually do not choose their rulers, the governments frequently feel compelled to buy the support of the urban populace with pricing, foreign exchange and resource policies. As a result, the interests of the scattered and politically weak rural population is subjugated creating disincentives for agricultural production. These same policies are key roadblocks to the economic reform needed to grow out of the debt crisis. When the governments try to take these subsidies away, the urban population expresses its views through the only available mechanisms: violence or flouting the unpopular laws. Since most states lack the means to effectively control widespread and sustained public discontent, meaningful policy changes often are held hostage to urban opinion that is often uninformed about and alienated from the overall interests of the nation. Despite the high economic cost which they incur by attempting to placate the urban populace, Africa governments remain the least stable in the world with several ongoing civil wars and over seventy coups attempts of varying success in the last twenty-five years.

The present picture of external debt

The total debt over by African nations to foreign creditors in 1987 is estimated at $118.3 billion (including Nigeria's $26.65 billion debt). According to Table 5.1 below which uses International Monetary Fund (IMF) statistics on 'Sub-Saharan Africa' ('SSA'), total debt in 1989 was $103.8 billion excluding that of Nigeria. This represented more than a doubling from the $48.5 billion level of 1981, and the Fund expects these liabilities to grow to $113.9 billion in 1989. In 1989, this debt represented 8 per cent of all external debt of the developing countries. That percentage has been rising slowly through the decade, reflecting in part the progress in debt reduction or deceleration made by some non-African debtors. Almost all (92 per cent in 1989) SSA debt is long

Table 5.1 Sub-Saharan African external debt by maturity (in billions of dollars)*

Year Compared total	Short-term	Long-term	Total	Compared to LDC total
1981	5.0	43.6	48.5	6.5%
1982	5.3	48.4	53.7	6.3%
1983	5.0	51.0	56.0	6.2%
1984	4.8	53.8	58.6	6.2%
1985	6.0	62.7	68.8	6.7%
1986	6.6	73.0	79.5	7.1%
1987	7.4	85.3	92.7	7.5%
1988	7.7	89.2	96.9	7.8%
1989(e)	8.0	95.8	103.8	8.1%
1990(f)	8.8	105.1	113.9	8.5%

*Excludes Nigeria.
N.B. (e) indicates estimate; (f) indicates forecast.
Source: IMF, *World Economic Outlook: A Survey by the Staff of the International Monetary Fund [April 1989]* (Washington, D.C.: The Fund, 1989), pp. 187, 190

Table 5.2 Sub-Saharan African external debt relative to exports and gross domestic product* (in per cent)

Year	Compared to exports		Compared to GDP	
	Africa	All LDCs	Africa	All LDCs
1981	178.6	95.8	45.2	27.8
1982	212.5	120.0	51.0	31.0
1983	225.3	134.8	53.4	32.8
1984	221.6	134.3	57.8	34.1
1985	269.6	150.8	66.0	36.0
1986	300.6	170.8	72.2	38.1
1987	328.2	158.7	69.0	37.7
1988	331.0	141.9	69.1	35.6
1989*	330.8	132.1	71.9	33.7
1990′	338.2	126.6	72.6	32.3

* Excludes Nigeria. Exports are exports of goods and services.
Source: IMF, *World Economic Outlook*, op. cit., pp. 192–3

term compared with 84 per cent for all developing nations. This difference reflects is largely a reflection of the mix of creditors and the greater reliance on development financing[2].

When Africa's debt is compared to its total and external economies, the true magnitude of the burden of that debt on the continent becomes clear (see Table 5.2). In 1988, SSA's external debt was equivalent to 331 per cent of the exports of goods and services and 69 per cent of GDP. This compares to 142 and 36 per cent respectively for all developing countries. The trend of these ratios is also worrisome. Developing country debt as a proportion of exports peaked at 171 per cent in 1987 and is projected to decline to 127 per cent in 1990; by contrast, the African ratio is still increasing and should reach 338 per cent by the latter year. The picture for debt as a proportion of the domestic economy is comparable: developing nations moderating from the 1986 peak of 38 per cent, but SSA edging upwards again after plateauing at 69 per cent in 1987–8.

The weight of foreign debt lies roughly twice as heavy on African domestic economies as on the developing world as a whole. Given the poor standards of living and stagnant economic performance discussed earlier, it is clear that it is these African countries which are among the least able to handle that debt burden. In fact this region of the world is perhaps the one most in need of growth stimuli to correct the existing problems and to compensate for the expected annual 3.1 per cent expansion in Africa's population in the years 1987–2000.

The debt to exports ratio is a key to understanding the growth the Africa's external debt and the ensuing crisis. As the IMF's Eduard Brau noted in 1986, the tale of Africa's debt crisis can be summarised by the doubling of its ratio of debt to exports in the five years to 1983 and the sharp worsening of the debt service ratio between 1980 and 1985. For the lowest income African nations, he added, this 'deterioration is without parallel among any other country grouping, including the large commercial borrowers in Latin America'.

Table 5.3 Debt service ratios (in per cent)

Year	Africa	All LDCs	Baker Plan 15
1981	20.3	16.2	40.7
1982	22.5	19.7	51.9
1983	21.9	18.6	41.8
1984	23.8	20.0	41.7
1985	26.5	21.3	40.7
1986	26.1	23.0	45.3
1987	23.4	20.3	35.5
1988	23.4	19.6	39.6
1989(e)	23.3	18.9	40.8
1990(f)	25.4	17.5	39.7

* SSA excludes Nigeria.
N.B. (e) indicated estimate; (f) indicates forecast.
Source: IMF, *World Economic Outlook*, op. cit., p. 194

Africa's debt service ratio[3] was about 1.2 times higher than that for the developing world in 1988 see Table 5.3) and the gap between the two is increasing. Although the debt payment burden faced by the fifteen middle-income debtors addressed by the 'Baker Plan' (including

Cote d'Ivoire and Nigeria) is even heavier, their ratios are moderating from a 1982 peak while the African debt service ratios are still rising. Although analysis of each case is necessary, a rule-of-thumb has been that a debt service ratio of 20 per cent or more signalled a potential rescheduling. By the IMF's statistics, Africa's debt service ratio has been running above that warning level since 1981.

However the limitations of the debt service statistic mask the full extent of the problem. A World Bank Staff Working Paper explained that when past due interest and principal is included in an examination of repayment burdens, the short-term debt service picture is 'even more dismal'. In 1984, the African debt service would have jumped $4.3 billion or 45 per cent if all arrears were repaid, even without considering Nigeria's commercial payments backlog of $4.6 billion. African Development Bank (ADB) President Babacar N'Diaye pointed out further limitations of the statistic: the debt service ratio was about 30 per cent in 1985, but if payments of short-term debt, arrears and IMF credit were included, the ratios for many African countries would escalate to 50 or even 100 per cent.

Table 5.4 Structure of long-term debt by creditor type* (in per cent of total debt)

Year LDCs	Africa Official	Africa Banks	Africa Other private	All LDCs Official
1981	65.4	22.2	12.2	37.0
1982	68.4	20.7	11.0	37.5
1983	69.8	19.4	11.0	37.6
1984	71.6	17.5	10.8	38.6
1985	72.2	16.3	11.5	40.2
1986	76.0	14.1	10.0	42.3
1987	77.6	13.2	9.0	45.1
1988	78.8	12.7	8.5	47.0
1989(e)	79.9	12.2	7.9	48.6
1989(f)	81.1	12.0	6.9	49.6

*SSA, excludes Nigeria.
N.B. (e) indicates estimate; (f) indicates forecast.
Source: IMF, *World Economic Outlook*, op. cit., pp. 187, 190

These debt service ratios would be even higher if it were not for the striking importance of official creditors extending credit on concessional terms. Sub-Saharan Africa looked to official creditors for over three-quarters of its borrowing in 1988, compared to less than half for all developing countries see Table 5.4; World Bank data on Africa's long-term debt through 1984 show that roughly one-half of official debt was concessional. This has four major ramifications. The first is that borrowings from official creditors tend to have lower interest rates and longer repayment schedules than commercial loans, easing the debt service burden per unit of debt. The impact of this 'soft' debt component can be illustrated by contrasting the average terms offered by official and private creditors in 1984 on new commitments of public and publicly guaranteed debt: an interest rate of 4.2 versus 10.4 per cent, a maturity of 29.2 versus 8.0 years, and a grace period during which no principal repayment would be due of 7.0 versus 1.7 years. The second ramification is that many bilateral lenders (outside of some export credit agencies) have been more sympathetic toward debt forgiveness than commercial creditors because these governments are already engaged in granting development assistance to Africa; they also may view their loan portfolio more as a policy tool than as an investment in contrast to most private lenders.

While the first two ramifications are positive, the second pair are problematic. One is that a larger proportion of external debt is ineligible for rescheduling under traditional guidelines because the World Bank and IMF are 'preferred creditors' who do not renegotiate the terms of their loans. This fact partially negates the benefit of concessional loan terms at times when even low payment cannot be met. While repayments by Africans to the World Bank are not yet large, this is not the case with scheduled repayments to the IMF which amount to more than $1.0 billion annually over the next several years. The other is that with African debt representing a relatively small part of their loan portfolio, the commercial banks tend to take a harder stance when negotiating African reschedulings. Nonetheless, the African nations probably have an even greater need for some of the concessions gained by key Latin American debtors such as rescheduling several years of maturities at a time, lower interest rates, the waiver of rescheduling fees, and lengthened grace and repayment periods.

Table 5.5 Concessional nature of long-term debt* (concessional debt as a percentage of)

Year	Total debt	Disbursements
1980	35.1	25.5
1981	34.8	26.4
1982	33.8	22.6
1983	32.8	21.0
1984	34.0	29.7

* Excludes South Africa and nine countries with less than 500,000 in population

Source: World Bank, *Toward Sustained Development in Sub-Saharan Africa* (Washington, D.C.: World Bank, 1984), pp. 81-3

Recent historical roots of the debt crisis

While the magnitude of the crisis in Africa has its roots in the characteristics discussed above, the run-up in foreign debt began in the 1970s, a decade which included short-lived commodity price booms, expanded public sector spending, and greater access to non-concessional foreign credit. The first oil price shock in 1973 set off a commodity price boom which included most of Africa's primary exports: cocoa, coffee, tea, groundnuts, sugar, sisal, phosphate and uranium. Seeing an increase in actual revenues through export duties, public marketing boards, and other taxes and projecting a continuation of this enhanced income stream, African governments increased their level of spending. To finance their new spending agendas, these states augmented their revenues with foreign bank loans which were extended on the presumption that existing relative price levels would hold.

Instead these price peaks proved transitory, moderating in the slower world economic pace of the mid-1970s. Nevertheless these countries remained committed to major development projects and current general spending levels which were financed to an increasing degree through foreign borrowing. As the World Bank's Kathie L. Krumm wrote: 'When the commodity price booms ended, most governments were reluctant to adjust their current and capital expenditures accordingly, which led to even more external borrowing.'

These new loans were extended to a much greater degree than ever before by western commercial banks rather than the traditional government or multilateral sources. These large financial institutions were looking for profitable places to reinvest the surplus funds which OPEC members had deposited in the western banking system. To these banks, a number of African governments seemed to be desirable borrowers, particularly given the appreciation of the value of their natural resources and farm products. But the new infusion of credit came at a cost: these loans carried stricter terms than those from official sources and were usually tied to an internationally-known interest rate such as the US prime lending rate or the London inter-bank offered rate (Libor). These rates 'floated' - they rose or fell in correlation with inflation and other interest rates - which placed the risk of changing interest rates on the borrowers themselves. This soon proved to be an expensive risk to bear in the inflationary cycle which coincided with the second oil price shock; the average interest rate on Africa's commercial debt rose from 9 per cent in 1973–8 to 13 per cent in 1979–82. Even when these commercial loans were extended at a 'fixed' rate of interest, new loan were pegged at the prevailing high market interest rates.

Commercial bank loans were extended for purposes which ranged from the construction of factories to roads to new capital cities. Some of the purposes were ill-suited for this type of borrowing since they could not generate the pounds, dollars or francs required to pay off the underlying loans by their typical eight-year maturity if at all. Thus the borrower was forced at the outset to rely on expanding revenue from other exports or a continued stream of fresh loans to repay these debts. In addition the anticipated proceeds from many of the apparently viable investments evaporated, falling victim to poor administration, a reliance on transitory price levels or graft.

Africa's export prices showed overall improvement in the 1970s even though commodities did not sustain the peak prices seen after the first oil shock. Ghana's cocoa price provides an illustration of this process. The London wholesale cocoa price went from an average of $0.27 (per pound) in the 1960s to $0.97 in the following decade with a peak of $2.14 in 1977. This export price betterment compensated for the sluggish (0.6 per cent annually in 1973–80) growth in the volume of merchandise exports. But in 1981 and 1983, these volumes dropped due to the international recession and the African drought. Further in 1981–2, the prices of non-oil commodity exports fell and did not fully regain their 1980 levels in 1983–4. Ghanian cocoa is again illustrative: already on a declining trend, the price bottomed out in 1982 at $0.86 and recovered to $1.16 in 1984, still short of the 1980 price of $1.27.

The relative prices of exports and imports deteriorated by an annual average of 0.9 per cent for Sub-Saharan Africa in the 1970s as import price rises (petroleum and industrial products) exceeded the 13.0 per cent annual export gain. With the 1981–2 export price slump, these 'terms of trade' fell on average 4.0 per cent both years, further eroding the purchasing power of Africa's exports. The price gains of 1983–4 were wiped out by a decline for the balance of the decade, especially by 1986s 17.1 per cent drop.

New lending to Africa slowed as worries about developing countries' economic performance were fulfilled with the 1982 Mexican moratorium and indications of debt servicing difficulties on the continent. While oil importing African nations received a boost in the form of new lending immediately after the second oil price shock, disbursements quickly fell from their 1980 peak of $6.8 billion to $5.1 billion in 1983. Not surprisingly, commercial banks nearly halved their new loans to these nations from $2.8 billion to $1.5 billion over those three years; perhaps less expected was that so did the bilateral creditors, from $2.1 billion to $1.9 billion. The slowdown in lending to oil exporters (especially Nigeria) was delayed by the lagged improvement in their trade prospects; this category boosted new drawings from $2.2 billion in 1980 to $5.3 billion in 1983, mirroring the rest of Africa's earlier commodity-based borrowing stage.

The deficit on the 'current account' of the balance of payments (which includes exports and imports of goods and services as well as private and official transfers) for Sub-Saharan Africa was widened to a low of $9.6 billion in 1981 see Table 5.6) by the unfavorable trade developments. This deficit on current transactions needed to be funded from new investment, new borrowing, or drawing on savings (in the form of 'reserves' of foreign exchange). With the slowing of new

Table 5.6 Sub-Saharan African current account balance of payments, interest payments and reserves* (in $ billions)

Year	Current account	Of which interest	reserves	Reserves' cover of imports (months)
1981	−9.6	−3.0	3.4	1.0
1982	−8.2	−3.1	2.8	0.9
1983	−5.6	−3.1	3.0	1.1
1984	−3.3	−3.7	3.1	1.1
1985	−3.3	−3.9	4.1	1.5
1986	−5.9	−4.3	5.1	1.6
1987	−6.7	−4.9	5.9	1.8
1988	−8.2	−5.6	6.3	1.7
1989(e)	−7.4	−5.6	7.4	1.9
1990(f)	−7.8	−6.0	9.8	2.4

* SSA, excludes Nigeria. Reserves to imports of goods and services in months.
N.B. (e) indicates estimate; (f) indicates forecast.
Source: IMF, *World Economic Outlook*, op. cit., pp. 170, 182–3

lending and the continued difficulty in attracting investment, reserves were drawn to a low of $2.8 billion in 1982, the equivalent of less than one month's worth of imports and roughly $300 million less than that year's foreign debt interest bill alone. Reserves were gradually rebuilt in the ensuing years, but still not to the typical comfort zone of three months' imports. Thus, there was little room for further contraction of reserves, particularly in 1982, to offset the reduction in export receipts and new loans.

By the beginning of the 1980s the prerequisites for a debt crisis were met. Debt servicing costs had escalated with the new generation of commercial bank debt which carried steeper principal repayment schedules and costlier interest charges. The ability to meet that service had deteriorated. Export receipts proved disappointing compared to the hopes engendered during the boom of the mid-1970s and recently had slumped even further. Reserves had been drawn down in that decade and now were insufficient to meet the even greater demands placed upon them. And the confidence required to induce lenders to extend fresh credit had been shaken by the deteriorating debt service ratios and shattered by the Mexican debt moratorium of 1982.

The result was to force the large majority of African nations into debt servicing difficulties in the 1980s. Not only did these countries need to limit payments on debt service, but also to reduce their imports of goods. From 1981–9, import volumes fell seven of the nine years, including a 7.9 per cent drop in 1983. Some of this reduction was certainly of luxury or non-productive items, but much of the reduction came in more vital goods such as the spare parts needed to keep existing machinery running.

In 1989, the smoldering debate over the blame for the African debt crisis was fanned into flame by the publication of a joint World Bank-United Nations Development Program (UNDP) study entitled *Africa's Adjustment and Growth in the 1980s*. The authors discerned 'a more complex, less dismal picture' in the recent economic statistics coming out of Africa: 'on average, countries where reforms have been implemented have also had better economic performance' and have attracted higher foreign aid flows which together 'appear to have helped offset unfavorable international economic conditions'.

The contention that African policy-makers who avoided World Bank and IMF-style reforms are largely responsible for the poor performance of their charges ruffled some feathers. Another arm of the UN, the Economic Commission for Africa (ECA), issued a report which took the same figures and reached the opposite conclusion. These divergent results arise largely from whether they included or excluded the oil-exporting countries (particularly Nigeria) and whether they used weighted or simple country averages. The ECA report also contends that much of the improvement found by the World Bank-UNDP is caused by the increased aid meted out to reformers rather than to the direct effects of the reforms themselves. While the quarrel continues, both sides probably could agree that realistic economic policy-making can only bring benefits to its practitioners and that it is a necessary - but not sufficient - condition for development given Africa's poor economic infrastructure. In any case, it is a sobering tribute to the tenacity of the difficulties facing Africa that the positive impacts of economic reform have not been significant enough to close all debate.

Country examples

The four countries reviewed in this section illustrate some key issues of importance to all of Africa. Sudan highlights the plight of a number of the poorest nations including the preoccupation with other concerns besides debt management. Nigeria reveals the impact that poor political choices have on the debt picture. The Cote d'Ivoire exemplifies the negative impact of international developments and the limitations of the structural adjustment regimen being proffered by the international development and monetary agencies. Kenya has been able to manage its external debt without rescheduling, but portrays the difficulties and dilemmas of attracting alternative sources of capital for development.

Sudan

Famine and civil war continue to plague this nation which has seen per capital GDP shrink by 0.2 per cent a year during the two decades to 1986. While not the poorest African nation, the Sudan is typical of

Table 5.7 1987 Summary indicators for country examples (in millions unless noted)

	Sudan	Nigeria	Côte d'Ivoire	Kenya
Population	23.1	106.6	11.1	22.1
- growth (1980-87)	3.1%	3.4%	4.2%	4.1%
GDP per capita*	$330	$370	$740	$330
- growth (1965-87)	−0.5%	1.1%	1.0%	1.9%
GDP	$8,210	$24,390	$7,650	$6,930
- growth (1980-87)	0.1%	−1.7%	2.2%	3.8%
Current account	−$422+	−$380	−$624+	−$497
Reserves	$12	$1,498	$30	$294
Official aid receipts	$902	$69	$254	$565
External debt	$11,126	$28,714	$13,555	$5,950
- to GNP	135.5%	117.7%	177.2%	84.4%
Debt service ratio	6.8%**	11.7%	40.8%	33.8%

* Not millions
** Public sector only
+ is estimate.
Source: World Bank, *World Development Report 1989*, op. cit., pp. 164, 166, 198, 202, 204, 210, 214

a number of states where the economic situation is desperate and is reflected in chronic debt servicing difficulties.

The Sudan began rescheduling its now $11.1 billion debt with the 'London Club' of commercial bank creditors with a $498 million agreement in 1981; it negotiated modifications to that accord and rescheduled another $2.6 billion in London Club debt over the next four years. Next the 'Paris Club' of western government creditors rescheduled $203 million of loans in 1982 and another $767 million the next two years. The Sudan is one of five African countries which could not service their rescheduled obligations and had to re-reschedule Paris Club debts in 1983 and 1984. As to the future, the World Bank's Kathie L. Krumm added that:

> prospects are especially bleak for certain groups of countries. For some of the extreme cases, the current debt level is not realistically serviceable over the medium term barring some extraordinary aggregate supply shocks, and the question of willingness to pay may not even be at issue. Certainly these include the Sudan, where the scheduled debt service exceeds current exports. . . . [I]t is difficult to imagine how the implied adjustment in consumption would be managed.

The ability of debt rescheduling to provide further relief is constrained by the sizeable component of IMF, multilateral, and previously-rescheduled commercial debt which is typically ineligible for restructuring. For the Sudan, debt service interest alone was equivalent to over 35 per cent of 1982 exports of goods and non-factor services.

In nations such as the Sudan, management of foreign debt does not and cannot head the list of priorities. For example, there is growing famine in the country's south caused by two drought years and the six-year old civil war. The combination of these ills has caused millions to flee their homes and has killed over 250,000 in 1988. The Sudanese crisis is compared to the start of Ethiopia's 1984–5 famine with the critical difference that food supplies are adequate in Sudan. However what food is available exists in the predominantly Arab and Moslem north. Tremendous difficulties have arisen in delivering it to mostly Black and Christian-Animist southern famine areas. The northern-based government of this largest African country has even been accused of treating food as one weapon in its arsenal against the rebellious south's Sudan People's Liberation Army.

The Sudan typifies the lowest income nations of Africa: per capita growth has been stagnant, official development assistance provides 13 per cent of GDP, foreign official creditors are virtually the only source of long-term finance, and the current level of debt and debt service appears unmanageable in the medium term. Reschedulings have reduced current debt service by pushing these payments into coming years but the room for future relief under traditional rules is limited. While the Sudan's plight of internal strife, civil war and famine is one of Africa's worst catastrophes, it is symbolic of the types of difficulties faced by many nations which cannot place the orderly servicing of external obligations at the top of their list of priorities.

Nigeria

Africa's most populous country could be used to illustrate several characteristics: it is the top oil exporter in Africa, it is a classic case of the instability of elected government, it made the unusual decision to service term debt at the expense of trade creditors, and until recently, it was a notable antagonist of the IMF. In this section, however Nigeria is chosen to illustrate how the use of foreign debt helped precipitate a debt crisis.

The oil glut that followed on the heels of the second OPEC price hike hit Nigeria hard. It caused petroleum-dominated merchandise exports to drop 30 per cent from 1980 to 1981 and swung the current account from a \$5.1 billion surplus to a \$6.2 billion deficit. While this current account had changed from a deficit to a moderate surplus in 1986 (before returning to the red by 1987), this improvement resulted from the reduction of trade activity as exports slipped to only 26 per cent of their 1980 peak and imports contracted to 22 per cent of their 1981 high. Beginning in 1981, Nigeria covered its foreign exchange needs by drawing on its reserves and by amassing payment arrears to trade creditors rather than take the conventional route of seeking a rescheduling of term debt. From 1980–86, this West African nation drew down its foreign exchange reserves from \$9.6 billion to \$1.1

billion and ran up arrears on trade-related payments of around $7 billion.

Nigeria's foreign debt is put at $28.7 billion in 1987 by the World Bank, the equivalent of 117.7 per cent of its GNP, although that nation only began large-scale borrowing in 1978. In December 1988, Nigeria reached an agreement on its economic policy with the IMF. This deal comes after several years of public refusal to sign with the Fund, a refusal punctuated by a public vote against any agreement. This accord clears the way for new loans from multilateral lenders and rescheduling accords from official and private creditors and supports the World Bank recovery program in place since 1986. Nonetheless this accord did not come in time to prevent Nigeria from being reclassified by the World Bank as a low-income rather than a middle-income country after its GDP per capita plummeted.

While the slashing of Nigerian oil receipts that accompanied the post-OPEC II oil glut was an important cause of its debt servicing difficulties, the ways in which the original borrowings were used also played a key contributing role. These fell into three categories: large projects which often earned the pejorative 'white elephants', theft and subsidies. The white elephants used large portions of debt for projects of questionable economic value and are symbolised by the government's attempts to create a national steel industry and construct a new national capital city. Other projects included a Nigeria-to-Benin divided expressway which is now filled with potholes and the Festac model housing project in Lagos which recently suffered from a typhoid outbreak when sewer pipes burst and contaminated drinking water.

The theft arose by corrupt officials and businessmen who circumvented the numerous trade restrictions and the exchange rate controls to their personal advantage. As *The Economist* noted in its trademark pithy manner: 'Nigeria's foreign debt is different from those of most black African countries. It has been amassed not by destitution but by incompetence and theft . . . by Nigerians who stole a lot of it.'

Subsidies benefited the politically powerful urban third of the population at the expense of two other sectors. One was the rural population which saw its income restricted by price controls on foodstuffs and by an exchange rate which earned it fewer nairas than would a market rate of exchange. These disincentives contributed to the decline in the agricultural sector in general and cash crops of cocoa, rubber, oil palm, groundnuts and cotton in particular. The other was the petroleum industry which saw domestic demand soar for gasoline at an official price of at $0.10 per liter. The oil companies, which rarely produce enough additional petroleum to fill the nation's OPEC export quotas, require subsidies from the government to remain viable. Moreover, the cheap oil encouraged domestic waste at the expense of potential exports, the importation of automobiles, and the smuggling of the cheap oil out of the country for sale at world prices. The military government of Major-General Ibrahim-Babangida which did away with many of price subsidies earlier, was loath to address this gasoline price subsidy until more recently. With the 1989 budget, the government agreed to boost gasoline prices 43 per cent for private use, although a 3 per cent April 1988 price increase was reversed after it sparked nationwide riots. Unless this increase holds and reduces consumption, the resource may be depleted within twenty years.

For Nigeria, the package of domestic policies was a key contributor to its debt difficulties. Prices and exchange rates encouraged consumption of imports while discouraging production for export. What foreign exchange did accrue from exports and borrowings was used to support subsidies, corruption and wasteful public projects rather than address the underlying problems. In a region characterised by nations without the means to improve their lot, Nigeria had the means, but chose to use them unwisely.

Cote d'Ivoire

This francophone West African nation was held up as the model of a pro-western state and became the darling of multilateral lenders and western governments. The Cote d'Ivoire (formerly also known as the Ivory Coast) built one of the strongest African economies on the basis of the infrastructure left from colonial days, continuing strong support from France, stability under the guidance of President Felix Houphouet-Boigny (who has dominated Ivorian politics since before independence), and pricing policies which continued to promote its agricultural base. Despite the accolades, the Cote d'Ivoire is now in serious financial difficulties arising from the sharp decline in world prices for cocoa and coffee which together make up 60 per cent of its exports.

The Cote d'Ivoire gained access to western commercial loans in the 1970s to finance the continuation of its ambitious development program when internal revenues faltered. The combination of lower prices for its main commodity exports, the effects of the drought, and some unsuccessful investments reduced export earnings by 31 per cent to $2.1 billion in 1980-83. The Cote d'Ivoire stepped up its external borrowing to cover its current account deficit which peaked at $1.8 billion in 1980. More importantly, the domestic budget moved to deficit with the public sector borrowing requirement above 13 per cent of GDP in 1983; this had the effect of restricting foreign exchange availability under the terms of its membership in the French financial zone. By 1983, with the debt service ratio at about 49 per cent, its exports shrunken, and its access to French francs limited, the Ivorians approached its external creditors for debt relief.

The Cote d'Ivoire managed to contain its current account deficit beginning in 1984, and even achieved a short-lived surplus in 1985. But cocoa and coffee prices remained weak, hindering further external account improvement and continuing pressures on the budget which in turn held down currency availability from France. The decline of

Ghana's cocoa price from its 1977 peak and partial rebound in 1983–4 was discussed above. The cocoa price continued to fall each year until 1988's price was just 66 per cent of the 1984 level and 42 per cent of the 1977 peak. Coffee followed a similar trend: Ugandan coffee peaked at $2.24 (per pound) in 1977, weakened through 1982, and then partially recovered in 1983–4. After an up year in 1986, coffee fell 36 per cent through 1988 to settle at 42 per cent of its 1977 peak.

Of course, there were domestic contributors to the Ivorian debt crisis as well. Current spending has been slow to come down, revenues have been constrained by tax fraud, and middlemen have boosted the public cost of cocoa production. While Cote d'Ivoire has continued to provide incentives to agricultural producers, the cost of those programs have mounted and the cocoa price stabilisation fund's deficit equals 4 per cent of government revenue. The capital budget also contained some unsuccessful agricultural ventures as well as several prestige projects. The most prominent 'white elephant' is a basilica being constructed of marble, ivory and gold in the president's hometown at an estimated cost of $280 million, about half of the government budget deficit; designed to rival St Peter's in the Vatican, it will probably be the tomb for President Houphouet-Boigny. Also noticeable is the high-rise skyline of the principal city of Abidjan.

In response to this debt crisis and as part of the rescheduling bargain, the Cote d'Ivoire committed itself to an austerity programme beginning in 1980, supported by a series of IMF, World Bank and French adjustment loans. The Paris Club rescheduled $813 million of maturities in 1984–6 and another $567 million which included some previously rescheduled amounts in 1987. The London Club renegotiated terms on $1.2 billion of debt in 1984 and 1986. In mid-1987, the president suspended foreign debt service payments citing low cocoa and coffee prices and a distaste for further austerity. Several months later he began to withhold Ivorian cocoa from the market as prices had fallen below Ivorian production costs. While he blamed the difficulties on international price speculation, experts pointed to the costs of the Cote d'Ivoire's producer price and marketing board structure. A new round of rescheduling and fresh loan negotiations was completed with the London and Paris Clubs to end this debt moratorium and stockpiling of cocoa. The accords were designed to enable the country to service its loans, but in spite of liberal terms such as the Paris Club's rescheduling 95 per cent of interest due between January 1988 and April 1989, the Cote d'Ivoire did not resume debt payments as expected. However, in January 1989, after long negotiations with France, the IMF and a commodities house, two agreements were announced: a 400 million franc loan from the French government and the delivery to the commodities house Sucre et Denrees of the 400,000 tons of cocoa which had accumulated.

These accords should lead to further agreements with the multilateral agencies and foreign creditor banks and governments for new adjustment programs, rescheduling and loans. Perhaps this medicine, will prompt *The Economist* to moderate its earlier note: 'A death is awaited in the Ivory Coast . . . that of the economy, which is bankrupt.' As the Cote d'Ivoire entered the 1990s, a new rescheduling agreement did not exist.

Kenya

This East African state has been successful in avoiding the debt restructuring endemic in the region despite a foreign debt of $6.0 billion and a debt service ratio of 33.8 per cent. However Kenya has not completely shaken the specter of future difficulties even though its future debt repayment profile is relatively well spread out. The key to its continued financial success may be how much existing foreign investment it can retain and how much new overseas investment it can attract. The political leadership faces the twin dilemmas that attracting this capital is at odds with the official goal of increasing indigenous control of the economic base and the unofficial goal of many bureaucrats of building their personal wealth through corruption. Nevertheless without this capital infusion, Kenya could find itself forced to overextend its borrowing in spite of its goal of lower development project spending and concomitant concessional loans as it faces political and economic pressures from Africa's most rapidly expanding population.

Africa has seen a decline in foreign investment capital which parallels the shrinkage of debt capital. According to the World Bank, net private investment in Africa, which was $6.0 billion in 1980, turned to a $1.0 billion net disinvestment in 1985. To counter this disturbing trend, many African governments have embraced western capitalism as a cure for the current economic malaise and as a means to shed their image of inefficient, inhospitable and corrupt places for the foreign investor to conduct business. In a representative response, the Kenyan government of President Daniel arap Moi recently took out a $112 million World Bank industrial sector loan to implement reforms to spur exports and new foreign investment including a 'one-stop' office for interested investors. Kenya hopes that this will dispel the fears engendered in June 1986 when President Moi reaffirmed his economic nationalist bias with a declaration that new joint ventures needed majority Kenyan ownership; while this declaration was quickly reversed and the liberal foreign investment act was retained, foreign investors' concerns over latent xenophobia were not.

Despite the recent public efforts to encourage investment, doubts remains whether governments are willing to back up their words by attacking investment obstacles. A *Washington Post* article cited a report by the Kenya Association of Manufacturers:

> Foreign investment in Kenya[n] manufacturing ceased in the late 1970s and shows no sign of being rejuvenated. . . . While the threat of price control is

paramount in such decisions [other problems include], access to foreign exchange for purchasing needed inputs and repatriation of capital and dividends; obtaining work permits for skilled and management positions; the risk of indigenisation of ownership; and the horrendous maze of bureaucratic licences and permits required.

The association was polite enough not to mention explicitly the problem of government corruption which further complicates these difficulties. In fact, according to an article in *The Wall Street Journal*, 'corruption and inefficient bureaucracy are having a profound impact here, torpedoing Kenya's reputation as one African nation that works'. With companies seeking to relocate out of South Africa, this would appear to be an ideal time to attract new investors, but Kenya has not been able to take advantage of the situation. One lost opportunity is Eastman Kodak, Co. which after almost two years of study decided against Kenya when it had to move its regional distribution centre out of South Africa.

In 1976–80, Kenya averaged \$57 million in new foreign direct investment annually, but this level tailed off to \$6 million in 1981–4, before rising to \$28 million in 1986. Few foreign firms have made significant new investments in Kenya (except for a late 1970s General Motors assembly plant and oil exploration by Amoco in the 1980s) while existing companies retrenched or reduced their presence. While Kenya has not suffered the disinvestment which has occurred in Africa as a whole, the trend of the early 1980s coupled with some of the negative comments from the business community is cause for concern. Hopefully the government will implement concrete incentives to build on the 1985-6 upturn in investment. Without this capital, Kenya and Africa will find it increasingly difficult to emerge from the debt and aid trap in which it is now caught.

Options

Before considering the options to cope with the African version of the debt crisis it is crucial to realise that in the majority of cases, African nations are unable to repay their foreign debt under the rescheduling structures now commonly in place and certainly not on its original terms. As *The Economist* opines:

> The big Latin American debtors can eventually grow out of their debts if they adopt sensible economic policies. The poorest of Africa's poor cannot realistically be expected ever to service their debts in full. . . .Conventional rescheduling can do little to help. Most [African] countries are paying no debt back anyway; to give relief, either interest rates must be cut or some of their debt written off.

Most African nations are in desperate need of an increased net inflow of financial resources either in the form of new lending or relief from debt repayment. In the past several years, new loans have done little more than cover debt service obligations. A report compiled for the United Nations in early 1988 by a committee headed by former permanent secretary of the British Treasury Sir Douglas Wass warned that for Africa to begin to recover, it needed at least an additional $5 billion annually for the next few years. The 'Wass report' estimated that interest relief could provide one-fifth of that shortfall with the remainder coming from increased bilateral aid and multilateral lending. With the reduction of new lending, alternative means of easing Africa's debt burden need to be found.

In the last few years, official debt relief for Africa has steadily gained acceptance in western capitals. As late as April 1987, the British Chancellor of the Exchequer Nigel Lawson's suggestion to provide this type of help to the most needy debtors was criticised. But attitudes changed rapidly. By the June 1988 Toronto summit of seven western nations, the provision of relief to the poorest African nations was chosen as an innocuous subject for discussion; a current issue of *The Economist* added that: 'Recently, rich countries have been falling all over one another to look generous. . .' as the seven nations agreed in principle that some form of debt relief was necessary. While the US would not endorse debt forgiveness, it did not object to such steps by other countries, including France's bilateral program which included forgiving about one-third of its debt owed by the poorest African nations. At their next summit held in West Berlin in September 1988, the Group of Seven endorsed the implementation of the Toronto accord. It gave thirty-four of the poorest countries which owe $43 billion to official creditors the option to choose forgiveness of one-third of their debt, reduced interest rates, or longer repayment periods; the total debt relief provided is estimated at $500 million a year.

On the debt which remains, innovative refinancing approaches are necessary to better match repayment capacities and schedules. One such proposal was advanced in December 1987 by ADB President N'Diaye. Using Zaire as a test case, the plan would give bilateral and commercial bank creditors of this central African nation twenty-year tradable securities for the face value of its $5.0 billion debt. Principal repayment would be supported by Zaire paying 2 per cent a year into savings (a 'sinking fund') under international administration. The securities would carry a concessional 4 per cent interest rate. As the plan was calculated from the actual payments which Zaire had been able to make in 1981-6, the terms would give Zaire a payment schedule based on its ability to pay without reducing the level of the debt service paid creditors.

Japan has begun to take initiatives in increasing assistance to Africa and in suggesting some alternative approaches to the debt crisis. At the Toronto summit, then-Minister of Finance Kiichi Miyazawa proposed that after debtors agreed to medium-term structural reform plans with the IMF, that part of their bank debt be converted into bonds. As with President N'Diaye's plan, principal would be guaranteed by the creation of a sinking fund financed in this instance by foreign-exchange reserves and proceeds from the privatisation of public assets. The remaining bank debt would be rescheduled with a five-year grace period of interest reduction or forgiveness.

Some plans would only work on the margin, but could be helpful nevertheless. The notion of forgiving debt in exchange for a debtor's agreement to spend a portion of the savings on wildlife conservation has been most visible in the Latin American nations of Costa Rica, Bolivia and Ecuador. In Summer 1989, Madagascar, the World Wildlife Fund, and the US Agency for International Development reached a $3 million debt-for-nature agreement modelled on similar programs in Latin America and the Philippines. Madagascar has shown more environmental concern than most African states, a fact largely attributable to the large number of unique and endangered species on that island. The swap notion can be applied to policy actions in other spheres as well. For example, Nigeria has received some debt forgiveness in exchange for undertaking more family planning efforts.

Trading existing debt for new equity investments in debtor countries could also provide marginal assistance, but the potential of these 'debt-equity swaps' to significantly reduce Africa's debt burden is limited by the size of Africa's capital base. According to an *African Economic Digest* table on emerging stock exchanges, the three African exchanges in Nigeria, Zimbabwe, and Kenya had a total market capitalisation of about $3.1 billion in 1985, compared to $29.2 billion in Malaysia, the largest exchange. However because of the deep discounts in the secondary markets for most African debt, swapping that debt for new investments in the borrowing country can be attractive. Countries including Niger, Sierra Leone and Zambia have used or considered swaps and Nigeria's President Babangida decreed a plan for the conversion of debt into as much as $4.8 billion in equity. The Nigerian programme will favor proposals which would stimulate employment and export earnings without the need for significant imported components.

A key fear of commercial and official lenders alike is that any concession offered to one debtor becomes the demand of every other borrower. This fear of 'contagion' is justified by the ratchet-like progress of debt rescheduling talks with the major debtors. Each country's concession is added to the shopping list of the next debtor facing the rescheduling committee. However, in recent years, the creditors have shown an ability to differentiate between debtors and rescheduling packages. If debt relief measures are provided on a non-discriminatory basis solely on the criterion of per capita income, then the most needy nations will benefit and the largest debtors will continue to be governed under the established rules of the game.

Conclusions

The condition of Africa today is the result of almost a generation of decline. As then-World Bank President A. W. Clausen noted in 1986, 'per capita output in low-income Africa has declined so drastically over the last fifteen years that most of the gains of the modern era have been wiped out. Today, low-income Africa is poorer than it was in 1960'. What is the outlook for Africa? Regardless of how external debt and economic reform are managed, the prospects for an adequate and sustained rate of economic growth and development are daunting.

The chances for success can be improved nevertheless by proper policy choices made in African nations, western capitals and corporate boardrooms. Any improvement of the African standard of living to some 'acceptable' level will only come as the result of a sustained and difficult effort by all parties. The need for such an endeavor is summarised by the recent statement of James Grant, an executive director of UNICEF, that the 'impact is so severe that more than 1,000 children are still dying every day in Africa as a consequence of our inability to put Africa[n] economics back on track'.

Certainly a major effort must come from the African nations themselves. Policies must be re-oriented to allow market forces to operate in determining domestic pricing and foreign exchange rates; this will remove the disincentives for agricultural and commodity production which persist. While these nations want to move into secondary and tertiary production, they cannot do so at the expense of the primary sector. They must instead build gradually upon the wealth produced by the farmers and miners. Such policies would effectively reverse the political favoritism shown to the urban population and to entrenched political elites. Governments will have to open up to allow for greater political expression by the mass of the population to avoid further political instability; without that voice, urbanites can only express their opposition to policy by illegal or violent means.

Africa will continue to rely on international aid and concessional lending particularly with the retreat of commercial lenders. Even more so than in the past, this aid can provide tangible support of those nations which are making positive economic and political reform. The multinational agencies and western governments must continue to find innovative ways to provide increased funds and to reduce the debt service requirement. The banks may be unable to justify new money to African debtors given their competitive mandates and regulatory environments; however, some of the more innovative debt relief alternatives reviewed above could be adopted by the banking community without any appreciable real reduction in cash inflow and income.

Africa's borrowing is a small portion of the global debt, but it looms large in relation to the region's economic output, foreign exchange earnings and international reserves. Innovative debt reduction and forgiveness based on debtor income levels can make a huge difference for the region's welfare. In the final analysis, reducing Africa's debt burden is a necessary, but not sufficient, condition for recovery.

Notes

1. The World Bank groups nations by their 1987 level of income measured as GNP per capita. There are four income categories. The lowest three in terms of income are dominated by developing nations, and are 'low-income economies,' 'lower-middle-income economies' and 'upper-middle-income economies.' The other category is 'high-income categories.'
2. IMF data was compiled on or before 20 March 1989. 1989 and 1990 figures are estimates and projections respectively. IMF debt figures exclude amounts owed to the Fund. Its regional categorization is not fully consistent with the rest this chapter. Its definition of 'Africa' includes Algeria, Morocco, Tunisia and South Africa and 'Sub-Saharan Africa' excludes Nigeria [and South Africa].
3. N.B.: The debt service ratio shows the proportion of foreign exchange earnings which are scheduled to be used to pay interest on all external debt and principal amortisation on medium- and long-term debt. Short-term debt principal is usually not included in calculating the ratio because these obligations are assumed to be self-liquidating trade transactions.

References

African Research Bulletin, Economic Series, 'Africa's Debt Burden, New Steps to Ease Crisis', 31 October 1988.

African Research Bulletin, Economic Series, 'Cote d'Ivoire, Budget (1989)', 31 January 1989.

African Research Bulletin, Economic Series, 'Cote d'Ivoire, Generous Creditors', 31 May 1988.

African Research Bulletin, Economic Series, 'Cote d'Ivoire, Unable to Pay Debts', 31 July 1988.

African Research Bulletin, Economic Series, 'Nigeria: IMF Endorses Plan', 31 December 1988.

Battiata, Mary, 'Sudanese Famine Rages Despite Supplies of Food', *Washington Post*, 14 October 1988.

Commonwealth Secretariat, *Mobilising Capital For Development: The Role of Private Flows. A Report by the Commonwealth Secretariat.* London: Commonwealth Secretariat, August 1988.

The Economist, 'Africa's Hard Road', 8 July 1989.

The Economist, 'African Debt: The Zaire Solution', 19 December 1987.

The Economist, 'African Economies: Reform on Trial', 19 April 1989.

The Economist, 'Greensback Debt', 6 August 1988.

The Economist, 'Ivory Coast: Felix in Wonderland', 15 October 1988.

The Economist, 'Madagascar: A Debt to Nature', 19 August 1989.

The Economist, 'The Miyazawa Plan: Any Interest from Debtors?', 6 August 1988.

The Economist, 'Nigeria: A Time of Pride and Pessimism', 7 January 1989.

The Economist, 'Out of Africa', 18 June 1988.

The Economist, 'Sudan: Just in Time?', 1 April 1989.

The Economist, 'Why General Babangida Takes his Democracy without Politics', 18 June 1988.

Financial Times [London], 'Tackling Africa's Debt Crisis', 10 June 1988.

Fitzgerald, Mary Anne, 'Kenya', *The Africa Review 1987*, Lincolnwood, Illinois:

NTC Business Book, 1986.
Harden, Blaine, 'African Nations on Long, Miserable Road to Economic Reform', *Washington Post*, 15 January 1989.
Harden, Blaine, 'As Economic Woes Worsen, Some Say Africa Must Share Blame', *Washington Post*, 8 October 1988.
Humphreys, Chris and William Jaeger, 'Africa's Adjustment and Growth', *Finance and Development*, June 1989.
International Monetary Fund, *International Financial Statistics, 1988 Yearbook.* Washington, D.C.: The Fund, 1989.
International Monetary Fund, *International Financial Statistics, February 1989.* Washington, D.C.: The Fund, 1989.
International Monetary Fund, *World Economic Outlook: A Survey by the Staff of the International Monetary Fund* [April 1989]. Washington, D.C.: The Fund, 1989.
Krumm, Kathie L., *The External Debt of Sub-Saharan Africa (Origins, Magnitude, and Implications for Action) (World Bank Staff Working Paper number 741).* Washington, D.C.: World Bank, 1986.
Lancaster, Carol and John Williamson, (ed.), *African Debt and Financing (Special Reports 5, May 1986).* Washington, D.C.: Institute for International Economics, 1986. (includes Eduard H. Brau, 'The Demand for External Finance: African Debt: Facts and Figures on the Current Situation'; Lancaster and Williams, 'Africa's Economic Predicament'; and Richard M. Moose, 'Alternative Sources of Capital'.)
New York Times, 'In Lagos, Economic Dream is Now Nightmare', 14 August 1988, p. 15.
Rocco, Fiammetta, 'The Last, Best Hope for Black Africa?', *Institutional Investor*, May 1988.
Stephens, Phillip, 'Britain Will Urge Action on African Debt Crisis', *Financial Times*, 10 June 1988.
Swaps: The Newsletter of New Financial Instruments, 'Building Coalitions for African Development', July 1989.
Swaps: The Newsletter of New Financial Instruments, 'Selected Operational Debt-Equity Swap Programs (Part 2)', January 1989.
Thurow, Roger, 'Capital Flight Strains Kenyan Economy', *Wall Street Journal*, 17 August 1989.
United Nations Development Programme and the World Bank, *African Economic and Financial Data.* Washington, D.C.: World Bank, 1989.
Weerasinge, Nissanke, 'External Debt Position of Sub-Saharan Africa has Worsened Considerably', *IMF Survey*, June 1988.
World Bank, *Financing Adjustment with Growth in Sub-Saharan Africa, 1986–90.* Washington, D.C.: World Bank, 1986.
World Bank, *Toward Sustained Development in Sub-Saharan Africa.* Washington, D.C.: World Bank, 1984.
World Bank, *World Development Report 1989.* New York: Oxford University Press, 1989.

Chapter 6

South Africa

Scott B. MacDonald

Introduction

South Africa poses an interesting question in regard to the global debt crisis. As Andrew Nagorski, then an editor for *Newsweek*, noted in 1978:

> In southern Africa, the line between perceptions of political realities and the realities themselves is a hazy one at best; more often than not, the perceptions become a major component of the situation, influencing events in a very direct fashion.

This was clearly the case with how external debt as well as economic relations have been handled between South Africa and the outside world.

Why separate South Africa from an analysis of the rest of the African continent or, at the very least, the rest of Sub-Saharan Africa? The answer is to be found in the country's socio-political structure: only South Africa is governed by an official policy of racial segregation called apartheid, which has set it apart in how other nations treat it on the diplomatic stage. South Africa, in the words of historian Mary Benson

> is a microcosm of our world: in its races, its religions, its perilous division into 'haves' and 'have-nots'. Yet, alone in the world, it is a country in which a racial minority is committed to preserving power in its own hands - a policy which has brought successive South African governments into conflict with the world community.

And, it should be noted, conflict with itself.

At the close of the 1980s, South Africa has undergone considerable change. The debt question has played a part in those changes although the importance of indebtedness should not be overstated as a single, dominating factor, but one of many. Clearly, the major point in looking at South Africa's external debt is its highly politicised nature. Mao Zedong once noted: 'Power grows out of the barrel of a gun.' To this could be added, political objectives often override economic concerns, unless of course economic tools become a means to an end. Nevertheless, politics has reigned supreme over economics in South Africa.

The South African matrix of debt and race

In 1989 South Africa's external debt re-emerged as an issue of public concern in Western Europe, the United States and Commonwealth countries. The reason for this renewed concern was that almost all of South Africa's $21.6 billion debt was scheduled to come due in 1990 and 1991 and there was the hint that Pretoria might seek another rescheduling akin to the one of 1985. What greatly complicated the South African situation was that while it needed new infusions of outside capital to maintain economic growth, commercial banks were reluctant to lend any new money to a regime that had increasingly isolated itself. That reluctance stemmed from the South African government's adherence to the governing ideology of apartheid - a system of enforced racial segregation which maintains the supremacy of a relatively small white population over the other more numerous elements of a society officially broken down into Indians (also referred to as Asians), coloureds and blacks. With a total population of 35 million, the largest ethnic group is black (69.9 per cent). The white segment consists of 17.8 per cent of the population, while coloureds (mixed blood) constitute 9.4 per cent and Indians 2.9 per cent.

South Africa is located at the southernmost tip of the African continent, being slightly less than twice the size of the US state of Texas. In terms of natural resources, it is well-endowed, possessing gold, chromium, antimony, coal, iron ore, manganese, vanadium, salt and natural gas. This wealth of natural resources has been a major factor in the country's ability to survive a world that is largely hostile to its form of government.

White South African society - the bedrock of the apartheid system - has its roots in the Dutch and British immigrants who settled in South Africa from the seventeenth century onwards. Through the nineteenth and early twentieth centuries the majority of white South Africans held a self-perception that was, as Nagorski noted: 'as a snug Western enclave at the tip of Africa. Faithfully Christian, they staunchly opposed communism and governed themselves according to a Westminster model of parliamentary democracy'. Independent since 1910, South Africa operated with little interference from the outside until after the Second World War. The fundamental problem, in terms of self-perception and in the new world of post-colonial empires that came out of the Second World War, was the blatant exclusion of the majority of the population, which was black, from political participation. While general suffrage is extended to whites over eighteen as well as to coloureds and Indians (for separate legislatures) the black population has traditionally been excluded. One of the main points of hardline white resistance is opposition to one man, one vote which would provide black South Africans a handy majority.

The political inequality of South African society is also reflected in the quality of life. According to the US Central Intelligence Agency's *The World Factbook 1988*, in terms of life expectancy, whites can expect to live to 71 years of age, Indians to 67, coloureds to 61, and blacks to 58. Infant mortality rates are even more skewed: whites 11 deaths/1,000 births; Indians 18/1,000; coloureds 50/1,000; and blacks 75/1,000. And, in education, the division between white and black is a yawning gap: almost all of the white population is literate and only 50 per cent of blacks (according to the South African government) are able to read and write.

Considering the political context of apartheid, South Africa's economic foundation was based on agriculture and mining, the latter highly dependent on black labour. It is important to emphasise the structure of the economy has come to reflect the apartheid system. The manufacturing sector was established by government investment and fed by state subsidies. Its development since the 1920s was generally fostered by sizeable parastatal corporations which continue in the later part of the twentieth century to dominate heavy industry, especially in electricity, steel and transport.

Manufacturing began to expand following the First World War, grew briskly in the 1950s and even more rapidly in the 1960s. It is important to note that high tariffs and import substitution policies, initially launched in 1925 to support local manufacturing were, to pro-apartheid South Africans, justified by their country's growing isolation and trade sanctions imposed beginning in the 1970s in response to the country's racial policies. Manufacturing is the largest contributor to the economy, followed by mining and quarrying. The mining sector produces some of South Africa's best known exports - diamonds, gold and uranium.

South Africa's private industry, like its parastatals, is financially concentrated in the hands of a few large conglomerates. The majority of these were originally mining-based. Both private and state sector activity are geographically concentrated: a system of incentives to firms, initiated in the 1960s to decentralise industry into black 'homelands' as a means of racial segregation, has been largely unsuccessful. The result of this failure has been an excessive industrial build-up around the four major white urban centres of Cape Town, Port Elizabeth, Durban and Johannesburg. This has been one factor that has undermined apartheid's spinning off of black homelands: those that have been spun off and are theoretically independent (in the eyes of the South African government), are in reality economically weak, devoid of industrial base, and dependent on the South African government for financial assistance. There are four 'independent' homelands or 'states' which consist of Ciskei (about 750,000 people), Bophutha Tswana (1.5 million), Transkei (2.5 million) and Venda (500,000). Only Bophutha Tswana has anything resembling a viable economy, which is based on platinum mines, casinos and entertainment centres, a soft-porn commercial broadcasting station and easy access to the South African railway to the north. All four, however, are a source of political instability, adding security costs for the South African government that has on more than one occasion ended up playing referee to the various factions within the local ruling elites.

The South African public sector's deep involvement in the economy has led to substantial public spending and a history of large public deficits. This is underscored by the fact that the South African government has overshot its budget for each of the past fifteen years (as of 1988). Fiscal deficits have usually ranged over 5 per cent of gross national product, which constitutes a substantial drag on the economy as it reduces the amount of capital available for investment. The deficits, moreover, have fueled what has become chronic inflation, which has stood at between 12–18 per cent throughout the 1980s. This has meant that the central bank has frequently opted for monetary restraint by raising interest rates: interest rates have been as high as 20 per cent in the 1980s. The side-effects of high interest rates have been unimpressive domestic investment and significant capital flight. This also means that South Africa needs outside credits. Although efforts were launched in the late 1980s to restructure the economy to promote greater flexibility and higher growth rates, the cost of apartheid and related complications with external debt have brought the South African economy into a sustained period of difficulty.

The rise of external debt

South Africa's external borrowing increased rapidly in the period from 1980-83. This was due to the need to promote growth as the country was emerging from a difficult and prolonged recession, a drought and a slump in metals prices that had helped push up domestic interest rates. It was felt that economic growth would diffuse potential political turmoil and keep employment generation ahead of the population growth rate. The infusion of capital as well as improved international prices did result in an impressive 5.1 per cent growth rate in 1984. The size of external debt levelled off between 1983 and 1985, standing at $23.5 billion at the end of 1985. Of that, $3.9 billion was official debt, with the rest, $15.5 billion and $4.1 billion from commercial banks and non-bank creditors respectively.

What was to become problematic and launch South Africa into its own debt crisis was the size of short-term (of one year) debt. More than half of the total external debt - some $13.6 billion - was short-term, meaning that the country's creditors expected repayment. South Africa, in turn, expected to maintain its access to the international financial market and be able to take out new short-term loans to pay off the old ones, much as it had done through the 1970s and early 1980s. As long as South Africa had access to new money it avoided a financial squeeze.

South Africa was not able to avoid a financial squeeze in 1985. The South African debt crisis broke in mid-1985 when concern by commercial banks over the escalating racial violence, combined with mounting pressure from international anti-apartheid groups, induced banks in the United States and the United Kingdom to prematurely close credit lines and call in loans. The ugly face of apartheid was vividly brought to millions of living rooms around the world by the press when riots erupted in Soweto, making South Africa a point of public business. As one US banker noted of the reaction to the 1985 violence in his institution:

> There was a tremendous amount of activity to close down a small checking account for corporate customers operating in South Africa and a careful examination of all of our corresponding banks to make certain that none of them were publicly known to conduct business in the Republic of South Africa. Anything that could possibly tie our bank to South Africa was closed down. There was little discussion.

The South African response to the abrupt closing of the financial door in their face was to impose a moratorium on principal payments on $14 billion of its $24 billion debt. Excluded from the amortisation freeze were trade credits, publicly traded issues of parastatals, private debt (this was around 37 per cent of South Africa's total external debt) and International Monetary Fund and Paris Club obligations. The action made South Africa the first nation to default on interbank lines, which are lines of credit that one bank lends to another.

The decision to strike back at the banks was not an easy one for the National Party government of Prime Minister P.W. Botha. The political turmoil in 1985 hurt productivity and reduced access to badly needed foreign capital. Moreover, the economy drifted into a recession as the real gross domestic product contracted by 1.2 per cent. Although payments on principal were halted, the situation was moderated by Reserve Bank Governor Gerhard de Kock, who made certain that the country continued to pay interest and that a full-scale repudiation of debt was avoided. A rescheduling was eventually hammered out in early 1986 and is referred to as the First Interim Agreement. This allowed South Africa to roll over all of the frozen debt until June 1987. An initial payment of $420 million was required by April 1986, with a further repayment of 5 per cent of the total debt outstanding by April 1987. It is important to note that although South Africa was able to come to an agreement with its creditors on its debt, because of the unpopularity of the country with the public it never formed a regular bank advisory committee. Unlike other countries that have undergone the rescheduling process, South Africa's public image problem led the banks to the creation of a 'technical committee': the banks did not wish to convey the impression that were advising the current regime in any capacity.

South Africa's external debt did not conveniently disappear and a Second Interim Agreement was reached in March 1987 between the country and its major commercial bank creditors. The new agreement stipulated that $1.4 billion of the remaining $13 billion of debt subject to the moratorium be repaid over the three-year period. Lenders were offered the option of converting up to $5 billion of the debt into ten-year bonds, maturing in 1997, with a five-year grace period. By the end of 1988, repayments under the Second Interim Agreement as well as revaluation effects from the fall of the dollar had reduced South Africa's total external debt to around $21.6 billion. The debt amounted to only 84 per cent of 1988 exports and the debt service ratio (the ratio of interest to exports) was a healthy 7.5 per cent, both strong indicators of creditworthiness.

During the period up to 1985, South Africa had no history of problems as a debtor along the lines of Argentina or Mexico. Whenever short-term borrowing became too high and creditworthiness was threatened, fiscal discipline was quickly imposed to adjust the economy. Under the agreements made after 1985, South Africa was exemplary in keeping current on interest payments. The current account has also managed to keep apace with principal payment requirements, registering a surplus of 6.15 billion rand in 1987 and a 2.8 billion rand surplus in 1988 despite a surge in domestic demand. Thus, by all financial and economic indicators, South Africa is under-borrowed, especially when compared to Latin America and the rest of Africa.

Political pressure, official sanctions and public protest have nonetheless made it impossible for South Africa to participate regularly in international credit markets. The price of South African debt on the secondary market, where debt paper is bought and sold around the globe, fell as low as 62 cents on the dollar (bid price, 14 June 1989), primarily because of public attitudes towards bank involvement with South Africa and uncertainty surrounding the availability of rescheduling over the next few years. The price of apartheid has been that while limited short-term trade credit is available from both private and official bilateral sources, it is almost impossible for South Africa to raise medium- and long-term loans.

The bond issue

The South African debt problem has lingered into the 1990s because of the ongoing concerns about the country's political future and the 1987 bond option. The 1986 Anti-Apartheid Act in the United States greatly reduced the scope of new investments and loans to South Africa. However, the act specifically avoided restrictions against continued ownership of investments or loans acquired before passage of the law, reinvestment of profits, or investment needed to insure the ongoing profitability of existing operations. It also excluded restrictions on the renegotiation of current claims or on the transfer of such investments as long as no additional credit or payment would be made to a South African entity or the South African government. The bond option, therefore, became an attractive exit strategy for commercial banks that wished to avoid another rescheduling. It was also attractive from the South African side, allowing them to reduce the amount of pressure on the country's finances.

In 1989 anti-apartheid groups around the world took issue with the bond option and sought to pressure commercial banks into not accepting it. As Terry Crawford Brown, financial advisor to Archbishop Tutu, commented before the US Congress on 1 August 1989: 'The bond issue lets the South African government off the hook.' He also noted that the purpose of international sanctions is to promote constitutional change, not destroy the economy. The bond issue, in Brown's eyes, allowed the South African government to put off payments for several years, reducing the financial pressure, hence the pressure from the outside to implement anti-apartheid reforms.

Anti-apartheid activists argued that the banks should go for maximum payment under current agreements to continue to drain the country of its hard-earned foreign exchange reserves. The message was simple: if the banks pushed for and obtained a maximum payment from South Africa, the system of apartheid would be further undermined. Howard Preece noted of the new pressure on commercial banks in 1989: 'creditor banks, including the Swiss, are under heavy pressure from anti-apartheid lobbies to keep demanding repayment of existing debt.'

The position of commercial banks in 1989 was awkward. The majority of banks had made no new loans to South Africa and any publicity related to the issue was shunned. At the same time, what the banks did have in South Africa they wanted to see a return on. This, in part, was complicated by the state of troubled developing country debt, against which banks were forced to put reserves. The idea of taking a hit on South African debt to please anti-apartheid groups had little appeal nor made any commercial sense. For those institutions that had already converted their loans into ten-year bonds, like Citibank, the deed was done.

One adverse development the new push against bank involvement did accomplish was to drive a number of banks to sell South African debt on the secondary market at less than its full value. Most of the buyers were South African firms: in a sense further pressure on banks pushed some to sell on the market at a lower price, hence providing South Africa a cheap way of buying back some of its debt and further reducing the burden.

In early October 1989 South Africa and its creditors reached an agreement to reschedule repayment of $8 billion. This action took many by surprise, especially as it came before the Commonwealth heads of government meeting in Kuala Lumpur, where the issue of economic sanctions was to be discussed. Abdul S. Minty, a representative for the Anti-Apartheid Movement to be attending the conference stated: 'The South African announcement [about the rescheduling] is clearly intended to provoke the Commonwealth. It means that the banks have decided to extend a lifeline to the apartheid system.'

The ongoing nature of South African debt management is largely political in nature. South Africa, with principal payments of $1.7 billion in 1989, nearly $2.1 billion in 1990 and $1.5 billion in 1991, was to be hard pressed to meet all its obligations. While the current account is likely to remain in surplus, it was not expected to be able to bridge the difference of what is owed and what exists even if foreign exchange reserves were largely depleted. However, under the new accord, the second interim agreement which ended in June 1990, was extended to 31 December 1993. The new agreement is expected to allow South Africa to get over the 'debt hump' in the early 1990s by stretching out the repayment schedule.

The South African economy, caught by the socio-political crisis of apartheid, is reaching the 1990s in a state of disarray. The political situation is characterised by widespread unrest, growing dissension within the white community, and tremendous pressure, both externally and internally, for change. Economically, apartheid is proving to have substantial costs, being a drag on growth, complicating access to foreign capital, and driving out investment.

There appears to be a long way before collapse, yet the rise of black union power and the strike as an economic weapon, coupled with the regime's lack of international support raises serious questions about the so-called autarkic South African system. Although some white South Africans are willing to withdraw into their laagar, it is doubtful that all white South Africans feel that same way. The politics of race will clearly continue to cast a long shadow over South Africa's ability to repay its external debt.

Leaks in the sanctions

The maintenance of the apartheid system has come with a large cost because of the impact of economic sanctions. Following the unrest in 1985 official trade sanctions were imposed by the European Community and most trading partners. US trade and investment sanctions were codified in the Comprehensive Anti-Apartheid Act of 1986. The drying up of international credit markets to South Africa is part of the impact of those sanctions.

Unfortunately, sanctions have a tendency to leak. While trade between South Africa and the United States and United Kingdom have fallen off since the mid-1980s, trade has increased with Japan and Taiwan (which has rejected imposing economic sanctions). In 1987, Japan emerged as the number one trade partner with South Africa, followed by West Germany. This changed in 1988 as Japanese companies were called upon by their government to reduce trade linkages. Japanese restraint meant that West Germany became South Africa's leading trade partner in that year and 1989.

One area beyond international finance that anti-apartheid forces have sought to hit hard on is South Africa's ability to import oil. In 1979 an oil embargo was launched against South Africa, which continues with various leaks to the present-day. Initially the lucrative business of delivering oil to South Africa was controlled by Norwegian shippers. However, in July 1987 Norway banned its shipping companies from engaging in the trade. While the closing down of Norwegian operations hurt, South Africa was not daunted. The Amsterdam based monitoring group, the Shipping Research Bureau, conducted a study released in 1989 that revealed that Hong Kong became the next base of operations for oil shipments to South Africa. As Hong Kong does not operate any restrictions on its shippers' oil deliveries, a company named Hong Kong World-Wide Shipping Group has shipped an estimated 4.7 million tons of oil to South Africa between October 1986 and December 1988.

The difficulty in making sanctions airtight is further complicated by the stranglehold South Africa has on southern Africa's railways. Because of the political turmoil in Angola and Mozambique, railways built through those countries to provide outlets for countries in the interior, such as Botswana, Zambia and Malawi, have been disrupted, and the landlocked countries have been forced to send much of their produce through South Africa, something which is distasteful, but an economic necessity. The 29 July 1989 edition of *The Economist* noted:

> At present roughly three-fifths of Zimbabwe's trade goes through South Africa, though the port of Durban is three times as far from Harare as is Beria, in Mozambique. Malawi, even further from South Africa, sends more than 90 per cent of its trade through Durban.

Add this to what David Lamb in *The Africans* wrote in 1983:

> Only one African nation, Malawi, has diplomatic relations with South Africa, and virtually none admits to doing business with South Africa. But what goes through back doors is another matter. Each year at least twenty African countries indirectly support apartheid by purchasing more than $1 billion worth of South African goods and services. Kenya buys South African maize, which it says comes from Mozambique. Zambia buys South African beef, which it says comes from Botswana. Gabon buys South African construction equipment, which it says comes from Europe. Zaire gets 50 per cent of its food from South Africa; 80 per cent of Zimbabwe's trade goes through South Africa; Malawi built its new capital at Lilongwe with the help of a $12 million South African loan; Mozambique keeps its ports and railroads running with South African technicians and administrators; six neighboring countries supply 182,000 laborers for the South African mines.

Although peace may be coming to Angola and Mozambique in the early 1990s, the situation of a number of other countries sending their chief exports through South Africa has made it more difficult to keep track of exactly what South Africa exports and imports. South African involvement in Mozambique, where a technical team is active in restoring the harbor at Maputo, could lead to a further leak in sanctions if the neighboring province of Transvaal makes use of that port. This would obviously put the leftist government in Mozambique in a difficult situation as it needs South African assistance in ending its decades long civil war, which the white regime helped continue by supporting the rebel forces.

As there are leaks in sanctions on trade and oil imports, there are undoubtedly leaks in sanctions, moral or officially imposed, prohibiting international finance. While credit availability has declined considerably in the United States, the United Kingdom and Commonwealth countries, short-term credit continues to come from a number of sources, especially for trade finance. Japan was initially willing to fill the gap left by the United States and European banks (except the Swiss), but international pressure and the embarrassment of becoming South Africa's number one trade partner caused a decline in lending on the part of Japanese financial institutions. Swiss banks, according to United Nations data, were the most notable lenders to South Africa after 1985: Swiss bank loans rose from $1.2 billion in 1985 to $1.8 billion in 1986, before falling to $1.6 billion in 1987. However, in 1988 and 1989, public pressure mounted on the Swiss to follow suit in reducing their exposure to South Africa.

There have also been allegations that the South Africans use shadow accounts, operating through New York and London. Under this scenario, transactions, such as arms deals, are disguised by using foreign banks or operating through other countries. Wire transfers, the high tech part of international banking, operate in huge sums of money and in different currencies daily, making it easy for South African enterprises to conceal financial transactions.

Is there a way forward?

While international pressure in the form of economic and diplomatic sanctions have played a large role in South Africa's debt problem, internal politics must also be considered with two points in mind. These are:

1. politics within the white political elite in regard to the threshold for the cost of apartheid and the need for change; and
2. politics within the black political elite in consideration of the impact of sanctions, boycotts, and eventually, how to deal with the debt situation in the hereafter of apartheid.

The ruling white elite has reached the 1990s divided on which path to follow in the future. Elements of white South African society are desirous of political and economic reform: if reform is not enacted, it will eventually lead to revolution based on ideology and, above all, race. This has been the plank of the liberal element of white politics. Other elements of white society, especially supporters of the far-right Conservative Party, remain opposed to the dismantlement of apartheid. They quickly point to economic problems of black Africa and imply that if the blacks are given political rights, especially the vote, South Africa will lurch in the same direction as countries like Uganda and Zambia.

The polarisation in South African white society has made a clear path forward difficult for the ruling National Party. F.W. de Klerk, who replaced P.W. Botha and led his party to an electoral victory in September 1989 appears to be leading the National Party into uncharted waters. The need for change is pressing and de Klerk is keenly aware of the threat of new sanctions in international finance as well as the heavy and growing cost of apartheid such as the boycott of white shops by blacks. A number of diplomatic visits, including a photo session with Zambian president, Kenneth Kuanda, were aimed at signalling to the outside world that change was on its way. De Klerk has also embarked upon a policy of opening discussions with members of the outlawed African National Congress, an easing of apartheid restrictions and amnesty (in December 1989) of some 'political' prisoners. One of the most dramatic steps was a 13 December 1989 meeting between de Klerk and Nelson Mandela, the jailed leader of the ANC. The meeting was held to discuss the country's political future and could possibly be the opening round of preliminary discussions on a new constitution for South Africa. Even more dramatic was Mandela's release from prison in early 1990.

Has white society reached its threshold tolerance for the cost of apartheid? The answer will be reflected in whether or not there is any meaningful political reform in the country in the 1990s. What is certain is that the government spends nearly 20 per cent of its annual budget or around $3 billion on defense. Additionally, all healthy white males must serve in the armed forces. One of the reasons for South Africa's willingness to negotiate a settlement over Namibia and Angola was the cost of military equipment and men. How will the cost be borne when the fighting draws closer to home? Another cost is disinvestment of foreign companies: net divestment caused a substantial capital outflow of $6 billion in 1988. The loss of such capital hurts white society as well as black society.

The other crucial element in the South African drama is the black political leadership. One of the problems here is that it is badly fragmented along regional, ideological and tribal lines. John de St Jorre, a former journalist for *The Observer* (London) noted:

> Unity of spirit does not conceal disunity of method. Black divisions are manifest in the banners that advertise the UDF, the ANC, AZAPO, the South African Communist Party (the Soviet Communist Party), the different trade union federations, and a host of local groups.

While the overwhelming majority of black South Africans would like to see an end of apartheid, the state's highly efficient security apparatus and different perceptions on approach have left divisions, some of which have had violent undertones.

In looking to the future, it will be essential for a black leadership to emerge which has a higher degree of unity. The stakes are high: South Africa without apartheid will remain Africa's only industrialised society, capable of maintaining a higher standard of living than found elsewhere on the continent as well as having the technological sophistication of being able to generate nuclear power. There must be a concern, therefore, that economic sanctions imposed by anti-apartheid allies around the world do not destroy the country's economy. There is a delicate line to be walked between bringing apartheid to its knees and leaving the economy intact enough for a post-apartheid system to be successful. This is clearly the heaviest burden facing South Africa's black leadership.

Conclusion

South Africa's external debt is a financial issue that has become a political football between anti-apartheid forces and the South African government. While South Africa's economic fundamentals do not preclude it from international credit, its political system and the sanctions that it has incurred have effectively put it beyond the touch of both official and commercial financial sources. Hence, South Africa's debt problem will remain closely tied to the fortunes of apartheid. Without resolving the apartheid problem South Africa will remain a country apart from the rest of Africa and the international community. The danger in the 1990s is that if change is too slow, the country will reach a post-apartheid period with an economy ruined by sanctions on the outside and disruption from within. External debt will be as it was in the past - one of many problems overridden by political concerns.

References

Benson, Mary, *South Africa: The Struggle for a Birthright*. New York: Minerva Press, 1969.

Carter, Gwendolen M. and Patrick O'Meara (ed.), *Southern Africa: The Continuing Crisis*. Bloomington: Indiana University Press, 1979.

Central Intelligence Agency, *The World Factbook 1988*. Washington, D.C.: US Government Printing Office, 1988.

de St Jorre, John, 'South Africa: A Reporter's Notebook', in Helen Kitchen (ed.), *South Africa: In Transition to What?*. New York: Praeger Books/CSIS Washington Paper, 1988.

The Economist, 'Southern Africa, back on the rails', 29 July 1989, p. 35.

The Economist Intelligence Unit, *South Africa Country Report*, No.2 1989.

Gavshon, Arthur, *Crisis in Africa: Battleground of East and West*. Harmondsworth, England: Penguin Books, 1981.

Harris, Nigel, *The End of the Third World: Newly Industrializing Countries and the Decline of an Ideology*. Harmondsworth, England: Penguin Books, 1986.

Kitchen, Helen (ed.), *South Africa: In Transition to What?* New York: Praeger, 1988.

Lamb, David, *The Africans*. New York: Vintage Books, 1983, 1984.

Preece, Howard, 'Feeling the pinch?', *The Banker*, August 1989.

Waldmeir, Patti, 'Mandela and de Klerk hold first meeting', *Financial Times*, 14 December 1989.

Waldmeir, Patti, 'South Africa reschedules debt on eve of sanctions debate', *Financial Times*, 19 October 1989.

Whitaker, Jennifer Seymour, *Africa and the United States: Vital Interests*. New York: University of New York Press, 1978.

World Bank, *World Development Report 1989*. New York: Oxford University Press, January 1989.

Chapter 7

Asia

David Maslin

The economic environment of the late 1970s and early 1980s was punctuated by major economic disturbances. These included two substantial oil price increases in 1974 and 1980, accelerating global inflation climaxed by a deep and prolonged world recession and a collapse of commodity prices between 1983-86. These events were instrumental in changing the way in which Asian countries financed their growth and development. Of greatest significance has been a substantial rise in international lending by private financial institutions such as banks, accompanied by a decline in the growth of official foreign assistance flows. The debt crisis focused mainly on Latin America and engendered a sharp reversal in the overall growth of international lending to the developing countries, especially by US banks. Yet, despite a slowing in the growth rate of bank lending to Asian countries since 1982, most borrowers in the region now have greater access to external commercial financing than at the beginning of the decade.

Despite commonalities in economic performance and overall policy orientation, the developing economies in Asia are at quite different stages of development. The spectrum of countries in the area can be categorised into four types. The first group is the newly industrialising countries (NICs) which include South Korea, Taiwan and the city states of Hong Kong and Singapore. They are natural resource poor, have a solid industrial base that is export-driven and in the case of the city states, rather sophisticated financial sectors.

The second group of Asian economies are the commodity exporting countries of South-East Asia which constitute the Association of South-East Asian nations (ASEAN) - minus Singapore. Those nations are Indonesia, Malaysia, the Philippines, Thailand and Brunei. These countries are natural resource rich but only semi-industrialised. Their export orientation is comparatively recent and growing and their financial sectors are generally less deep than among the NICs. However, this group of countries potentially represents the next wave of rapid Asian development in the 1990s.

The third group of Asian economies is that of the heavily populated countries of China (the People's Republic) and India. They have been less vigorous performers, but have embarked on modernisation drives that include liberalising heavily controlled domestic markets and increasing openness to external trade and capital flows.

The fourth and final group of economies includes Vietnam, Cambodia, Laos and North Korea. These are economies are, to varying degrees, centrally planned, rigid and with little or no local capital market development. Politics not economics is in command, especially in the near-totalitarian Kim Il-song regime in North Korea. Despite the rigid facade, changes are being made in these economies as the 1990s begin. Vietnam's military withdrawal from Cambodia is a reflection of the tired nature of the larger country's economy. Burma has only recently emerged from a long dormant period, with a stagnant economy. Having spent the last three decades under the dictatorial Ne Win, Burma reemerged in 1988 and 1989 when Ne Win was overthrown and efforts were made to develop international ties for financial assistance and trade.

The transition from official and largely concessional long-term funds to commercially priced credits of short- and medium-term maturity has been critical to sustaining Asia's rapid growth pace, which has led to a shift in the centre of gravity of the world economy toward this region. But for all the developing countries in Asia, regardless of their circumstances, the changing nature of external finance presents significant new development and debt management challenges.

Rapid growth and external deficits, 1970–82

The decade of the 1970s observed a sharp acceleration in the pace of economic growth among the developing, market-orientated countries of Asia. This was accompanied by a steady widening of current account deficits, particularly from 1978 through the early 1980s. The more rapid increase in economic activity, much of it investment-based, greatly increased the growth of imports. Moreover, with the rise in oil prices beginning in the mid-1970s, the cost of energy imports rose markedly. An additional factor was the increase in prices for manufactured goods reflected in the general inflation in the United States and other industrial countries as well as the depreciation of most Asian currencies against the yen and major European currencies in the late 1970s and early 1980s.

The consequence of these factors was substantial in the volume of external financing and an extraordinary enlargement of gross and net external debt. For the eight major developing Asian countries in the following table, gross external debt owed to international banks had grown considerably from $13.1 billion in 1975 to $38.96 billion in 1980, more than doubling to $103 billion in 1985.

By 1985 South Korea's external debt had risen to $47.2 billion; Indonesia continued to add to its debt which rose to nearly $31 billion. The Philippines' use of debt slowed sharply in the case of commercial borrowings after 1983, while Malaysia and Thailand embarked upon

Table 7.1 International bank claims of the eight major Asian countries (in $ millions)

	1975	1980	1985
Korea	3,329	14,001	34,353
Taiwan	2,061	5,097	5,533
Philippines	2,036	6,977	13,414
Indonesia	2,480	4,280	15,169
Malaysia	690	2,286	11,174
Thailand	1,234	3,179	7,591
China	863	2,225	9,590
India	430	917	6,209
Total Asia	13,123	38,962	103,033

Source: Bank of International Settlements

more aggressive borrowing. China, with new found access to external funds following the dramatic opening of its economy, saw its debt grow from $4.5 billion to $16.7 billion in 1985. Most Asian economies, hungry for capital needed for infrastructure modernisation, actively sought financing from not only commercial banks, but also from multilateral institutions such as the World Bank and Asian Development Bank. China and India were especially attracted to these official aid agencies, considering the soft terms of loans issued.

The role of banks in expanding Asia's use of debt between 1978–85 was paramount. As demonstrated by Table 5.1, claims by international banks on developing countries of Asia (excluding Vietnam, Laos, Cambodia and North Korea) grew from $13 billion in 1975 to $39 billion in 1980, rising to $103 billion by 1985. Lending to South Korea alone accounted for just about one-third of this growth. Debt owed to banks by Indonesia jumped to $15 billion in 1985 from $4 billion in 1980, while Philippine liabilities to financial institutions doubled from $7 billion to over $13 billion in the same period. Between 1980 and 1985 China and India, despite their extensive usage of soft loans from multilateral agencies, began to use commercial borrowing to a much more significant extent, although their total borrowing remained low in comparison to most of the rest of Asia.

The cumulative increases in external debt among Asian developing countries led by 1980–81 to a rising concern over the continuing ability to repay principal and interest obligations and doubts about whether aggressive use of debt finance could continue to be an effective means of economic development. These doubts were given concrete substance in the aftermath of the second oil crisis, as inflation spiralled upward and the developed countries, especially the United States, moved into recession. The failure of Mexico in August 1982 to service its debt in a timely manner marked the emergence of the 'debt crisis', and put a chill on the willingness of banks to readily advance long-term credits, especially for balance of payments support. This further compelled most Asian nations to embrace a more cautious development policy emphasising price stabilisation, fiscal deficit reduction and a lowering of external imbalances.

Successful adjustment in the 1980s

Policy adjustment among Asian countries was in most cases swift and substantial, especially in comparison to Latin America (see chapter 2). Only in the Philippines, largely because of social and political problems compounded by dependence on commodity exports (sugar and coconuts), did economic deterioration overtake debt servicing requirements. Indonesia skirted the edges of debt servicing difficulties, in part because of an exceptionally high reliance on yen denominated financing, which boosted the dollar value of debt and debt servicing when the dollar depreciated against the yen. But strong fiscal adjustment efforts and currency depreciation, coupled with major support from traditional donors (through the Inter-Governmental Group for Indonesia) helped that country avoid rescheduling.

Asian countries have generally been able to sustain high rates of economic growth, which in large measure have been export-based especially since the recovery of the US economy since 1983. Since that period Asian economies reflect a general improvement in savings performance of business, government and households throughout the region. Investment, which had reached quite high rates in the NICs prior to 1981, also declined in those countries, although they remained strong in South-East Asia into the mid-1980s.

The improvements in the savings-investment balances occurred for a number of reasons. First, improved exports and effective currency depreciation boosted corporate earnings. Second, price stabilisation efforts through monetary policy significantly reduced inflation expectations and led to an increase in real interest rates, which rationalised investment spending and encouraged consumer thrift. Government expenditures, especially for projects of questionable economic return, were curtailed and fiscal balances improved. The exceptions to these developments, of course, remained the centrally planned economies of Vietnam, Cambodia, Laos and North Korea. Burma, still under the dictatorial Ne Win regime, remained dormant and its economy stagnant.

The adjustment among the NICs was especially rapid. As exporters mainly of competitive manufactured goods to North America they were particularly well placed to capitalise on the expansion of the US economy. Indeed, the combination of reduced investment and government spending, currency depreciation against the yen and the voracious US appetite for consumer and capital goods propelled South Korean and Taiwanese exports to unprecedented rates of expansion, creating in the process new, world class industries in the space of a few years' time.

Among South-East Asian countries, the pace of adjustment was initially slower due to their substantial reliance on commodity exports. Prices for most commodities continued to languish well into late 1987, despite the vigorous US recovery. As terms of trade deteriorated, income continued to be transferred abroad, partially offsetting early increases in domestic savings performance.

Since the Mexican default, sixty-one countries have experienced debt servicing difficulties. A comparison of those countries, especially in the large Latin American debtors, with the Asian group is revealing. The countries that have had debt serving problems entered the global recession with significantly higher ratios of external debt to exports, even though many had lower debt to GDP ratios than the average of borrowing countries. In large part this can be traced to a legacy of import substitution policies (especially in Latin America) that led to protected, uncompetitive domestic markets. In many cases this was compounded by the existence of large inefficient state enterprises that dominate local markets and resources.

Table 7.2 External debt per cent of GDP

	1975	1980	1985	1988
Korea	34	44	64	29
Taiwan	-	17	15	15
Philippines	23	56	94	84
Indonesia	33	27	40	71
Malaysia	18	23	63	64
Thailand	15	24	47	38
China	-	2	7	13
India	15	11	16	18
Total Asia	-	25	43	41
Mexico	21	28	53	59
Brazil	25	28	51	37
Argentina	21	16	75	59
Chile	72	36	130	93
Colombia	26	20	38	46
Venezuela	16	50	56	48
Total Latin America	30	29	67	57

Source: Morgan Guaranty Bank Economics Department

Higher trade barriers in the protectionist-orientated countries also contributed to making local industries less competitive globally and thus retarded export growth. This meant that interest payments absorbed a higher proportion of export earnings, making them particularly vulnerable to the rise in short-term interest rates that took place.

A further distinction is in the extent to which economic policy was effective in controlling monetary expansion and inflation. Where money growth was excessive and inflation rose to damaging levels (as in much of Latin America), currency overvaluation occurred, further undermining export competitiveness. In comparing Asia (Korea, Taiwan, the Philippines, Indonesia, Malaysia, Thailand, China and India) to Latin America (Argentina, Brazil, Chile, Colombia, Mexico and Venezuela) this is vividly demonstrated: between 1983–8 the average M2 growth was 17.83 per cent and inflation stood at 5.95 per cent for Asia. (M2 is a measure of the US money supply which includes cash and coin in circulation, demand deposits, savings accounts and small-denomination time deposits.) Asian export growth stood at 10.07 per cent. In comparison, Latin America's average M2 growth was 126.82 per cent and inflation an average 87.4 per cent. Latin America's average export growth was 3.75 per cent, considerably lower than Asia's.

In the instances of high M2 growth and inflation confidence in the currency and opportunities for profitable domestic investment were reduced, prompting capital flight that drained foreign exchange reserves and exacerbated the situation of external financing.

Growth of private external financing

The successful adjustment to a changed environment that facilitated continued stable growth with reduced demands for external financing, enabled Asian countries to resume quickly access to commercial credit markets. With the exception of North Korea which defaulted in 1979, Asian countries generally have enjoyed more favourable financing when compared to other developing country borrowers, especially in Latin America, and have even improved their financing terms since the onset of the debt crisis. Lending spreads for Asian borrowers have declined steadily since 1983–4 to an average of less than forty basis points, putting them on a basis with many industrial borrowers.

Longer-term funds are more readily available to lower risk Asian borrowers owing to innovations in the international financial markets and increasing competition among global financial institutions. Asian countries have been at the forefront of developing country utilisation of such new instruments, note issuance facilities and other types of 'securitised' lending. A number of Asian borrowers have also begun to issue bonds in the Euromarket and major national bond markets and to operate commercial paper programmes.

Asian countries have also realised a significant increase in non-debt creating capital inflows, consisting of foreign direct and portfolio investment. One significant source of increasing direct investment has been Japan. In response to the rapid appreciation of the yen since 1985, Japanese corporations have urgently sought out hospitable, low wage production sites to out-source component manufacture or final assembly for import back to Japan or as a means of maintaining export competitiveness. Foreign investment regulations have also been liberalised in a number of countries, such as South Korea, Thailand,

Malaysia and Indonesia, chief destination for Japanese foreign direct investment.

The emergence of domestic securities markets in both debt and equity instruments is also behind the increase in portfolio investment. Financial deepening and modernisation, coupled with relaxation of capital and exchange controls has facilitated an increase in the flow of private capital both in and out of a number of Asian countries, reflecting the maturity of corporate sectors, particularly in the NICs, and the current capital surpluses of South Korea and Taiwan.

Four flashpoints

Four specific countries loom large in the 1990s with potential external debt problems - the Philippines, China, India and Vietnam. Each already has a substantial debt burden and will require new capital inflows in the future. The 1 December 1989 coup attempt in the Philippines, the crushing of the democratic movement in China earlier in the year, the change in government in India in December, and the problem of ageing leadership in Vietnam all point to relatively uncertain political development in these Asian countries, that could well have serious economic consequences.

The Philippines, with a total external debt of around $29 billion (1988 World Bank figure), ended the 1980s with the prospects of a Brady Plan debt reduction programme almost uprooted by a military coup that came close to unseating President Corazon Aquino. Earlier in the year, the Philippines and its commercial and official creditors had worked out an agreement: new money would be provided by a number of countries, led by Japan and the United States, part of which would be made available for a debt buy-back of $1.3 billion of Philippine debt at 50 per cent of face value. The combined assistance from the IMF, World Bank, and other bilateral donors was expected to allow the Asian country to reduce the annual cost of financing its external debt.

Although the December coup attempt almost disrupted the process, the US government provided $95 million in grant funds later in the month to support the Philippine government's buy-back programme. The demonstration of US support for the Philippines was crucial, considering the political baggage the country took into the 1990s. While 'people power' helped bring down the Marcos dictatorship, Mrs Aquino's administration largely failed to deliver many of its promises of cleaner government, a more pluralistic system, and a responsible national leadership. Six coup attempts in four years failed to unseat the democratically-elected government, but serious problems loom with the people's expectations.

The sad truth is that corruption continues to exist and many of those elected to the nation's legislative body favoured the President's removal, even if it were to happen by a coup. The economic overlap of the questionable political future in the Philippines - that also includes an insurrection on the part of the Marxist-orientated New People's Army - is a coolness on the part of investors to put their money, factories and other operations in the country. Considering the need for foreign investment, the ripples from the December 1989 coup have the potential of derailing or postponing the country's recovery in the early 1990s.

China underwent considerable growth in its external debt in the 1980s. Total external debt stood at a hefty $42 billion at the end of 1988. Although the political storm that swept out of the massacre in Tiananmen Square in June 1989 decapitated the democracy movement and preserved the political power in the hands of hardliners, foreign investment rapidly cooled off. It was only at the very end of 1989 that Japanese banks indicated that the capital tap was to be turned on again. Considering the potential for further political turmoil and the economic tightening that China faces in the early 1990s due to import expansion, the size of the external debt and the question about the ability to pay cannot be far from the thoughts of the country's leadership.

India has long been considered relatively untroubled by debt problems. However, China's entry into the World Bank and growing competition from poorer countries for soft loans, pushed India to seek more commercial funds. In the aftermath of the December 1989 general parliamentary elections which observed the fall of Rajiv Gandhi's administration, the new National Front government of Prime Minister V.P. Singh announced that the country's external debt had been underestimated, which in mid-1989 stood at $61 billion.

The major concerns for the National Front government will be maintaining unity, dealing with economic imbalances in the country and dealing with the debt build-up. Prime Minister Singh's Janata Dal party only has 147 seats in the 529 member house. Its coalition partners are the Hindu revivalist party (BJP) with 88 seats and the Communist with 44 seats. Forging an economic policy will be difficult: even within his Janata Dal party Singh must contend with conflicting views of those favouring ongoing trade liberalisation and industrialisation with a place for foreign investment and those opposed to foreign investment with a preference for promoting cottage industries and rural development.

On the debt front, Singh must deal with the rise of private commercial creditor debt. In 1980 this stood at $2 billion; in 1988 it was $18.6 billion. Moreover, the interest payments have risen from $503 million in 1980 to $2.6 billion in 1988. What may complicate matters for India is the dual rise in imports and the debt service in the 1990s. India stands to have problems with both simultaneously if prudent measures are not taken in the short term.

While Vietnam lacks the same access to international capital markets enjoyed by China and India, its economy limps into the 1990s with an external debt, according to the Economist Intelligence Unit, of around $8 billion (1986), low growth and a distribution system incapable of dealing with its tasks. As early as 1987 it was acknowledged that the economy was in dire straits. The troop withdrawal in 1988 and 1989 from Cambodia further underlined this point: the ongoing war with the Khmer Rouge and other Cambodian resistance groups was a tremendous cost on Hanoi's budget and isolated it from both foreign aid and international lending. In the 1990s Vietnam will badly need international assistance to modernise its economy. The way ahead will be difficult and the temptation to overborrow may well exist.

Challenges for the 1990s

Economic growth in the Asia-Pacific area is expected to remain above that of any other region and trade growth has already surpassed that between North America and Europe. A development of major importance is the rise of new creditor nations in the area; most significantly Japan, but followed by South Korea and Taiwan. Apart from these saving intensive economies, the need for continued foreign financing for growth and development is likely to remain high. Asian countries continue to face substantial infrastructure needs to accommodate increasing trade. The growing emphasis on improving general welfare as per capita GNP rises, and the demand for upgraded technology needed to remain competitive, argue for continued growth in investment in the region.

Domestic savings as a source of development finance can be expected to grow steadily as incomes in the region rise and financial deepening takes place. But savings performance in most countries remains low in comparison to more developed economies and the high saving Asian countries and is not expected to close the gap with investment for some time. Consequently there will be a continuing demand for external sources of savings to meet the requirements for domestic investment.

While the role of official finance, particularly through multilateral channels can be expected to remain important, significant increases from current levels, at least in real terms, seems unlikely. To a large extent, this reflects the move to reduce fiscal deficits in the main donor countries as well as competing demands from other, needier borrowers. A number of previously major claimants to bilateral assistance in Asia are being 'graduated' toward more commercially based financing. Another reason for the levelling off is the reluctance of many borrowing countries to avail themselves of assistance which is restricted to the purchase of donor country exports (called tied aid). Some donor countries redirected their assistance through multilateral institutions which to a certain degree has supplanted some bilateral flows.

One important exception to this may be the role that Japan can play in furthering development through a substantial augmentation of its foreign development assistance. Indeed, Japan has pledged itself to a significant increase in the level of its Official Development Assistance (ODA), although questions remain as to the means by which such assistance will be made available, to which countries and on what terms. Japanese assistance has been criticised in the past for being overly tied to the import of Japanese goods. Even so, a rise in Japanese assistance in the region may be sufficient only to offset a diversion of overall assistance to the poorer nations of Latin America and Africa and the least developed countries in Asia itself.

The relative decline in official financing means that commercial channels are likely to continue to grow in importance. This means that the process of economic adjustment to market forces and the integration into the global economy that this implies will remain a compelling force for Asian economies (especially in the command economies and China). Access to commercial financing puts a premium on achieving higher degrees of creditworthiness. This is a self-reinforcing cycle. Sound economic policies that achieve favourable conditions for private financing create the environment for the most efficient use of investment funds. Furthermore, political stability is an essential precondition to attract and retain access to private funds. In this respect the broad trend toward regional accommodation and reapprochment among longstanding antagonists is highly encouraging.

In the commodity dependent countries of South-East Asia, there is a continuing need to improve the structure of the balance of payments by reducing vulnerability to volatile commodity prices. This means establishing the proper framework for the growth of non primary product exports through appropriate exchange rate valuation, elimination of trade distortions and import substitution bias to investment. In these more traditionally rural economies, the role that financial deepening can play in improving savings behaviour and resource allocation stands to improve significantly from better policies.

Increasing dependence on commercial financing puts a larger burden on governments and markets to access carefully the volume, cost and maturity structure of offshore borrowing, so that the growth of external debt remains compatible with the expansion in debt servicing capacity. In particular, over-reliance on short-term financing can be especially risky by increasing the rollover requirement, which could become difficult in the event of adverse developments or shocks to the financial system.

Additional risks arising from increased reliance on commercial financing have to do with exchange rate and interest rate volatility. The former is of increasing importance in Asia with the growth of yen-based lending from Japan. In the event of dollar depreciation, the dollar value of outstanding debt can rise, perhaps precipitously, along with the debt servicing burden. If there is a mismatch in the original or denomination of export earnings against debt service obligations, key indicators of creditworthiness can be substantially and swiftly affected. Increased reliance on commercial finance also tends to expose the borrower to higher risks from interest rate repricing. The changing structure of money and capital markets has led to greater volatility in interest rates, particularly under a system of more widely fluctuating exchange rates and divergent monetary and fiscal policies. As the world's capital markets become more closely interconnected, these fluctuations are quickly translated into interest rate movements.

Clearly, the outlook for continued economic growth and advancement in Asia will be highly influenced by developments in the major industrial economies. The US, in particular, faces the task of restructuring its own economy to become more competitive, in order to reduce its unsustainable trade deficit, while avoiding a turn toward protectionist policies that could severely harm Asia's trade-based and outward looking development strategy. Therefore, Japan needs to continue opening its domestic economy in order to reverse the potentially unmanageable build-up of foreign assets and to provide markets for Asia's and other regions' developing economies' exports. The shift of the locomotive burden from the United States to Japan as well as Europe, is critical to avoid a potentially damaging world recession.

In turn Asia's developing economies, particularly South Korea and Taiwan, have become important players in the world economy, which entails the need for these high savings economies to accelerate the pace of their own trade and financial liberalisation. In the first instance, liberalisation is needed to improve the efficiency of industries supporting key export sectors, in order to broaden industrial integration. Trade liberalisation would also ensure that the benefits of economic progress are more equitably distributed to the population and that standards of living improve. It is also important that these countries begin to play a constructive role in ensuring the integrity of the global trading system, from which they have benefited and to avoid protectionist actions by the US and other countries aimed at forcibly prying open their markets. Likewise, financial liberalisation may be necessary to prevent an unproductive use of accumulating foreign assets, distortions to the exchange rate, of an increase in inflationary pressures that could ultimately damage competitiveness.

References

Collins, Susan M. and Won-Am Park, 'External Debt and Macroeconomic Performance in South Korea', in Jeffery Sachs (ed.), *Developing Country Debt and the World Economy*. Chicago: University of Chicago Press, 1989.

The Economist, 'The Odds against V.P. Singh', 23 December 1989.

The Economist Intelligence Unit, *World Outlook 1989*. London: The Economist Intelligence Unit, January 1989.

Kelly, Brian and Mark London, *The Four Little Dragons: Inside Korea, Taiwan, Hong Kong and Singapore at the Dawn of the Pacific Century*. New York: Simon and Schuster, 1989.

Loong, Pauline, 'Singapore leaves the door ajar', *Euromoney*, July 1987.

McBeth, John, 'Aquino's position seriously weakened by rebellion: Gunning for Cory', *The Far East Economic Review*, 14 December 1989.

Rowan, Roy, 'A Strategic Look at the Rim', *Fortune*, Fall 1989.

Rowley, Anthony, 'Indonesia Struggles with Rival Paths to Progress: Economic Schizophrenia', *The Far Eastern Economic Review*, 10 September 1987.

Tiglao, Rigoberto, 'Instability Threatens already Weakened Economy: Shattered Confidence', *Far Eastern Economic Review*, 14 December 1989.

Woo, Wing Thye and Anwar Nasution, 'The Conduct of Economic Policies in Indonesia and Its Impact on External Debt', in Jeffery Sachs (ed.), *Developing Country Debt and the World Economy*. Chicago: The University of Chicago Press, 1989.

World Bank, *World Debt Tables 1989–90: External Debt of Developing Countries*. Washington, D.C.: World Bank, 1989.

Chapter 8

Southern Europe

*Scott B. MacDonald**

Introduction

There have been riots in the streets, power struggles within ruling leadership elites, downfalls of governments and electoral losses associated with it. Austerity has been one of its results, and many people feel they have been unfairly targeted to pay the cost. This is the 'debt crisis' and its impact on the Southern European countries of Portugal, Greece, Turkey and Yugoslavia. (The other Balkan countries are covered in the Eastern Europe chapter.)

Although often overlooked in discourses on the debt problem, Southern European nations have been through their 'own time of troubles'. It is frequently forgotten that Turkey was one of the first of the major non-industrialised countries in the late 1970s to reschedule its external debt and undergo a far-reaching and painful economic restructuring. More recently, Yugoslavia continues to have problems with its external debt, a situation exacerbated by political factors. Greece and Portugal, though more economically advanced (according to World Bank criteria), carry heavy debt burdens that could potentially complicate their ongoing process of integration with the European Community (EC).

This chapter examines the debt crisis in Southern Europe with two specific questions in mind: what was the balance between external factors and the strategies adopted by the four Southern European countries that led them into the debt crisis, and conversely, how did other strategies lead some of the countries out of the debt crisis? The experiences of these countries show that debt problems did not begin in 1982 nor are they limited to Latin America, but to a wider set of countries. The Southern European experience, moreover, demonstrates that for all nations affected, debt problems have been and are complex and that each country is different in its response.

The Southern European countries occupy a rather odd place in discussions about economic development: are they part of the so-called Third World or are they part of the industrialised group of nations? Clearly, in a broader definition of 'Southern Europe' that encompasses Italy and Spain, the group is more industrialised and has a higher

---

* Mr. MacDonald is an official of the Office of the Comptroller of the Currency. The views expressed in this chapter, however, are solely his and do not necessarily represent those of the Office of the Comptroller of the Currency.

standard of living than most developing countries. Unemployment is not a severe problem, poverty exists but not in a widespread manner, and economic inequality has steadily declined from high levels.

However, subtracting Italy and Spain changes the picture. The remaining four have similarities to both groups of nations, but in the late 1980s and into the 1990s have drawn increasingly closer as a group to the industrialised countries, a process enchanced by Greece's and Portugal's entry into the European Community. In many respects, the Southern European countries occupy a peculiar developmental niche. While they have, in general, modernised their industrial infrastructures, made advances in the standard of living and per capita income, and developed greater market sophistication, external debt continues to be a drag and structural problems related to distribution and inflationary pressures linger. In this Greece, Portugal and Turkey advanced the furthest. At the other extreme, Yugoslavia's economic crisis in the late 1980s and early 1990s has put that multi-ethnic country under considerable strain. From the experiences of these four countries, there are perhaps some lessons to be drawn for the developing world.

Any discussion on Southern Europe and its debt problem would be remiss without acknowledgement of the importance of political developments. In the 1980s Southern Europe underwent considerable changes in the political realm, a process that continues into the 1990s. Greek and Portuguese democracies are beginning to mature after their rebirths in the 1970s; Turkey too, has re-embarked down the democratic path in the 1980s. Even Yugoslavia has made tentative steps towards this goal, although the ethnic and economic tensions that boiled over in the late 1980s cast a shadow over the potential for full political liberalisation along western lines. Despite the varying levels of political development, the 'will of the people' has emerged as a factor to be taken into consideration when implementing austerity programmes or devaluing the currency. Political systems, especially those in Yugoslavia and Turkey, have been hard-pressed at different periods to meet the demands of the population while keeping international creditors content. Therefore, in the broad scope of the discussion about the debt problem in Southern Europe, political factors are also given credence.

Turkey: evolution of a crisis

Of the four countries under examination, the debt crisis crept into the Turkish economy first. It was, in fact, the first of the major non-industrialised countries forced to reschedule its external debt. As two economists, Merih Celasun and Dani Rodrik, noted:

> Turkey's debt reschedulings prior to 1982 were the largest ever undertaken, and accounted for nearly 70 per cent of the total volume of debt renegotiated by all LDCs [Less Developed Countries] in 1978-80.

Turkey's difficult situation with its external debt reflected a convergence of crises. Turkey in the post-World War II period has gone through several 'ten-year cycles'. In very broad terms, this means that every decade (1960, 1971, 1980) a democratic government undergoes economic and political crises. The economic crisis is characterised by rising inflation, adverse international conditions for exports and rising costs of imports, and an inability of the elected government to implement the measures needed to rectify the situation. The failed economic management also has an important political component: as the economy sours, political forces polarise. Turkey provides a rather fertile ground for the polarisation of political groups. It has traditionally been pulled between divergent forces: Europe and the Middle East, secularism and Islam, as well as communism and right-wing nationalism. Furthermore, Turkey has a sizeable Kurdish population, who have frequently sought to create their own nation in the south-eastern part of the country.

The recurring crisis in Turkey's political economy did not come overnight in 1980, but was the product of a number of factors which were in nature structural as well as external. The Turkish economy has traditionally been state-driven with public enterprises playing an important role, while development policies have favoured import substitution over exports and industry over agriculture. This process has its roots in the very founding of the Republic following the collapse of the Ottoman Empire.

In many ways the Turks followed the concept of 'étatisme', in which the state guided the economy from the 'commanding heights'. This basic concept was evident in the programme of Kemal Ataturk's government party and inscribed in the Republic's constitution. The result was that by the 1940s, the government, through its numerous organs, became the nation's major industrial producer, largest employer and leading exporter. By the early 1970s the state-driven Turkish economy was characterised by rapid expansion stimulated by strong industrial growth. This was reflected in 1972 and 1973 by the country's first current account surpluses in over two decades. But there were emerging problems. Import substitution and heavy industrialisation required a high level of capital investment because of the need for sophisticated technology and large-scale production. This resulted in high cost manufacturing in what was a limited domestic market.

In the early 1970s, investment productivity declined, raising questions about the country's ability to sustain high cost manufacturing. The decline in investment productivity was temporarily offset by rapid increases in workers' remittances, helping Turkey to avoid a decrease in its rapid rate of economic growth. At the same time, the benefits of higher growth were not passed on to the population in terms of substantial per capita income increases because of rapid population growth.

Turkey's inward-looking development model was also structurally fragile. As long as imported inputs, such as energy, remained at relatively low prices, and workers' wages continued to be lower than those in the developed countries in the rest of Europe, there was forward momentum. The quadrupling of oil prices related to the Arab oil embargo in 1973–74 and the ensuing world recession threatened to end that forward momentum.

Turkey was faced with a difficult situation in 1974. The rapid rise in imports, due primarily to oil, necessitated greater revenue for continued industrialisation and for payment of the external account deficits. There were three paths open to the government: it could either seek to

1. devalue the Turkish lira, control domestic demand and expand exports;
2. seek greater US foreign aid; or
3. turn to the foreign commercial banks.

The first option would be politically unpopular and require a substantial change in economic policy. Meanwhile, the avenue of seeking greater US assistance was closed by the 1974 Turkish invasion of Cyprus. This was undertaken in response to Greek attempts to force a political unification of the island with the mainland. The only remaining option was increased foreign borrowing, and commercial banks in Europe and the United States were more than willing to lend, driven by the need to recycle petro-dollars.

Foreign borrowing provided the Turkish economy with the needed capital to continue rapid expansion. Economic growth accelerated in the years immediately following 1973, which was demonstrated by an average 7.5 per cent GDP expansion during the 1974–7 period. This ongoing pace of expansion increased the need for imported inputs. At the same time, export expansion was inconsistent and adversely affected by the appreciation of the real exchange rate.

The result of heavy borrowing, rapid economic growth and substantial import expansion was a widening current account deficit. A substantial amount of the borrowing was short term and interest payments mounted rapidly. Turkey's current account balance of payments shifted from a surplus in 1973 of $660 million to a deficit of $3.1 billion in 1977. While the economy overheated, the pressure on the country's resources to meet its international obligations increased substantially: the debt service ratio - the ratio of interest payments and amortisation to merchandise exports - increased from 14 per cent in 1974 to 33 per cent in 1977 as a result, raising questions as to Turkey's creditworthiness.

In the 1977–9 period, the civilian government responsible for leading the country found the situation increasingly beyond its control. Although two large parties, the centre-left Social Democrats and the right-wing Justice Party, respectively led by Bulent Ecevit and Suleyman Demirel, rotated in and out of office, they were dependent on the support of a bewildering assortment of small-party alliances. The fragmentation of political parties in Turkey during the 1970s led to a situation in which the major parties were largely ineffective in forming governments that could provide sustained policy direction. The parliamentary parties remained more concerned with political survival, hidden agendas and the destruction of opponents than in resolving the country's growing array of economic problems.

The situation deteriorated further with the second oil price rise in 1979 and 1980. The price of Saudi Ras Tanuro, one of the major oil grades, rose from $12.70 a barrel in 1978 to $28.67 a barrel in 1980, almost doubling Turkey's energy import bill. Other commodities also cost more. Coffee, which occupies an important cultural niche in Turkish life, rose from 41.2 cents a pound in 1973 to $1.52 a pound in 1977. These factors, combined with the government's difficulty in reducing the import flow, was bad news for Turkey. The negative trend in the current account continued in 1978 with a deficit of $1.27 billion, followed by $1.4 billion in 1979.

Turkey was also hit by the steady increase in interest rates in the late 1970s, which added to its external debt servicing burden. As the international creditor community began to have doubts about Turkey, difficulties with further borrowing made debt management increasingly problematic. Foreign creditors, in large part, were increasingly apprehensive about Turkey because of the country's growing political instability. Lending became short term.

The lynchpin to Turkey's downfall was a device referred to as 'convertible Turkish lira deposits'. These were short-term loans in the form of deposits by foreign banks in Turkish banks. The problem with this scheme was noted by Pedro-Pablo Kuczynski:

> since these loans were officially in the form of deposits, convertible into foreign exchange, they were not counted as debts and, therefore, were not subject to witholding taxes on the interest paid abroad. For a while, everyone, including the international agencies, was fooled; then, in early 1977, Turkish foreign exchange reserves ran out.

Although Turkey managed to survive 1977 with economic growth and inflation at 27 per cent, the day of reckoning came in 1978 when the economy contracted by 2.9 per cent and inflation rose to 45.6 per cent. Turkey's debt crisis slowly unfolded in 1978–9 as the country had stacked up $2.3 billion in short-term debt by the end of 1979. The country was forced in 1978 to begin the rescheduling process, which was to ultimately cover some $5.5 billion. This was to be a protracted and painful process: it was not until 1980 that negotiations were successfully concluded. The country's political slide complicated matters, especially the period of chaos leading up to the 12 September 1980 military coup. This was the third military intervention in Turkish politics since the establishment of a multiparty system after World War II. The 1980 coup was a departure from earlier putches (1960 and 1971): the country's political system had not been as badly polarised and many observers felt that the country was on the brink of a civil war between the left and right.

The new military government was headed by General Kenan Evren, a strong nationalist committed to returning his country back to stable government and economic growth. While the military moved rapidly to de-politicise the country by disbanding the old political parties (on 16 October 1981) and banning a number of leaders from political activities, Turgut Ozal, who handled economic affairs in the last pre-coup civilian government, was given responsibility for reforming the economy.

The new government's impact

Although General Evran was the head of state, elected automatically by a clause in the 1982 constitutional referendum, it was Ozal who was to emerge as the pivotal figure in Turkish history in the 1980s. An engineer by training, Ozal soon proved to be an able politician, making significant transformations in the economy while distancing himself from the military's attempt to establish a new political order.

Within three years, Ozal created the Motherland Party (ANAPO) and was elected Prime Minister in 1983. Although only three out of the country's fifteen parties participated in the 1983 elections, and the ban on certain politicians remained in effect, Ozal took his place as an elected head of government.

Mr Ozal's economic reforms were the main achievement he could offer to the Turkish people when they went to the polls in 1983 and again in 1987. He was convinced that the country needed to undertake extensive and fundamental reforms that would change the structure of the Turkish economy. As Rusdu Saracoglu, Governor of the Central Bank of the Republic of Turkey in 1989 noted:

> The programme was based on principles of a free market economy. Import substitution was discarded as the basic strategy for economic growth. Instead the government adopted an outward-oriented growth strategy based on export promotion.

The overarching policies (implemented between 1981–4) that encompassed this change of direction were export and import liberalisation, a flexible exchange rate policy, a series of mini-devaluations and new directions in fiscal and financial services sectors oriented at enhancing the export sector.

The results of the change in direction were significant, especially considering Turkey's historical bent for a restrictive trade regime. The real GDP expanded at an average annual rate of over 6 per cent during the 1984–6 period, while inflation declined from 50 per cent in 1984 to below 30 per cent in 1986. There was also a steady improvement in the external accounts. In 1980 total exports were $2.9 billion; by 1984 they had expanded vigorously to $7.4 billion and up to $10.3 billion in 1987.

In 1988, Turkey's economy grew by 3.4 per cent (slowed by anti-inflationary measures) and the current account showed a surplus of $1.5 billion, the first since 1973. The shift was in large part credited to the development of the country's tourist sector which contributed around $2 billion in earnings and an increase in merchandise exports. Low oil exports also helped.

The export growth model has meant diversification of goods exported as well as markets. The composition of exports has continued to shift from agricultural goods to manufactured products and while the US and European markets are significant, the Middle East and North Africa have emerged in the 1980s as important areas for Turkish commerce. The particular growth areas in industry have been leather goods, textiles and machinery.

Sound economic management allowed Turkey to return to international capital markets after an absence of several years. While capital for African and Latin American countries dried up after 1982, Turkey cautiously re-entered the market in 1983 when it obtained eurocredits. The expansion of Turkish external debt from $18.4 billion in 1983 to around $42 billion (including foreign military debt) in 1988 is a crucial factor in the country's relative success in structural adjustment. Although the stabilisation and adjustment processes were painful for large parts of the population, the renewed access to outside funds provided badly needed investment. Renewed capital flows allowed the government to carry through its reforms of trade liberalisation, the development of non-traditional export products, regional development projects as in the south-east, and infrastructural improvements. While many capital-deprived developing countries were forced to neglect and 'devour' their own infrastructures, Turkey was actively improving its, which in part explains how the first of the major debtors to reschedule was one of the first to re-emerge from the debt crisis.

Turkey also benefits from direct foreign investment, attracted by the improved economic and political environment. In 1987, the Turkish government authorised a record $536 million in foreign-investment applications, nearly double the total for all the years 1954–80. In 1988, the figure climbed to $800 million and is expected to rise to $1 billion in 1989. The capital inflow of multinational companies helps the country in terms of employment and reduces the need for new loans.

For all of Turkey's advances, there are problems. Inflation continues to be a concern. At the end of 1988, it rose to its highest level in several years, reaching 77 per cent. Although inflation was brought down, below 70 per cent in 1989, it remains problematic due to greater money supply related to the wage settlement agreement reached with public workers in May 1989 and higher domestic demand. The wage settlement was estimated to cost around $1.6 billion, forcing the government to increase domestic borrowing throughout the year. This put considerable strain on the government's policies of reducing inflation and holding the budget deficit down. The growth of domestic debt also complicates Turkey's ability to develop a more cohesive debt strategy.

Although Turkey has used its new credits for development, debt accumulation has a downside. There can be no hiding the fact that Turkey still has a large external debt. Although it declined from $42.8 billion in 1987 to $42.3 billion in 1988 (due in part to dollar depreciation), projections for 1989 are $43 billion.

Concerns continue about the country's future ability to repay an annual debt service of around $7 billion (average annual interest and amortisation payments in 1987-91). Unlike South Korea in the 1980s, which was able to grow out of its external debt through trade and current account surpluses, Turkey's growth has not led to significant net debt reduction. As long as the external debt remains high, the potential for problems will continue. What happens if Turkey falls into a deep recession or exports fall off because of rising protectionism? Would cutting imports and new austerity measures be enough to keep the financial wolf of insolvency from the door? And, what would the political backlash be - riots in the streets, strikes and societal polarisation cut by inequalities.

Turkey has emerged from the 1980s with a stronger economic base, founded on the export growth model. Throughout most the decade until 1988, the economy has expanded at an average of 6 per cent, which gives it the highest growth rate among OECD (Organisation for Economic Cooperation and Development) members. Turkey has clearly made substantial progress in its external debt management. The country went from near political and economic collapse to a phase of painful structural adjustment and military government to renewed access to commercial bank lending and parliamentary government. There are no guarantees that Turkey will become a Newly Industrialising Economy or 'catch up' with Western Europe in the immediate future, but progress has been made. Although the GDP growth rate in 1989 slowed to 1.5 per cent due to anti-inflationary measures and drought, in September Turkey paid back the last segment of its rescheduled debt. It is the first troubled major debtor to have done so. In the 1990s, the possibility does exist that Turkey will grow its way out of its debt problem.

Parallels

Turkey's experience with the debt crisis has many parallels in Portugal, Greece and Yugoslavia. Each of these countries pursued, to various degrees, similar development policies in the 1970s. While Turkey has appeared to have made significant progress in the 1980s, the only other country to have the same such advances has been Portugal.

Portugal's crisis

Portugal sits at the end of the Iberian Peninsula, has a population of 10.4 million and one of the lowest standards of living in the EC. Portugal's traditional economic and political thrust has been outwards into the Atlantic and not towards Europe. This partially explains the country's relative isolation from the mainstream of European development, such as the breakup of colonial empires, the creation of the European Community and consolidation of democratic governments throughout Western Europe. Portugal remained a corporist state through the 1950s and 1960s with limited natural resources, yet carrying with it the legacy of the Portuguese Empire in the form of a number of costly colonial wars in Africa.

The Portuguese economy, like Turkey's before the 1980s, was largely inward-looking, with the exception of strong trade links to the African empire. Agriculture was the dominant sector of the economy, although there were some efforts to stimulate industrial development. By 1973, the eve of the corporate regime's demise, Portugal lagged far behind the rest of Europe in its economic status and, in some respects, had more in common with the more advanced parts of the developing world.

On 25 April 1974 a popular military coup ended Portugal's corporatist regime. Although there were concerns about the revolution's initial leftist direction, centrist forces emerged. By July 1976 the first democratically elected government took office in what has proven to be an unbroken return to constitutional government. Despite the emergence of a democratic government, stability eluded the country: from July 1980, when the Socialist Mario Soares took office, to October 1985, Portugal had eight different heads of government.

The corporatist government had belatedly set in motion an industrialisation programme that rapidly gained momentum in the 1970s under the various 'revolutionary' administrations. Portugal's industrialisation, however, was hard hit by the second oil price hike in 1979-80 and the international recession in the early 1980s. Comfortable foreign exchange reserves, which had built up to $930 million in 1979, declined to $391 million in 1982. The economy struggled against the global recession, mirrored by a slowdown in GDP growth from 4.8 per cent in 1980 to 1.3 per cent in 1981. Although the economy witnessed a shortlived growth spurt in 1982, it was stagnant in 1983. The current account revealed the growing crisis: following the second oil price rise, the deficit widened from $54 million in 1979 to $3.3 billion in 1982.

Like many countries caught in similar circumstances, Portugal turned to external borrowing to finance its current account deficits. In 1982 alone there was a 16 per cent increase in external borrowing. The country's total external debt shot upwards from $8.9 billion in 1980 to $13.6 billion in 1982. Although not as critical as in many developing countries, the debt service rose from $1.6 billion in 1980 to $2.3 billion in 1982. It was the debt service ratio that underlined why there was concern about the country's debt management: it rose from 24 per cent in 1980 to 39 per cent in 1982.

The country's ongoing political instability discouraged direct foreign investment. At the same time, the widening current account and budget deficits as well as a growing external debt burden increased inflationary pressure. Inflation remained stubbornly above the European norm, rising from 16.7 per cent in 1980 to 22.8 per cent in 1982. Moreover, the widespread sectoral nationalisations in the 1970s created a bloated state sector that ranged from banks to breweries, while most agricultural production was collectivised. In general, the state-owned businesses were inefficient and over-staffed, while the labour market was complicated by revolutionary-inspired legislation that made it exceedingly difficult to reduce employees in troubled industries. Recorded unemployment was high, hovering at an average of more than 7 per cent for the 1980–82 period.

The Portuguese economy was heading for a serious crisis. The increase in short-term debt was becoming problematic and although the country eluded a rescheduling in the late 1970s, it was forced to arrange loans with the Switzerland-based Bank of International Settlements in the early 1980s amounting to $1 billion. Seven hundred million dollars was repaid in 1982 by gold sales, but the government was forced to extend the remaining payments due to mounting economic pressures.

Portugal avoided the systemic political breakdown that afflicted Turkey by a shift in the 'revolution's' direction. In 1982 Socialist President Mario Soares took the country to the right by revising the leftist Constitution of 1974 to allow the establishment of more private enterprise. Soares' ability to move the country further right in terms of economic reform was greatly strengthened by the formation of a centrist coalition government following the April 1983 elections.

The coalition between the Socialists (*Partido Socialista* or PS) and Social Democrats (*Partido Social Democrata* or PSD) gave Soares the largest parliamentary majority of any of Portugal's numerous short-lived governments. This allowed him to implement badly-needed yet painful economic reforms that aimed at stabilising a deteriorating situation. It also set the stage for an extensive restructuring that would diminish the state's role in the economy, enhance the private sector and place a greater emphasis on exports.

Soares, like Turgut Ozal, was a pivotal figure on his country's political-economic landscape. The Socialist leader was staunchly opposed to communism, looked to European integration as a means of strengthening the democratic experience, and made considerable progress in bridging Portugal's deep political and social divisions. The PS reflected its leader: it was pragmatic, favouring a mixed economy in which market mechanisms were linked to national plans of limited guidance. The PS favoured a reduction of the public sector, feeling that social equity was achievable by broad policy measures rather than state-induced (or forced) income distribution.

The immediate measures of the Soares government's economic programme included the implementation of a retroactive tax package, the slashing of food and gasoline subsidies, and an increase in interest rates to 30 per cent. These measures, though politically unpopular, were linked to a $480 million IMF standby loan and agreement. The IMF loan went for projects oriented at preparing the structurally weak economy for entry into the EC.

The results of the 'new economic wave' were impressive. Though the economy marginally contracted in 1983 and in 1984, exports rose from $4.1 billion in 1982 to $5.2 billion in 1983, improving the trade balance from a $4.85 billion deficit to a $2.4 billion surplus over the same period. The current account deficit also began to shrink after three consecutive years of expansion: in 1982 it was $3.3 billion; by 1985, it shifted to a surplus of $410 million.

Despite the expansion of total external debt from $14.5 billion in 1983 (70 per cent of GDP) and $15 billion in 1984 (77.5 per cent of GDP), the structure of that debt changed significantly. Portugal's major problem with its debt management, as in Turkey, was its short-term debt. This had risen to substantial $3.8 billion in 1982. However, by 1985 it was reduced to $2.6 billion, which was far easier to handle. At the same time, Portugal began to enjoy greater access to international capital markets, providing another source of funds for the country's modernisation.

Soares steered the country through one of its most difficult periods, but failed to hold his coalition together. By June 1985 the coalition government dissolved and Portugal, with an improving economy, headed for the polls. Ironically, the PS-PSD alliance ended because of growing differences over economic policy.

The PSD, which had been the junior partner, wanted more rapid economic changes. While they concurred with the PS on EC membership, the PSD favoured a more sweeping economic liberalisation and placed a greater emphasis on the role of the private sector. In particular, the PSD wanted the elimination of the 'revolutionary' and 'socialist' articles in the 1974 Constitution, which they perceived as impediments to local businesses and created a poor environment for attracting foreign direct investment.

The PSD, led by economist Anibal Cavaco Silva, won the largest number of seats in the 6 October 1985 election, capturing 88 of a total of 250 seats (or 34 per cent). Soares' PS lost considerable ground, falling from 101 seats to 57. The rightist Democratic Renewal Party (PRD) won 45 seats and the rest was divided between smaller parties, including the Communists. The PSD then formed a minority government, with Cavaco Silva as prime minister.

The Cavaco Silva government took office on 6 November 1985 with a tacit agreement with the PRD. The PSD minority government quickly surprised most critics as it passed its budget, continued the economic restructuring, and took Portugal into the European Community on 1 January 1986. Furthermore, in July 1986, Cavaco

Silva led his PSD to an overwhelming victory at the polls, providing it with a substantial majority in parliament - the first time a party had done so in over a decade.

Under the Soares and Cavaco Silva governments Portugal stabilised economically and in the aftermath of the 1983-4 adjustment period, made considerable gains. Economic growth was constant in the late 1980s and inflation fell under 10 per cent. Foreign direct investment was increasingly drawn to the improving business environment: it rose from a low of $123 million in 1983 to $327 million in 1987. There were also improvements in the country's standards of living: according to the World Bank, Portugal made advances in health and nutrition standards, such as a greater number of doctors per person and daily calorie supply per capita. Portugal, in fact, ended the decade with a better population per physician ratio than Ireland, Australia and New Zealand.

Portugal's major concerns no longer include debt repayment, despite some deterioration in the current account related to EC membership adjustment. The movement to a single market within the Community by the end of 1992 has steadily gained in importance for the country's economic planners, a remarkable transformation from the time when an inward-looking country was forced to go to the IMF. In fact, total external debt fell from $18.4 billion to $17.2 billion in 1988.

Key factors in Portugal's success were responsible leadership and greater access to international capital markets, especially Eurobonds. The country's leadership demonstrated the political will to steer the country out of what was rapidly becoming a debt trap. The policies adopted by Soares and Cavaco Silva were pragmatic and flexible, emphasising export growth, liberalisation of the trade regime, and promotion of the private sector over ideological rigidity and rhetoric. State control over the economy was gradually reduced. Although Portugal's debt remains a concern in the early 1990s, the country's overall economic performance has improved considerably.

Greece - against the tide

Greece shares many commonalities with Portugal and Turkey in its recent economic development: the country of ten million fell victim to the same problem of rising oil prices, external account pressure and growth of external debt. Greece, however, differed in one outstanding respect: at a period when the debt crisis was becoming a problem for other countries, the government of Prime Minister Andreas Papandreou (1981-9) came to office with an ambitious programme of state spending and intervention in the economy. While the other countries in Southern Europe, including Yugoslavia, implemented economic liberalisation programmes, Greece moved in the opposite direction. The timing could not have been worse and by late 1985, the Panhellenic Socialist Movement (PASOK) government was forced to impose a stabilisation programme, with considerable assistance from the EC.

To understand why the Greek government turned to heavier state involvement in the economy in the 1980s, it is necessary to understand PASOK's ideology. The twentieth-century Greek political system was traditionally divided into three competing camps: the communist left, the liberal centre and the conservative right. In the early post-war period, the country was torn apart in a brutal civil war between the left and right. From that time, the three political forces evolved, surviving the downfall of the constitutional monarchy and several failed democracies. In 1974, the Greek political scene changed with the birth of PASOK. Led by Andreas Papandreou, PASOK rapidly became an important force, overshadowing both the communist left and the centrists.

PASOK's ideology, which was to play an important role in the evolution of the country's debt crisis, had a distinctively Third World tone to it. Panayote E. Dimitras, in a 1985 *Foreign Policy* article noted:

> From the outset, PASOK assumed a posture and espoused an ideological line closely resembling those of African and Asian liberation movements. In fact, PASOK's declared aim was the 'national liberation' of Greece from foreign political and economic domination. In international politics, PASOK opposed both military blocs and what it called 'the logic of Yalta and Potsdam'. That opposition, however, was not evenhanded. Like many Third World movements, PASOK's criticism of the Soviet Union was rare and relatively gentle, while criticism of the United States was unrelenting and violent.

PASOK regarded capitalism with disdain and linked to the military might of the United States, especially after Washington had supported the authoritarian regime of the Colonels in the early 1970s. In a speech delivered in 1984 Prime Minister Papandreou stated:

> A levelling consumerist model has invaded our country and . . . threatens to transform us into a cultural colony. The main vehicle of that invasion is the mass media. They have created the well-known culture: the culture of exhibition and of hedonism, based on acceptance and not on critical processes. It is a pompous, parasitic, faked, tasteless, standardised subculture created with the least common denominator as a criterion . . . It threatens our physiognomy, our specificity, our heritage, our very existence . . . Our traditional popular culture, with its fighting resistance character is . . . our aggressive confrontation to the imported capitalist model.

Considering PASOK's dislike of capitalism, which policies did the newly elected government in October 1981 embark upon? The Greek economy had already slowed from 2 per cent growth in 1980 to −0.2 per cent in 1981, a trend related to the international recession and higher oil prices. Like many countries the austerity option was unappealing as it did not fit the new administration's desire for new social spending and income redistribution. Despite the economic slowdown, there was still wealth in the country – the private sector – and there was external borrowing. The PASOK government would seek to tap both and stimulate domestic demand.

PASOK's approach renewed the discussion about state involvement. Anti-capitalistic, the new government perceived the state as being able to mobilise the resources and possess the political will needed to break through the bottlenecks, bend the inflexibilities and force the pace of growth. The reform of Greece's political economy would be top-down and imposed.

Much of PASOK's approach was summarised in its preliminary Five Year Plan for Economic and Social Development (1983–7) submitted to the Greek Parliament in June 1983. Within the framework of a mixed economy a greater role was given to the public sector and an emphasis was placed on the 'socialisation' of certain activities through participation of local authorities, workers' representatives and public interest groups. The state's role was to be strengthened in the industrial sector in particular. The private sector was notified that it should observe 'the rules of the game'. This meant that the government recognised the importance of profits in the productive process, but it was against anything that smacked of oligopolistic practices (except for the government) and speculative profits (something certain members of the party appear to have forgotten in later scandals).

The new government quickly set to expanding the public sector, stimulating domestic demand, and launching or widening social programmes for health, education, welfare, labour conditions and environment. Initially in 1982 the costs were covered by higher corporate taxes. The situation changed the next year when government spending, as mirrored by a rising budget deficit, began to spiral upwards, climbing from 175 billion drachmas in 1982 to 283 billion drachmas in 1983.

Although PASOK did not create Greece's economic difficulties, it certainly poured fuel on the flames. Its anti-capitalist mentality and policies led to capital flight, a further sag in private sector activity and a steep decline in foreign direct investment. Direct investment in the Greek economy fell from a high of $672 million in 1980 to $436 million and $439 million in 1982 and 1983 respectively.

Greece was also hurt by its entrance into the EC, which as Nicholis Gianaris noted, 'caught protected sleepy Greek firms unprepared by the imported European products that flooded the home markets.' This new wave of imports even outsold Greek food products in Greece, causing the country's food trade surpluses to turn into deficits. Greek reforms, including a 15.5 per cent devaluation of the drachma at the beginning of 1983 and invocation of a clause in the accession agreement to restrict imports from the EC to 1980 levels, did little to halt the deterioration in the external accounts.

The Greek economy failed to resume substantial growth despite the government's efforts: GDP growth was only 0.4 per cent in 1983. This led the government to rely more heavily on increased foreign borrowing to stimulate domestic growth. These efforts were in part rewarded in 1984 and 1985 as the growth rate picked up to 2.7 per cent and 3.2 per cent respectively. Economic growth was regarded as a priority because of elections held in February 1985.

PASOK maintained a comfortable majority of 157 seats in the 1985 elections, but its dominance was eroded. The conservative and pro-business New Democracy Party captured 110 seats and won 41 per cent of the total vote, an increase from 1981's 37 per cent. While PASOK's political hold was weakened, the party's expansive spending policies brought the country to a major crossroads.

By the end of 1985 the budget deficit reached a then historic high of 587 billion drachmas and further growth-orientated, yet state-led polities threatened to turn Greece into a troubled debtor. The structure of the country's debt reflected the broad dimensions of the problem: by the end of 1985, after four years of PASOK, total external debt had expanded to $18.7 billion, with the expansion coming from the public sector. Private sector borrowing actually had fallen from 16.8 per cent of the total debt in 1980 to around 9 per cent in 1985.

By the end of 1985 there were three major problems for PASOK and both were related to debt management. The country's short-term debt had risen to $4.5 billion, the debt service ratio had shot upwards from 11 per cent in 1981 to 25 per cent, and 1985's current account deficit was a record $3.3 billion. Additionally, the net public sector debt had reached a hefty 80 per cent of gross national product, one of the highest ratios for OECD countries. Although this was not yet a full-blown crisis, it indicated that the government's policies had increased Greece's dependency on imported capital, most of which ironically came from West European and US commercial banks.

Greece's deteriorating economy pushed the PASOK government into accepting an austerity programme in October 1985. Greece could have turned to the IMF, as other Southern European countries had, or as a member of the EC (since 1 January 1981) could turn to that organisation. Ideologically, the PASOK government regarded the IMF with suspicion, especially as it emphasised structural adjustment programmes that liberalised trade, reduced state spending and subsidies and promoted the development of private sector. The IMF also favoured direct foreign investment; PASOK looked upon this with suspicion, especially if it came from the United States. The EC provided an alternative path out of the debt crisis that other Southern European countries lacked.

The October 1985 Stabilisation Programme was a comprehensive two-year package that included fiscal and economic measures as well as a six-year ECU 1.75 billion loan from the EC for current account balance of payments assistance. There were clear targets attached to the loan which included a reduced public sector borrowing requirement; a reduction of the external deficit from 10 per cent of GNP to 3 per cent; and a fall in inflation from 25 per cent at the end of 1985 to 10 per cent by the end of 1987. The programme's tools included price and wage controls, monetary restrictions, curbs on tax evasion and public expenditure growth, a 15 per cent devaluation of the drachma and higher prices for public services.

The intitial reaction to the austerity programme was manifested by street demonstrations and a wave of strikes. Hardline PASOK supporters felt betrayed and there were a number of defections from the ruling party. At the same time, support from labour unions diminished. The problem for PASOK was as journalist Kerin Hope noted: 'To many Greeks, lulled by the Socialists' election promises of "Even better days", the restrictions came as an unpleasant surprise.'

The Stabilisation Programme which ended in 1987 did have some successes and helped reduce the possibility of Greece rescheduling. The current account deficit was reduced from 1985's $3.3 billion to $1.3 billion in 1987. The budget deficit, which accounted for 17.6 per cent of GNP in 1985, was brought down to 13 per cent in 1987 (despite being a record 1.16 trillion drachmas). Inflation was also reduced from a high of 22.5 per cent in 1985 to 16.3 per cent in 1987.

Papandreou's change in direction from expansion to restraint helped stabilise the country. This also meant that PASOK pragmatically retreated from its antagonistic approach to the private sector. An OECD report commented: 'the government appears to have shown greater recognition of the key role of the private sector has to play in moving the economy back to a sustainable path of rapid growth, thereby serving to improve the business climate'. This was reflected by a greater inflow of direct investment which rose from $471 million in 1986 to $683 million in 1987.

By the end of 1988 Greece had weathered the financial storm without a rescheduling of its external debt. The combination of austerity and EC assistance, including the disbursement of the second half of the ECU 1.75 billion loan in early 1987 had guaranteed that. The EC loan allowed the government to repay foreign debt early and build up its international reserves, which stood at $2.7 billion at the end of 1987. Greece's creditworthiness improved, which gave it access to $1.5 billion of new loans from commercial banks in 1987 and about the same in 1988. Greece's total external debt stood at $24.5 billion in 1988. Although the size of the debt grew moderately, the economy expanded by 3.1 per cent in 1988 and the improvement of most sectors, enhanced the country's debt service capacity. It appeared that Greece was on its way out of the debt problem.

At the end of the decade, a number of factors once again militated against the Greek economy. PASOK was hurt by Papandreou's ill health and a number of scandals that included his affair with a younger woman (whom he eventually married after divorcing his wife). One of the most damaging affairs was a multi-million dollar banking scandal involving the Bank of Crete: revealed in October 1988, it eventually led to the resignation of five cabinet ministers. The combination of these factors brought the opposition New Democracy Party victory at the polls in June 1989, but without the necessary 151 seats to make an outright majority. After a brief period of uncertainty in which none of the three major parties was able to form a government, New Democracy (with 146 seats) and the communist Alliance (with 29 seats) agreed to form a coalition interim government. The new government was led by the larger party's Tzannis Tzannetakis as prime minister and its three-month mandate was to investigate corruption in the Papandreou administration.

Greece's economy drifted under the right-left coalition government and Papandreou continued to be a force in the country's politics despite corruption probes. A second election was held three months later, which continued the deadlock between the three major parties. With a background of rising inflation, a swelling budget deficit, and declining foreign exchange reserves, the three major parties agreed to form a National Unity government on 21 November 1989. Xenophon Zolotas, eighty-five years of age, was made prime minister. He was a distinguished economist and a former Bank of Greece governor with conservative leanings.

Greece in the early 1990s runs the danger of returning to the difficulties of 1985–6, especially considering the political deadlock and the airing of corruption under PASOK. One of the biggest concerns is the widening budget deficit. In a Bank of Greece (central bank) memorandum leaked to the press in July 1989, it was revealed the government's budget deficit would substantially exceed what PASOK's budget projected, which was already at a historic high.

The National Unity government that brought Greece into the last decade of the twentieth century carried with it a wide range of political views. That wide range of views on economic and social policy complicates the situation as lengthy discussion has the potential to further delay badly-needed reforms. The danger is that the economic slide will not be checked by a stop-gap government with a limited life-span and the temptation to borrow may once more appear to be an option with political motives obscuring economic sense.

Yugoslavia's slide into the debt crisis

Yugoslavia, with a population of 23.4 million, is the newest state of the four, having been established in the aftermath of the First World War under the Karadjordjevic dynasty in 1918. The formation of a state was greatly complicated by the friction between the various ethnic groups. The Serbians were the dominant group in terms of population and military power, but they were forced to share power with the Croats, Slovenes, Bosnians and Montenegrins. Relations between these groups were not always cordial and ethnic tensions continued through the years of the dynasty and the Second World War, only being muted by the rise of communist Marshal Josip Broz Tito.

By the time of Tito's death in 1980, Yugoslavia had survived the Soviet Union's hostility, developed a more broadly-based economy and had close relations with the United States and Western Europe. Political scientist and Yugoslav watcher Bruce McFarlane also noted: 'From the viewpoint of "delivering" a higher material living standard for a majority of citizens, the record of the Yugoslav regime since the 1950s, while erratic, remains impressive.'

Despite Yugoslavia's advances up until General Tito's death, a number of structural problems lingered which would be greatly exacerbated by the international recession and then the global debt crisis. The primary problems confronting Yugoslavia in the two years before the debt crisis hit were uneven regional development; ongoing problems with rising deficits on the external accounts; inflation (18 per cent annually 1976–80); and unemployment. Added to this was the ongoing experimental nature with economic management that had gradually emerged in the 1950s and was further refined in the 1960s and 1970s.

Central to Yugoslavia's approach was the system of workers' self-management, which according to a World Bank study, 'was to create an institutional environment that would provide workers with control over their workplaces and the economy'. Added to this was the perception that the state was to decentralise the economic controls and, in time, destatify as self-management socialism gained momentum. The shift of decision-making power was to transcend private capitalism and state capitalism and institute direct democracy in economic matters to individuals without the intervention of autonomous intermediaries. In many respects, this system instilled a degree of freedom in the economic realm, providing a way to deal with the ethnic pluralism of Yugoslav society. Or, as one study noted, 'enabled different regional interests to be voiced, considered and harmonised'.

As early as 1979, a World Bank report was critical of the self-management model. As the Yugoslav economy came under pressure from rising oil prices in 1979 and 1980 and the global recession, a critical prop was revealed as missing. The central government, which was traditionally the decision-maker, found that the decentralisation process had greatly weakened its ability to formulate and, more significantly, implement a coherent macro-economic policy to deal with the expanding plethora of problems. In particular, the drive for decentralisation stripped the state of two key functions – fiscal policy and planning. A World Bank report in 1979 noted:

> The consequences of these changes could be observed in the inflationary pressures that developed and the stop-go policy cycles that ensued. The momentum of economic growth flagged; import dependency increased; balance of payments difficulties recurred.

But that was in 1979. The *real* crisis would come later. The 1979–81 period was marked by concern, but despite the emergence of such problems, overall performance was relatively satisfactory and leadership succession following Tito's death in 1980 weighed more heavily on the agendas of the national and regional elites.

In 1982 Yugoslavia's problems mounted as the trade deficit was a substantial $2.8 billion and the current account deficit was an equally onerous $1.6 billion. The country's debt service was $3.8 billion, which could not be covered by the foreign exchange reserves of $775 million. To make its international payments, Yugoslavia had to borrow. Considering that the economy only grew by 0.6 per cent in 1982, the country was entering a crisis zone. A number of measures were taken in 1982–3 to stop the slide: policies of demand restraint were pursued, the dinar was depreciated to help the external accounts and a flexible exchange rate policy was adopted.

At the end of 1983 results were mixed. While the economy contracted by 1.3 per cent and inflation rose from 30.4 per cent to 58.3 per cent, import compression helped reduce the trade deficit to a little over $1 billion and shifted the current account from the deficit column to a small surplus of $246 million. Nonetheless, Yugoslavia indicated to its creditors that it had to reschedule. Its first official multi-year debt rescheduling agreement was signed on 4 May 1984 and accounted for $500 million.

The Yugoslav economy continued to be plagued by problems in the 1984–8 period. While the central government struggled to make sense of economic conditions, the various republics sought to preserve their autonomy. This state of affairs undermined efforts to reduce inflation, which climbed steadily from 92 per cent in 1987 to over 250 per cent in 1988. Economic growth continued to elude the country: although 1986 was a good year (partially due to lower oil prices) with a 3.6 per cent expansion, in 1987 it contracted by 0.5 per cent and grew an anaemic 1.0 per cent in 1988. Although the current account was in a surplus throughout the period, Yugoslavia was continuously under pressure to make both interest and principal payments. Problems began when Yugoslavia missed $245 million of interest payments in June 1987 due to a currency shortage. The government asked for delays, opening the door to new rescheduling talks in 1988.

By 1988 Yugoslavia had undergone structural adjustment (with the assistance of the World Bank) since the beginning of the decade. The country had achieved current account surpluses every year since 1983 and had neither sought nor obtained new money (under a rescheduling) from the commercial banks since 1983. Moreover, $262 million of the $600 million of new money provided in 1983 was prepaid in 1986 and 30 per cent remained outstanding at the time of the new request in 1988. Yugolsavia had also worked hard to reduce commercial bank exposure, part of which was accounted for in the more than $1 billion in principal the country repaid in 1986 and 1987. Despite all of the sacrifices, Yugoslavia could not grow out of the debt trap.

Yugoslavia has two major problems:

1. There is a pressing need for a clear line of authority in terms of economic policy between the federal government and republics
2. Ethnic tensions continue to simmer beneath the surface, externalised at times of crisis.

Part of the problem was structural and directly related to the workers' self-management model. Nora Beloff, a noted Yugoslav watcher, referred to it as a 'Holy Grail' and noted that 'efforts to manage the market diverted the pressures of demand and supply into such anti-social practices as high inflation, black markets in currency and commodities, smuggling, speculation, almost ubiquitous corruption, and massive moonlighting in working hours'. These problems were brought home in 1987 with the Agrokomerc scandal which saddled the country with $920 million in bad debt.

Throughout 1988, the federal government sought to implement a sweeping economic reform programme that included liberalisation in trade, prices and foreign exchange allocation. It also included wage controls and a strict bankruptcy law, measures which were unpopular and resulted in demonstrations and over 800 strikes. The demonstrations culminated with workers storming the legislature in Belgrade in June. The difficult economic situation, which occurred simultaneously with new negotiations with the country's creditors also led to an attempt in September to unseat the federal government headed by Prime Minister Branko Mikulic in the country's legislative body.

Although the Mikulic government survived a vote of no confidence and signed a new agreement with its creditors in September that provided Yugoslavia with a little over $1.2 billion ($300 million from commercial banks), October proved to an explosive month. Slobodan Milosevic, Serbia's Communist party leader, blended discontent with the country's economic management and revived Serbian nationalism into a powerful mixture in a bid to assume greater power within the federation.

Milosevic came close to uprooting the system Tito left behind of rotating leadership in both party and government posts that distributed power among national groups and prevented the emergence of a strongman, especially one from Serbia. In May 1987, Milosevic, a former banker, had become Serbia's Communist party leader. His major efforts in that post were to change the 1980 Constitution that gave Serbia only limited authority over the autonomous regions of Vojvodina to the north and Kosovo to the south.

Kosovo, home to a sizeable Albanian minority and cradle of Serbian nationalism, had long been a region of ethnic tensions. Throughout the summer of 1988 Serbs and Montenegrins staged militant protests against alleged persecution of Slavs by ethnic Albanians in Kosovo. Milosevic's role was noted by the *Washington Post*'s Peter Humphrey: 'The Serbs have been egged on by praise from Serbian regional Communist Party leader Slobodan Milosevic, whose supporters have hailed him on the streets as a new Tito.' His critics called him a new Stalin.

Milosevic's attempt to gain greater power was partially successful. Although the October 1988 party congress observed the purge of some his supporters, he did obtain the changes in the constitution that gave Serbia greater authority over the two autonomous regions.

The party's central committee also sought to address the economy. The main thrust of the reforms that came out of the October meeting were the reduction of the party's control over the state and, in a sense, reduction of the control of the state over the economy. In the past, party and state officials were one and the same. Under the new legislation, party officials could not hold both positions and the same was true for state officials. There were two areas to be affected by this change. First, the Federal government, in theory, is strengthened by an enhanced ability to pass economic reforms applicable to all republics and autonomous regions. The second area, as the *Financial Times*' Judy Dempsey noted 'was to claw back some authority for the state and reduce the party's role in the running of the economy.'

Yugoslavia's political rollercoaster did not stop despite what appeared to be a check in Serbian nationalism and the advancement of new economic reforms. In late December, the Mikulic government fell after the Prime Minister failed in the Federal Assembly to pass the 1989 budget that included enterprise legislation and a foreign investment law, both designed to introduce a more market-orientated approach. Resistance came from the republics because the new measures, combined with those from the October plenum, would strengthen the federal government's hand at the expense of local interests. A complicating factor was that the opposition to the proposed 1989 federal budget came from Croatia and Slovenia (the country's most developed republics) due to their apprehension about greater pressures on their resources. The issues raised by anti-Mikulic forces in the Federal Assembly also included the Prime Minister's inability to stem inflation and halt the decline in living standards and his possible ties to scandals in his native Bosnia.

Yugoslavia entered 1989 a nation troubled by ethnic and economic problems. The new prime minister, Ante Markovic, a Croatian, faced a daunting task. The danger of renewed Serbian nationalism and the Mikulic's government fall indicated that sharpened national rivalries continued to be a dictating force in a country whose cohesion threatened to evaporate just as it faced one of the most severe economic crises. Despite Markovic's efforts at economic reform, including the launching of a debt-equity conversion programme, industrial strife continued and inflation climbed upwards past the 2,000 per cent mark.

By December 1989 the political situation was defined by a new offensive of Serbian nationalism launched by Milosevic and a new wave of expanding pluralism driven by events in Slovenia and Croatia. Eastern Europe's democratic thaw reinforced pro-democratic forces throughout Yugoslavia. However, ethnic tensions resulted in a Serbian embargo of trade with Slovenia. Additionally, 650,000 workers in Serbia staged a brief strike on 20 December against new changes proposed by Markovic. Markovic's December economic proposals included a wage freeze aimed at inflation and, significantly, the establishment of an internationally convertible currency. The latter step was radical and indicated that Markovic's programme intended to push Yugoslavia further into becoming part of the global economy.

Throughout 1989 and into 1990, the twin issues of ethnic nationalism and democratic reform became entwined: the greater the push of Milosevic and his allies for Serbian domination (which carried with it a distinctively anti-democratic tendency), the faster the pace of political liberalisation in Slovenia. By early 1990, Slovenia was potentially well advanced to establishing a western-style parliamentary system. Croatia was not far behind. At the other extreme, Milosevic, backed by elements of the military, tightened his grip over Serbia and Kosovo.

Considering the ongoing tensions between the federal government and the republics as well as between the Serbians and Slovenes and Croatians, it is likely that unless strong measures are taken Yugoslavia will spend the 1990s with its development retarded by the debt burden of around $20 billion and political tensions. The country needs new capital to modernise its industrial infrastructure. Without new capital infusions the country will continue to loose its international competitiveness. Yugoslavia also runs the problem that West European economic largesse that was usually available, could well be earmarked for Eastern European countries, like East Germany, Poland and Hungary, that are moving far more rapidly with both political and economic liberalisation. The ongoing erosion of the country's ability to generate capital will greatly diminish Yugoslavia's prospects for escaping the debt trap. With that comes an increasing deterioration of the population's standard of living.

Conclusion

The four Southern European countries examined in this chapter demonstrate a number of commonalities in how they entered the debt crisis. These commonalities were

1. Relatively similar economies in terms of traditional orientation (industrialisation) and the role of the state (interventionist).
2. A costly absence of oil.
3. A turn to external borrowing to overcome the rise in oil and commodity prices in the 1970s and early 1980s.

These three similarities had a corresponding impact on each country's political system. In Greece and Portugal problems with debt and economic management became part of electoral politics. In Turkey the debt crisis was a factor in the demise and rebirth of that country's democratic government, and in Yugoslavia the debt crisis has been an ongoing dilemma that has opened the door for the vocalising of ethnic tensions.

The exit process to the debt crisis is more difficult and there has been a differentiation process that has separated Portugal and Turkey from Greece, and those three from Yugoslavia. Although none of the countries has reached the point where debt management is a minor concern (if there is ever such a point for any country, e.g. the US), Portugal and Turkey have made considerable strides in that direction. Greece has also made some painful adjustments, but has benefited from EC membership to avoid the embarassment of being forced to deal with the IMF. The other three nations have worked closely with the IMF and World Bank.

What has made the difference between Greece, Portual and Turkey vis-à-vis Yugoslavia has been the ability of the three to carry out stabilisation and adjustment programmes. This has meant that the three were either able to regain or maintain access to commercial lending.

Yugoslavia was the only one of the four Southern European countries to be placed under the auspices of the Baker Plan (1985–9), which became the US debt policy. The US plan placed an emphasis on self-sustained growth through a package of liberalisation and supply-side economic reforms. A crucial part of the Baker Plan that did not materialise was the renewal of commercial bank lending to the fifteen countries on the list. It was correctly understood that new lending was necessary to help speed along structural reforms and stimulate growth. Unlike Greece, Portugal and Turkey, Yugoslavia has had considerable difficulty in obtaining new money, even being forced to seek financial help from the European Free Trade Association countries (Austria, Finland, Iceland, Norway, Sweden and Switzerland) in 1989. Yugoslavia's status under the Brady Plan, the Baker Plan's successor, was unclear in 1989, especially when considering the country's problems with inflation. The new plan placed an emphasis on debt reduction.

An additional factor that separates Yugoslavia from the other Southern European countries is that financial support is needed from the collective group of private banks, governments and multilateral agencies. Both Greece and Portugal benefit from EC membership. Turkey's major creditor governments, especially West Germany, Japan and the United States, have worked with the World Bank and commercial banks as well as through the OECD to keep that country from backsliding into a rescheduling. At the same time, each of these countries has made the effort to make changes more conducive to integration in the international economic system.

Ultimately the element that divides Yugoslavia from the others is a political factor. Beyond the obvious differences of ideology, the three countries have political centres orbiting the chief executive who is able to impose the government's economic policies. Yugoslavia's political system has fragmented power and at best the chief executive is the first among equals. At the worst, he is at the mercy of regional and ethnic interest and unable to carry out the economic reforms needed to improve the country's ability to obtain new loans. Until Yugoslavia resolves its political crisis, its economic crisis will continue and the walls of the debt trap will remain unscaleable.

In looking ahead to the mid-1990s, debt will continue to be a concern to varying degrees to the Southern European economies. None of the four countries has achieved substantial debt reduction, but most have an enhanced debt service capacity. At some stage, debt reduction will have to be considered. A related factor is debt fatigue, which directly relates to political stability. New rounds of austerity measures, especially in Yugoslavia and Turkey, have the potential to be counter-productive as such measures undermine political and economic stability. As in any geographical region where the debt crisis has been profound, the growing danger is debt fatigue and a gradual erosion of political will to carry out difficult economic reforms.

The lesson to be learned from the Southern European experience is that structural adjustment can succeed, but that access to foreign capital is crucial. Without restored access in some form, such as trade finance, economic growth becomes difficult and the costs of the crisis become increasingly political as populations reach their limits of tolerance. Greece, Portugal and Turkey appear to be moving in the direction of a post-debt crisis world, while Yugoslavia remains transfixed between ethnic tensions of the past and the debt burden of the present.

References

ABECOR Country Report, 'Greece', London: Barclays Bank, February 1988.

Beloff, Nora, *Tito's Flawed Legacy: Yugoslavia and the West Since 1939*. Boulder: Westview Press, 1985.

Birand, Mehemt Ali, *The Generals' Coup in Turkey: An Inside Story of 12 September 1980*. London: Brassey's, 1987.

Celasun, Merih and Dani Radrik, 'Turkish Experience with Debt: Macroeconomic Policy and Performance', in Jeffery D. Sachs (ed.), *Developing Country Debt and the World Economy*. Chicago: The University of Chicago Press, 1989.

Central Bank of Turkey in collaboration with the State Planning Organization and the Undersecretriat of Treasury and Foreign Trade, *Turkey: Economic Developments, Policies and Prospects*. Ankara: Central Bank of Turkey, April 1988.

Demirsar, Metin, 'Foreign Investors Flooding Into Turkey, Though Inflation, Borrowing Costs High', *Wall Street Journal*, 20 December 1988.

Dempsey, Judy, 'Mikulic may turn to emergency measures', *Financial Times*, 30 December 1988.

Dimitras, Panayote E., 'Greece: A New Danger', *Foreign Policy* no. 58 Spring 1985.

Gianaris, Nicholis V., *Greece and Turkey: Economic and Geopolitical Perspectives*. New York: Praeger, 1988.

Hope, Kerin, 'Greece', *The Europe Review*. Lincolnwood, Illinois: NTC Business Books, 1987.

Humphrey, Peter, 'Emergency Looms, Says Top Yugoslav', *Washington Post*, 30 December 1988.

International Monetary Fund, *International Financial Statistics Yearbook 1988*. Washington, D.C.: International Monetary Fund, 1988.

Keyder, Caglar, *State and Class in Turkey: A Study in Capitalist Development*. London: Verso, 1987.

Kuczynski, Pedro-Pablo, *Latin American Debt.* Baltimore: The Johns Hopkins University Press, 1988.

McFarlane, Bruce, *Yugoslavia: Politics, Economics and Society.* London: Pinter Publishers, 1988.

Morgan, Dan, 'Yugoslavia's Makeup Could Lead to Its Unraveling', *Washington Post*, 17 December 1989.

Morgan Guaranty Trust Company, International Economics Department, *Morgan International Data.* New York: Morgan Guaranty Trust Company, June 1985.

Opello, Walter C. Jr., *Portugal's Political Development: A Comparative Approach.* Boulder: Westview Press, 1985.

Organisation for Economic Development and Cooperation, *Greece Economic Survey 1983/1984.* Paris: Organisation for Economic Development and Cooperation, November 1983.

Organisation for Economic Development and Cooperation, Portugal Economic Survey 1983-1984. Paris: Organisation for Economic Development and Cooperation, June 1984.

Organisation for Economic Development and Cooperation, *Greece Economic Survey 1986/1987.* Paris: Organisation for Economic Development and Cooperation, July 1987.

Rustow, Dankwart A., *Turkey: America's Forgotten Ally.* New York: Council on Foreign Relations, 1987.

Saracoglu, Rusdu, 'Economic Stabilization and Structural Adjustment: The Case of Turkey', in Vittorio Corbo, Morris Goldstein and Moshin Khan (ed.), *Growth-Oriented Adjustment Programs.* Washington, D.C.: International Monetary Fund and World Bank, 1987.

Saraiva, José Hermano, *Historia conçisa de Portugal.* Lisbon: Publicaçoes Europa-America, 1979.

Schrenk, Martin, Cyrus Ardalan and Nawal A. El Tataway, *Yugoslavia: Self-Management Socialism and the Challenges of Development.* Baltimore: The Johns Hopkins University Press, 1979.

Steinbach, Udo, 'Turkey's Third Republic', *Aussenpolitik*, vol. 39, no.3, 1988.

Suro, Roberto, 'A Serb Patriot to the Core, but Is It Enough?', *New York Times*, 29 November 1988.

World Bank, *World Bank Debt Tables: External Debt of Developing Countries, Vol. II Country Tables.* Washington, D.C.: World Bank, January 1988.

World Bank, *Turkey: Industrialization and Trade Strategy.* Washington, D.C.: World Bank, 1982.

Chapter 9

Eastern Europe

Margie Lindsay

Introduction

On the threshold of the 1990s, Eastern Europe finally broke from its forty-odd year past of Communist suppression. The economic chaos that those years of central planning have caused, and will continue to cause for some time yet, make the future of the region far from stable. The peaceful revolution of 1989 began with the formation of a Solidarity-led government in Poland - the first non-Communist government installed in Eastern Europe since the end of World War II. This was the first concrete sign that the Communist rule was crumbling. Poland's dash for freedom was followed closely by Hungary, which threw off its socialist past, denouncing the brutal suppression of the 1956 revolution and declaring the country simply a republic. Most dramatic in its bid for freedom to that point was East Germany, where massed demonstrations that began in churches flooded out into the street, until the entire Politburo had resigned and the hated Berlin Wall was breached. Czechoslovakia followed soon after, but with more of a struggle; its old-guard communists did not want to leave the stage. Even tiny Bulgaria, after 35 years of rule by Todor Zhivkov, the longest serving East European leader, began the long road to a new system of government and economy. In Romania the change, when it came, was a bloody revolution with a chaotic and confusing start to the 1990s.

All these events were made possible by the vision and daring of one man - Mikhail Gorbachev, general secretary of the Communist Party of the Soviet Union and its president. Gorbachev's substitution of the Brezhnev Doctrine - which gave the Soviet Union the right to interfere in its 'sphere of influence' throughout Eastern Europe - was replaced by the much more subtle and lenient 'Sinatra Doctrine'. This allowed East European countries to 'do it their way', even if it means the possible disintegration of the Warsaw Pact. His decision to relinquish control over Eastern Europe, however, coincided with an equally dramatic loss of control at home; as the Soviet Union began the 1990s, it faced ethnic, nationalistic, racial, religious, economic and ideological problems that threatened to tear it apart before Gorbachev's

Table 9.1 Hard currency debt of European Comecon countries ($ bn, at end-year)*

	1982	1983	1984	1985	1986	1987	1988**
Gross debt							
Bulgaria	2.9	2.4	2.1	3.5	4.9	6.2	6.9
Czechoslovakia	3.7	3.5	3.1	3.3	3.9	5.1	5.2
East Germany	12.6	12.1	11.6	13.6	16.1	19.2	19.1
Hungary	7.7	8.3	8.8	11.8	15.1	17.7	17.0
Poland	25.9	26.3	26.9	29.7	33.5	29.2	28.7
Romania	9.8	8.9	7.2	6.6	6.4	5.7	3.1
Group of six	62.5	61.4	59.7	68.5	79.8	93.2	90.0
Soviet Union and Comecon banks	28.4	26.9	25.6	31.4	37.4	40.2	40.1
Total	90.9	88.3	85.3	99.9	117.2	133.4	130.2
Net debt							
Bulgaria	1.9	1.2	0.7	1.4	3.5	5.1	6.5
Czechoslovakia	3.0	2.6	2.1	2.3	2.7	3.5	3.8
East Germany	10.7	8.7	7.1	7.1	8.6	10.2	10.3
Hungary	7.0	6.9	7.3	9.5	12.9	16.2	15.5
Poland	24.9	25.1	25.4	28.1	31.8	36.2	35.7
Romania	9.5	8.4	6.6	6.3	5.8	4.3	2.1
Group of six	56.9	52.9	49.0	54.6	65.3	75.5	73.9
Soviet Union and Comecon banks	18.4	16.0	14.2	18.3	22.5	26.0	25.1
Total	75.3	68.8	63.2	72.9	87.8	101.7	99.0

*Less deposits held at BIS banks
***EEC Economic Bulletin for Europe*, Vol. 40.
Source: Planned Economies in the World Economic Trends, Spring, 1989, Institute for Economy, Market Research and Informatics, Budapest

perestroika (restructuring) programme could heal the rifts caused by a combination of years of strangling central planning and Stalinist suppression.

Never a homogeneous grouping, Eastern Europe as it enters the 1990s, is even in less of a coherent state than previously. More questions than answers face each of the countries, and the range of questions is very broad indeed. However, there are some common features:

Transformation from central planning to market economics

As it has been pointed out at various meetings, seminars, discussion groups and high-level meetings, no one has ever tried to change a centrally planned system back into a market one. The process, as one despairing Soviet economist pointed out, is like trying to unscramble an egg and put it back into the shell. The pessimism surrounding the transitional period is well founded. The few East European countries

Table 9.2 East European borrowing on international financial markets ($ m)

	1983	1984	1985	1986	1987	1988	1989 Jan–May
Bulgaria	-	-	475	45	260	194	38
Czecholovakia	50	-	100	279	242	330	-
East Germany	386	936	1,173	81	209	-	-
Hungary	567	1,166	1,642	1,315	1,951	1,016	629
Poland	-	260	-	-	30	-	163
Romania	-	-	150	-	-	-	-
Eastern Europe	1,004	2,362	3,540	1,720	2,692	1,540	830
Soviet Union	68	867	1,508	1,821	1,003	2,679	631
Comecon banks	-	140	250	400	20	75	-
Eastern Europe*	1,071	3,369	5,298	3,941	3,716	4,294	1,461
of which**							
International medium- and long-term bank loans+	889	2,676	4,200	2,664	2,144	1,050	488
Foreign medium- and long-term banks loans++	111	358	339	404	729	1,652	-

* Funds raised on the international markets.
** Includes also bonds, bank facilities, including 'bankers acceptance'.
+ Without officially guaranteed credits, without debt rescheduling.
++ In currencies of the creditor countries, without officially guaranteed credits.
Source: OECD, *Financial Statistics*, Part 1

that have begun the transition in earnest so far - Hungary, Poland and the Soviet Union - have found that the process is fraught with dangers and pitfalls, not least of them increasing the indebtedness of the country.

All the reforming economies need to face devaluation of currencies which have been consistently over-valued against world currencies, such as the dollar, for the past twenty years; deteriorating environmental conditions including air, water and ground pollution; industrial restructuring which aims at lowering energy and raw material input and replacement of obsolete equipment; infrastructural investment, particularly in telecommunications and transport; and a need for a mixed ownership structure with a heavy emphasis on private ownership.

No one has yet come up with a strategy for an effective - and relatively painless - transition to a market economy. Standard reform programmes usually contain an imposing array of reform measures but do not have a clear focus on key problems of macroeconomic policies and institutional determinates for the behaviour of the economy. There is usually no ordering or sequencing of linked reform measures and in the course of implementation, the transition to free prices and more realistic exchange rates, as well as liberalisation of foreign trade are usually postponed because of fears as far as social consequences of such steps are concerned. Doing that, however, is the same as postponing actual systematic changes.

The first step should be sound money and financial disciplines. This means tightening money. But to do that without effecting institutional change - including changes in ownership - is impossible. This also means that inefficient factories and industries have to be closed down and a redistribution process take place. But getting prices right remains the trickiest as well as the most crucial point of the transition.

Non-convertible currency

At the beginning of 1990, Poland was the only country to attempt convertibility of its currency and the limited convertibility that Poland has put in place has been possible only with substantial balance of payments support and a lot of good will as well as money from West European countries anxious to see the country succeed. Having a non-convertible - or even an internally convertible one with tight exchange control regulation - hinders the reform process in two ways. First it makes western investors think twice about entering a market where it is difficult or sometimes impossible to repatriate profits. Second, the continuing inability of the country to give its population access to hard currency heightens political and social tensions while at the same time making the break towards free pricing which reflects world market levels that much more difficult.

Poor infrastructure

Trying to telephone almost anywhere within an East European country is a frustrating and time-consuming exercise. Attempting international connections is equally a nightmare for a company. Modern telecommunications is one of the priority areas for investment in the region, not least because this is needed in order to support foreign investment in Eastern Europe. At the same time, transportation is difficult. These physical barriers to trade restrict the speed of development of the region as a whole and for individual countries to a greater or lesser extent serve as a disincentive for economic development and foreign investment.

Added to this is a lack of a wholesale and retail distribution system that can cope with the (hopefully) increased production output that a move towards market economics will mean. The remnants of the centrally planned distribution systems are unable to cope with the influx of new capital and investment from both at home and abroad. Too many monopolies remain in the transitional phases and so serve to restrict economic development as well as hindering internal and external trading.

Lack of capital market development

Not only are telecommunications and transport in a mess, there is hardly any development of the banking or capital markets sector. Hungary, which was the most advanced in this respect, having started its banking reform in the mid-1980s, could still not equal West European developments at the beginnings of the 1990s. The small, but growing stock exchange, should expand as privatisation grows, but the process will be a slow one. Elsewhere in the region, banking reform was lagging even further behind, but there are hopes that once coherent economic reform programmes are introduced - particularly in Poland, Czechoslovakia and East Germany - the pace of development in this sector will increase. Nevertheless, in the interim period, the lack of a strong banking sector hinders economic development and makes the switch to market economics more difficult.

Training and educational deficiencies

One of the first things that needs to change in Eastern Europe is the educational system. For over forty years, education has been subjugated to the plan and ideology. Until children begin to learn the truth about their own country's history, as well as the truth about world history and other subjects, it will be difficult to change the systems governing these countries. Not only does the entire educational system - from primary to higher level - need a complete overhaul, there is a great need for training facilities. Some management training centres have already opened - the first were in Hungary - but even more will be needed. All levels of management need to be trained in the techniques that many western managers take almost for granted: labour negotiations, budgeting, cash-flow analysis, pricing, inventory control, production profiles, corporate planning and others. At the same time, the restructuring of industries means that there will be a need for re-training of many for new or changed professions.

Need for large injections of foreign capital, know-how and expertise

The transition to market economics can be made less bumpy with injections of foreign investment. Needed perhaps just as much, however, is western know-how and expertise. The transfer of technology from West to East can be most easily achieved through investment - but the scale of the task is daunting.

Albania

Albania remains the most isolated of all the East European countries. After the death of its leader since the end of World War II, Enver

Table 9.3 Change in East European indebtedness with western banks

	Gross			Assets			Net		
	1986	1987	1988	1986	1987	1988	1986	1987	1988
	(change against preceding year in $ bn)								
Eastern Europe									
Total	+5.0	+8.2	−1.1	+0.7	+3.1	+1.6	+4.3	+5.0	−2.7
in real terms*	−0.2	+2.0	+2.5	−0.9	+1.2	+2.7	+0.7	+0.8	−0.2
exchange rate effect	+5.2	+6.2	−3.6	+1.6	+1.9	−1.1	+3.6	+4.2	−2.5
USSR									
Total	+6.4	+4.3	+3.5	+1.8	−0.7	+1.1	+4.6	+5.0	+2.4
in real terms*	+3.6	+0.3	+5.5	+0.8	−1.9	+1.7	+2.8	+2.2	+3.8
exchange rate effect	+27	+4.0	−2.0	+1.0	+1.2	−0.6	+1.8	+2.8	−1.4
Eastern countries									
Total	−11.4	+12.5	+2.4	+2.5	+2.4	+2.7	+8.9	+10.0	−0.3
in real terms*	+3.4	+2.3	+8.0	−0.1	−0.7	+4.4	+3.5	+3.0	+3.6
exchange rate effect	+8.0	+10.2	−5.6	+2.6	+3.1	−1.7	+5.4	+7.0	−3.9

* Exchange rate adjusted.
Source: Planned Economies in the World Economic Trends, Spring 1989, Institute for Economy, Market Research and Informatics, Budapest

Hoxha, there has been some signs of liberalisation - relative to Albania - under the new leader, Ramiz Alia. A thaw in relations with the West has been noticeable, with meetings taking place with Greek and West German officials in particular. The isolationist policies, however, appear deep. Suspicion about the Soviet Union and China - both of which Hoxha broke relations with sometime before his death - continue, although Alia has been able to push through some, albeit modest, reforms aimed at trying to loosen the stranglehold of central planning. Part of this new policy has taken the form of increased trade with the West, reflected in increases in assets held by the country with the Bank for International Settlements.

In 1988, trade with the West increased significantly compared to previous years, with exports to West Germany alone increasing by over 80 per cent (from very low levels). Increases were also seen in trade with Italy and Greece and overall trade with Western Europe and the OECD area also increased. This reflects Albania's need to start replacing its obsolete factories and to provide its people with food and consumer goods. Although the country still maintains its policy of 'no debt', it is stretching the definition of credit to its linguistic limits. For example, Albania and West Germany signed in 1989 an agreement on technical and financial co-operation. The deal was worth DM 20 million. The money it is understood is not repayable, but still presents the Albanian government with a problem: under its constitution, the acceptance of foreign credits is forbidden. It appears that the Albanian authorities get around this problem by 'financing development

Table 9.4 Albania's position with BIS banks ($m, end of period)

	1987			1988		
	March	September	December	March	June	September
Assets	21	35	100	120	223	216
Liabilities	3	2	83	113	171	187
Balance	18	33	17	7	52	29

Source: Economist Intelligence Unit, *Country Report 2*, 1989, Albania

projects'; these, they maintain are not credits in the traditional sense, although it is hard to spot the difference.

In any event, it is unlikely that Albania will begin a borrowing spree. Although its debt position (none) is enviable, it does need to start modernisation, particularly in its export-earning, hard currency sectors such as chrome mining, nickel, iron and steel industries. However, an increased borrowing programme will only be possible once the country's tight political control is relaxed and economic and political reforms are introduced. Neither appeared likely at the beginning of the 1990s, but considering the pace of change in the rest of the region, it is possible that by the end of the decade, Albania, too, could be looking for world market financing for industrial development.

Bulgaria

At the beginning of the 1990s, Bulgaria was in a state of economic and political turmoil. With the end of thirty-five years of rule by Todor Zhivkov came political uncertainty and economic reality. The cracks in the mismanagement of the economy over the past few years could no longer be disguised and the government looked set at the beginning of 1990 to begin in earnest a reform programme which until then had been elaborated on paper but never implemented. Nevertheless, like other East European countries, transformation will not be swift or painless. Added to the general economic decline - which includes a decline in exports to the West - is an increasing debt burden which the hapless Zhivkov was being blamed for by the remnants of the communist party.

Bulgaria's debt problems, which were becoming clear at the end of 1989, came about through a combination of factors not uncommon in borrowing strategies in the rest of Eastern Europe: using western credits to fund investment projects which make little or no economic sense, are centrally administered and tend to fall well behind schedule as there is a lack of control over the administration of such funds and progress. At the same time, money was ill-spent to provide consumer goods and food items and the ability of the country to pay for hard currency debts declined. The result of Bulgaria's borrowing spree was a net debt at the end of 1988 of $6 billion.

Table 9.5 Bulgaria's hard currency debt and assets ($ bn, end of year)

	1980	1984	1985	1986	1987	1988
Gross debt*	3.5	2.3	3.6	5.0	6.2	7.2
Net debt*	2.7	0.9	1.5	3.4	5.1	6.1
Position vis-à-vis BIS banks						
Liabilities	2.6	1.6	2.9	4.1	5.3	6.4**
Assets	0.8	1.4	2.1	1.4	1.1	1.1**
Net liabilities	1.8	0.2	0.8	2.7	4.2	5.3**

* Estimates
** end-September.
Source: Economist Intelligence Unit, *Country Report 2*, 1989

Bulgaria, too, fared worse than other countries in the region in efforts to improve sales on hard currency markets. In 1987 exports to industrial countries at $1 billion were 35 per cent below the 1980 result and the deficit of $1.3 billion larger than the exports. Gross indebtedness at the same time doubled between 1984 and 1987. As one western analysis remarked, indebtedness was approaching a 'critical level.'

This had happened to Bulgaria once before in 1978 when the relation of new indebtedness and hard currency exports was about 288 per cent; in 1987 this was estimated at 211 per cent. The country got out of the debt hole in 1978 by boosting exports to the West in 1979 by 75 per cent and a further 28 per cent in 1980, using the re-export of Soviet oil in the main to earn the hard currency it needed for debt repayment. In the second quarter of 1985, Bulgaria's net debt to western commercial banks totalled only $152 million. But trouble was just around the corner. By the end of 1988 it was just over $6 billion - nearly twice the level of debt when it faced its debt crisis in mid-1979.

With the decline in exports and the overall fall in world crude oil and oil-related product prices, Bulgaria was heading for trouble at the beginning of the 1990s. Debt stabilisation was clearly necessary but would only be possible through a real and severe cut in imports. Assuming Bulgaria was able in the next few years to increase exports to the West by around 6 per cent, stabilisation of indebtedness, according to one estimate could only be achieved by cuts in imports - 24 per cent in nominal terms - over 1989 and 1990. This did not happen in 1989 and at the beginning of 1990 the country was embarking on radical reforms which could upset the economy as well as cause social tensions to increase.

Extraordinarily, no one noticed the gathering storm clouds over Bulgaria's debt until the end of the first quarter of 1990 when the country stopped principle payments. Until then western banks had continued to lend and Bulgarian bankers continued to claim that there was no problem. Until the second half of 1988 there was no sign that Bulgaria was taking its debt problem seriously. There was no sign of a sensible debt management strategy from the National Bank and

Table 9.6 Bulgaria - projection of current account and debt (in $m) (hard currency area/assuming low OECD growth)

	1989	1990	1991	1992	1993	1994
Exports to the West	1,213	1,286	1,363	1,445	1,532	1,624
Imports from the West	2,734	2,898	3,072	3,256	3,451	3,658
Gross debt	7,761	8,917	10,190	11,591	13,130	14,818
Net debt	6,558	7,642	8,839	10,158	11,611	13,209
Net debt per capita	724	841	970	1,111	1,266	1,436
Net debt to total exports in per cent	263	289	315	342	369	396
Debt service ratio in per cent	45	36	37	61	77	90

Source: Hard currency position of CMEA countries and Yugoslavia, Institute for Comparative Economic Studies, Vienna, November 1988

payments troubles are expected in the early 1990s. But the promise of radical reform from Bulgaria's retreating communist party could mean a more responsible debt management. This includes, amongst other elements, an application to join the IMF and World Bank, a move which could help the country's economic planners to plot a course to economic prosperity in the 1990s, despite the mismanagement of the 1980s.

Czechoslovakia

At the end of 1989, Czechoslovakia's hitherto silent and sullen population had shaken off the nightmare of 1968's suppression and defeated the stranglehold grip of the communist party. For Czechoslovakia, economic reform could not even begin to be implemented before radical political changes were seen. Although one of the last to follow the East European freedom and democracy bandwagon, Czechoslovakia was in an enviable position to begin its trek back to economic prosperity. Relative to other East European countries, Czechoslovakia's economy was prosperous: living standards were among the highest in the region and most people found life relatively comfortable if not dull and limited. Another added boost to Czechoslovakia's economic reform plans for the 1990s is its low debt. At the end of 1988, total hard currency debt to all creditors was estimated to be between $5.6–5.7 billion; at the end of 1989, official government figures had the figure rising to $6.9 billion - still Eastern Europe's lowest per capita borrower. By all measures, the country was in a comfortable debt position and was viewed by western bankers as a creditworthy country - even better than East Germany.

Valtr Komarek, First Deputy Prime Minister and head of the Institute of Prognostics in Prague, thinks Czechoslovakia could sustain a swift economic recovery. The economy, he modestly claimed, has

Table 9.7 Czechoslovakia - projection of current account and debt (in $m) (hard currency area/assuming low OECD growth)

	1989	1990	1991	1992	1993	1994
Exports to the West	4,053	4,296	4,554	4,827	5,117	5,424
Imports from the West	4,647	4,926	5,222	5,535	5,867	6,219
Gross debt	6,587	7,269	8,011	8,818	9,696	10,650
Net debt	4,775	5,348	5,975	6,660	7,408	8,224
Net debt per capita	300	340	378	420	466	516
Net debt to total exports in per cent	96	102	107	113	119	124
Debt service ratio in per cent	18	13	13	25	30	34

Source: Hard currency position of CMEA countries and Yugoslavia, Institute for Comparative Economic Studies, Vienna, November 1988

potential. 'We have a rather solid infrastructure and are a well-educated nation', he said in an interview with the western press.

Komarek's Institute is advocating a sharp reduction in heavy engineering, mining, basic chemicals and textile production. It wants more emphasis placed on consumer goods output and tourism - which could play a key role as a hard currency earner. According to Komerek's estimates, $40,000 will be needed to modernise one job in the processing industry - a total of $15 billion over a period of ten years. He thinks the country could easily pay for this by increasing significantly its exports to the West.

The Finance Minister, Vaclav Klaus, said at the end of 1989 that Czechoslovakia wants economic aid from the West on a credit basis only. 'I don't like the word "aid"', he said. To that he added: 'What we want are normal financial transactions on a credit basis.' Klaus wants to open the country to the international flow of information, goods, labour and capital, with a minimum of economic turmoil. Klaus wants to avoid economic destabilisation and inflation: 'The main thing . . . is to prevent the Government from carrying out policies which would be popular but unwise.'

More than the other countries, however, Czechoslovakia is in desperate need of western imports of capital goods in order to modernise and re-equip its obsolete energy and raw-material hungry industries. If such imports begin, by the early 1990s, Czechoslovakia's export potential to the West could, on one estimate, double or triple. Plans to join the IMF and World Bank had been put on hold in 1989, but a membership application was presented at the end of the year. (Czechoslovakia severed links with the IMF in 1954.) Czechoslovakia is expected to pursue a responsible and reasonable borrowing programme to bring its industries back up to the levels of pre-war prominence in Europe.

Table 9.8 East Germany - projection of current account and debt (in $m) (hard currency area/assuming low OECD growth)

	1989	1990	1991	1992	1993	1994
Exports to the West	8,973	9,511	10,082	10,687	11,328	12,008
Imports from the West	8,718	9,241	9,796	10,383	11,006	11,667
Gross debt	14,736	14,041	13,242	12,327	11,288	10,113
Net debt	4,623	3,322	1,879	283	−1,479	−3,420
Net debt per capita	278	200	113	17	−89	−207
Net debt to total exports in per cent	46	31	17	2	−12	−26
Debt service ratio in per cent	29	16	14	19	23	23

Source: Hard currency position of CMEA countries and Yugoslavia, Institute for Comparative Economic Studies, Vienna, November 1988

East Germany

With the crumbling of the Berlin Wall in November 1989, the demise of communism in Eastern Europe was signalled as well as the end of the comfortable certainties of European security since the end of World War II. A non-communist, reforming East Germany has presented not just Gorbachev as leader of the socialist nations with a major headache, but both the US and Western Europe need to grapple with the problem of reunited Germany in the middle of revolutionary changes throughout Eastern Europe. The future is unclear, but as one spokesman for the Kremlin remarked, the idea of two German states in the middle of Europe by the end of the 1990s is absurd; but when, how and what a single Germany will look like is another question and one on which no one wants to make predictions.

East Germany's total hard currency debt at the end of 1988 was estimated to have risen to between $21.7 billion–$22.2 billion from almost $20 billion at the end of 1987. By all accounts, the country's debt position was considered good at the beginning of the 1990s, with deposits in BIS-area banks up and other hard currency assets high in the West. Revelations of large-scale corruption and the transfer of state funds by discredited communist officials to secret bank accounts in Switzerland at the end of 1989, showed just how much better off the country's hard currency position could have been - and could possibly become if the funds can be transferred back.

Unlike the other countries in the region, East Germany has a big brother which is not only economically powerful but willing to help rebuild its eastern sister. West Germany's conditions for economic support and aid, however, are tied to economic reforms and the introduction of multi-party democracy. Since the reunification issue had become a hot topic by the end of 1989, such considerations may be academic. However, East Germany whether alone or as part of a reunited German state - will need money to help reform its aging industrial base, improve living standards and consumer goods production and clean up its environment which has been pumping out polluting elements for too long. Western banks are likely to favour lending to East Germany as economic reforms begin; the East German authorities have decided to draft laws to guarantee that foreign partners in joint ventures - banned under the communist leadership - can transfer earnings abroad. A cabinet working group had been formed at the end of 1989 to deal with economic problems and proposals for economic reforms which were to be presented to parliament early in 1990. A crash programme was likely, as prices were rising and consumer goods shortages appearing at the end of 1989 as a result of the opening of the border between the two Germanies. A devaluation of the East German mark was also thought likely, since the currency - overvalued and given parity with the Deutschemark - was coming under severe pressure at the end of 1989 because of an increase in black market activity and profiteering as a result of the open border. Monetary union, scheduled for the second half of 1990, should spread unification but has unknown implications for both Germanies.

Hungary

Early in 1989, Hungary made it clear it saw its economic future in the West. Already the leading reformer of Eastern Europe, its break with the communist past was slower than in Poland, but just as dramatic when it came. However, like Poland, Hungary also faced a massive debt - the highest per capita debt in the region. Hungary got into its debt problems through a combination of bad investment, rising dollar rates, continued subsidising of loss-making companies and poor debt management by the National Bank. The situation was exacerbated by not-quite-far-enough reforms and an interfering communist government which only gradually relinquished control over the economic mechanisms.

At the end of 1989, Hungary had still managed to avoid a rescheduling. It may be able to avoid rescheduling through the 1990s by pursuing a policy of rapid economic reform and severe austerity measures. Talks with the IMF looked more promising at the end of 1989 than they had at mid-year, when the IMF froze Hungary's $350 million one-year standby credit after the country's first quarter budget deficit soared to Ft 29 billion (approximately $490 million at the forint/dollar rate in May 1989). By the end of 1989, hard currency debt had risen to $20 billion, the budget deficit reached Ft 49 billion and inflation was running at about 17 per cent a year.

Hungary requested in December 1989 a bridging loan of $1 billion from the Bank of International Settlements; the country was also to receive a five-year Ecu 1 billion loan from the European Community (EC) to help ease balance of payments problems. The loan has three

Table 9.9 Hungary - projection of current account and debt (in $m) (hard currency area/assuming low OECD growth)

	1989	1990	1991	1992	1993	1994
Exports to the West	3,963	4,201	4,453	4,720	5,003	5,303
Imports from the West	4,499	4,724	4,960	5,209	5,469	5,742
Gross debt	19,621	20,553	21,468	22,357	23,212	24,020
Net debt	17,956	18,805	19,632	20,430	21,188	21,895
Net debt per capita	1,692	1,772	1,850	1,926	1,998	2,065
Net debt to total exports in per cent	315	311	306	301	294	287
Debt service ratio in per cent	42	42	44	61	70	76

Source: Hard currency position of CMEA countries and Yugoslavia, Institute for Comparative Economic Studies, Vienna, November 1988

preconditions attached to it: Hungary must agree to a credit and adjustment plan with the IMF and on the terms of supplementary economic restructuring with Brussels and the loan should not be used to replace commercial bank credits. The EC also set some 'micro-economic' conditions to encourage private enterprise, in addition to the traditional IMF aggregate targets. The EC loan is to be paid out in three tranches, supervised by the EC's Monetary Committee. The first tranche was expected to be released in the first quarter of 1990.

Some, however, argue that Hungary cannot hope to repay its loans without some debt relief. In order to reduce its indebtedness, Hungary needs to run a surplus on its hard currency current account balance. With the ability to boost exports to the West constrained by its real industrial base, Hungary can only do this by cutting imports. But more imports from the West are the key to restructuring industry and providing domestic producers with competition. Although exports to the West outstripped imports in 1989, the current account balance of payments at the end of the year was estimated to be in deficit by $1.3 billion to $1.4 billion.

Even under good conditions Hungary will find it difficult to reduce substantially its need to borrow to finance its current account deficit. Direct investment from the West and debt-equity swaps will only partially help. The only way for Hungary to get by in the coming years, conclude most analysts, will be to borrow - something that Hungary should not be doing, especially since most of this borrowing is simply to meet interest and amortisation payments on existing debts.

Even if Hungary does not borrow much in the early 1990s, which appears unlikely, its debt servicing burden will grow even heavier. The Economist Intelligence Unit (London) has estimated that the debt servicing burden will sky-rocket in the early 1990s when grace periods on loans taken out in the mad borrowing rush of 1985–7 begin to expire. Hungary may need to borrow $4 billion-$5 billion a year in 1992-3, A serious liquidity crisis could arise.

Such a path offers no hope of a brighter future. Even if Hungary's export sector can show massive growth, debt servicing will be an almost unbearable burden on the economy. Faced with such a future, some analysts are now advocating debt relief - the writing off of a substantial part of Hungary's debt burden.

Poland

This same argument is even more relevant for Poland, which even before the new Solidarity-led government introduced its radical economic reform package for the 1990s, found it could not meet interest payments. Indeed, in December 1989, as the IMF team, led by managing director of the Fund, Michel Camdessus, left Warsaw the prospect of such a plan was more than idle speculation. Camdessus said the Fund would undertake a debt reduction programme for Poland after 1990 similar to those being negotiated with some Latin American countries (see Chapters 2 & 3). Poland's Finance Minister, Leszek Balcerowicz - a respected economist - had gained approval from the IMF for his radical reform plans, but at the beginning of 1990 still had to convince the Polish parliament and population that his methods were the best. The blueprint for harsh economic austerity and sweeping reforms was targeted at reducing hyperinflation, introducing internal convertibility of the zloty (the national currency) and switching the economy to capitalism. Aid to the country for 1990 included an IMF standby loan of $700 million, a $500 million bridging loan from the Bank of International Settlements (BIS), restructuring loans worth $1.67 billion from the World Bank, debt rescheduling by the Paris Club of creditor nations and the London Club of commercial bank creditors and a $1 billion stabilisation loan by the Group of 24 developed western nations.

The IMF package was in place by the end of 1989 and the Fund was urging the Paris Club - which holds two-thirds of Poland's $38 billion debt - to give the country 'the most generous rescheduling' and asked the London Club to follow this lead, too. In 1990 $4 billion of Poland's debt due to the Paris Club and another $4 billion of arrears for 1988 and 1989 needed to be rescheduled. Once the IMF programme was in place, western nations went ahead with a $1 billion loan to support Poland's reforms. The IMF standby loan was $700 million, released over a thirteen-month period. The BIS $500 million bridging loan provided Poland with balance of payments support before the IMF loan came on stream in January 1990. The IMF was also maintaining its support for the Polish economy with a further three-year programme after the thirteen-month standby loan was used. 'This could be complemented with a debt reduction programme', confirmed Camdessus.

Table 9.10 Poland - projection of current account and debt (in $ m) (hard currency area/assuming low OECD growth)

	1989	1990	1991	1992	1993	1994
Exports to the West	5,664	6,004	6,364	6,746	7,151	7,580
Imports from the West	4,809	5,098	5,403	5,728	6,071	6,436
Gross debt	38,731	38,297	37,714	36,965	36,034	34,902
Net debt	35,364	34,729	33,931	32,955	31,784	30,397
Net debt per capita	915	890	862	829	792	750
Net debt to total exports in per cent	455	421	388	356	324	292
Debt service ratio in per cent	71	85	68	65	64	90

Source: Hard currency position of CMEA countries and Yugoslavia, Institute for Comparative Economic Studies, Vienna, November, 1988

Poland's debt problems began in the 1970s, when riots and demonstrations in Polish towns in December 1970 forced the then communist party leader, Wladyslaw Gomulka, to resign and be replaced by Edward Gierek. Gierek promised to modernise Poland's industry and he proposed to do this by borrowing massively from the West. The money was to finance imports of new technology and capital equipment. The loans were to be repaid in the late 1970s, funded by the increased hard currency exports that would result from this modernisation programme. Like most communist plans for Poland, Gierek's fell short of expectations. In order to keep the volatile population quiet, he had to increase living standards and the only way to do that was to import consumer goods.

The economy began to overheat in 1975–6 resulting in long delays in the completion of investment projects and shortages of consumer goods. The foreign debt, meanwhile, grew - from $1.2 billion at the end of 1971 to $11.2 billion at the end of 1976. It was clear by December 1976 that the economy was out of control and it was then decided to cut back investment spending, imports and wages growth. This was not as simple in practice as Gierek's government had hoped it would be. At first things appeared to go smoothly, but the economy did not respond to the cuts. Output slumped in 1979 for the first time in post-war history. As the 1970s drew to a close, Poland had to borrow heavily in order to just meet current debt repayment obligations. The trade deficits for most of the 1970s also added to the debt. But still, the West was eager to continue lending. The mood, however, changed by spring 1980. Western bankers by then were uneasy.

In or around April 1980 important revisions were made to the 1980 economic targets which few people were aware of at the time. In Poland all information on the country's debt was treated as a state secret; the first public announcement by a Polish government minister on the debt was not made until August 1980, when the debt stood at $20 billion.

As one report sumarised: in 1979, Poland failed to keep its promise to balance trade with the West. In 1980 it had large borrowing needs, but banks were less helpful than only a year earlier. The authorities tried to demonstrate to the bankers that economic order was being restored. This led to desperate action to increase exports, causing shortages of consumer goods on the home market. Poland's leaders seemed oblivious to the chaos and tension their import reductions and export drive were causing. Disturbances in Poland in the summer of 1980 badly affected production and exports. Credits began to flow again in late August 1980, just about the same time the authorities finally formally recognised the Solidarity trade union.

Leadership changes in September 1980, when Stanislaw Kania took over as party secretary, went hand-in-hand with dramatic changes in economic policy. At the beginning of 1980, economic policy was 'appeasement' - trying to keep the population happy and calm.

In March 1981 Poland suspended debt service and restricted exports to the West. Rescheduling agreements were concluded, but the situation did not improve. The bubble burst when martial law was imposed in December 1981. There then followed the disruption of Paris Club rescheduling negotiations when Poland suspended all payments on state guaranteed credits. Since then - until the Solidarity-led government was brought to power in late 1989 - western governments and commercial bank creditors has constantly been trying to manage debt repayments and a volatile political situation simultaneously.

Romania

The bloody and confused revolution at the end of 1989 which overthrew the unreformed Nicolae Ceausescu, plunged Romania in both an economic and political crisis. The worst legacy of the Ceausescu years is the economic mess his policies have created.

Perhaps the most damaging to the country was Mr Ceausescu's maniac insistence on paying off the country's remaining gross debt by the end of 1989, or the latest the end of 1990. Mr Ceausescu made this announcement in November 1988, when the government told western creditor banks it would make a major repayment on its external debt. Mr Ceausescu managed to do this, more or less. By the end of the first quarter of 1989, Romania's debt to western commercial banks declined to about $250 million. Deposits in BIS-area banks still stood at $809 million at the end of 1988.

World Bank statistics indicate that Romania's debt to it declined by two-thirds over 1988 and by the end of March 1989, the debt to the Bank was repaid completely. IMF statistics show that debt owed to it was repaid by the end of January 1989. Romania's debts to other creditors similarity declined. Total debt at the end of the first quarter 1989 was estimated to be anything up to $350 million.

The repayment of the country's debt, however, has seriously

Table 9.11 Romania - projection of current account and debt (in $m) (hard currency area/assuming low OECD growth)

	1989	1990	1991	1992	1993	1994
Exports to the West	4,157	4,407	4,671	4,951	5,249	5,563
Imports from the West	1,573	1,667	1,767	1,874	1,986	2,105
Gross debt	2,092	14	−2,323	−4,944	−7,874	−11,140
Net debt	739	−1,420	−3,844	−6,555	−9,582	−12,950
Net debt per capita	32	−61	−163	−276	−400	−538
Net debt to total exports in per cent	11	−20	−51	−82	−113	−145
Debt service ratio in per cent	18	9	5	0	−4	−11

Source: Hard currency position of CMEA countries and Yugoslavia, Institute for Comparative Economic Studies, Vienna, November 1988

disrupted the economy and had a dramatic and drastic effect on living standards for the majority of the population. Industry has been starved of capital investment, equipment and technology because of import cuts. At the same time, exports have been pushed to gain the needed hard currency leading to shortages - particularly of food. The emphasis on heavy industry, particularly petrochemicals, metallurgy and steel production, led to electricity cuts. Once the debt was paid, western observers estimated that the country would need at least $2 billion a year in fresh credits to restructure and modernise industry. But Ceausescu followed his break-neck repayment with a law outlawing foreign borrowing.

Romania will have an additional $2.5 billion a year at its disposal from 1990, if exports continue. This money could be used to cut exports of food and energy and help rebuild the crumbling economy and restore some degree of comfort to the long-suffering population. This possibility, however, seems to have been ruled out by announcements of a plan which sees exports growing by 10 per cent in 1989 and continuing into the 1990s. In the future, according to the plan, all foreign trade will be carried out on a countertrade basis, but it is unlikely that the country will be able to conduct all its foreign trade on this basis.

Romania's commercial and political isolation continued to grow at the end of 1989, with no sign of a crack in the hard-line Stalinist regime of Ceausescu. In 1988 Ceausescu decided to forego most favoured nation status with the US, rather than comply with American demands concerning human rights. Romania's efforts to distance itself from Moscow are seen as negative, rather than positive, factors in foreign relations with the West. Within Eastern Europe, Romania's isolation is also growing as it remains the only country refusing to begin political and economic reforms.

The approved draft programme for economic and social development for 1991-2010 proposes 'more moderate growth' rates than previous because of a lack of resources. The blame for this, however, is placed on the hardships imposed on Romania by foreign countries during the period 1975-89 during which Romania paid back its hard currency debt. The programme appears to suggest that Romania is now experiencing an economic crisis, brought on in part by its policy of pre-paying its debt. Despite Ceausescu's spectacular growth plans, the country never achieved anything close to them over the period of 1965-88. The shortfall caused by missing those targets - 40 to 44 per cent annual national income growth was planned - means that Ceausescu has had to postpone until 2010 his hopes of reaching the 'multilaterally developed socialist society' originally scheduled to be arrived at by 1990.

The 1991-2010 programme plans a reduction in the accumulation fund - money used to pay for economic development - from 30 per cent of national income to between 28 and 30 per cent. In theory this reduction could release more money to be spent on producing food and other consumer goods. This may not happen since the growth expectations are still unrealistically high, compared with Romania's actual abilities. For example, the draft plan expects 100 million tonnes a year of coal to be produced by 1995, although representing a growth rate below that previously planned, it is still a large increase over the 58.8 million tonnes produced in 1988. The projected growth rate of net industrial production - the value of newly created goods - is expected to be smaller during the 1991-5 period than between 1986-90. The production of steel, natural gas, aluminum and wood products is expected to stagnate. Production in steel in 1988 was actually 14.3 million tonnes, but under the new plan, overall steel production should rise by two-fifths by the year 2000 compared with 1988, despite the planned stagnation.

To save money and raw materials, the authorities plan savings in areas that affect living standards. Housing construction is to slow with 10 per cent fewer flats being built during 1991-5 than in the 1986-90 period, during which time construction targets were not met. Unless there is a political change, it appears that Romania is set to continue along its road of economic decline and falling living standards for the population.

Soviet Union

Officially, at the end of 1988, Soviet gross debt totalled $49.5 billion and net debt stood at $34.6 billion. These figures reflected the growing Soviet debt which continued to rise in 1989, mainly due - according to a report by the Washington-based economic forecasting group, PlanEcon - to three factors:

- a generally unfavourable external economic climate
- a large drop in the Soviet non-socialist trade surplus during the fourth quarter of 1988

Table 9.12 Soviet Union - projection of current account and debt (in $m) (hard currency area/assuming low OECD growth)

	1989	1990	1991	1992	1993	1994
Exports to the West	25,355	26,876	28,489	30,198	32,010	33,931
Imports from the West	24,797	26,285	27,862	29,533	31,305	33,184
Gross debt	25,039	22,032	18,567	14,597	10,074	4,946
Net debt	9,169	5,210	735	−4,305	−9,961	−16,291
Net debt per capita	32	18	3	−15	−33	−54
Net debt to total exports in per cent	28	15	2	−11	−24	−38
Debt service ratio in per cent	10	10	9	8	7	6

Source: Hard currency position of CMEA countries and Yugoslavia, Institute for Comparative Economic Studies, Vienna, November 1988

• an increase in Soviet deposits in BIS-area banks.

Despite this, however, Soviet indebtedness has always been thought to be moderate. The Soviet Union, despite the enormous economic and political problems facing Gorbachev, has large deposits of crude oil, natural gas, gold, other raw materials and a so far untapped potential as an exporter. Although hard currency debt may not appear a long-term problem, the country has an internal debt, put at R330 billion in mid-1989, which accounts for about 10 per cent of Soviet GNP. The finance ministry estimates that the annual budget deficit would be manageable if it ran at less than 2 or 3 per cent of GNP.

So far Gorbachev's *perestroika* (restructuring) programme has had little success. He admitted as much himself at the end of 1989, when addressing the parliament he said 'no positive changes have occurred in the economy'. Leonid Abalkin, the deputy prime minister in charge of economic reform and a respected Soviet economist, wants to implement a radical reform plan that could help bounce the Soviet Union out of its present difficulties and give it a new lease of life for the 1990s. Under this plan, the Soviet Union would adopt in 1990 a law on property which would create state, co-operative and private property rights. It would also begin to transfer at least 25–30 per cent of total assets of state enterprises to lease terms; form joint stock companies which would account for 30 to 40 per cent of total assets; allow 50 per cent of farms to be leased and mixed ownership; and begin to liquidate loss-making factories.

This process would be completed by the beginning of 1994. Meanwhile, the budget deficit should be reduced to between 3 and 4 per cent of GNP and money supply would be brought under control. Flexible interest rates would be begun to be introduced in 1992. The beginnings of a financial market would be created, with cuts in state investment starting in 1990, and a new banking law introduced in 1991 with tax reforms in 1992. A stock exchange would be set up over 1991-3. The key problem of price reform would at last be tackled with wholesale prices coming into line with demand - an attempt to balance the shortage economy - retail price reform begun in 1991.

Along with the price reform, the state would have to introduce unemployment benefits and an anti-monopoly law. Finally, foreign investment would be encouraged. Restrictions on foreign investment would begin to be eased in 1990 and new customs laws introduced in 1991. Meanwhile, the Soviet Union's integration into world financial markets and international trading would intensify.

Conclusion

Overall Eastern Europe was in a very volatile state at the beginning of the 1990s. Revolution - even under the best possible economic conditions and even if it is peaceful - is not easy for anyone. What is clear, however, is that all countries in the area will need western credits to help transform economies from central planning to market ones as well as put right years of misinvestment in industry and infrastructure. Western governments, credit institutions and commercial banks will be called upon to play an active role in this transition to market economics. At the same time, Western Europe needs to find a way of helping Eastern Europe - including the Soviet Union - integrate with it and begin to form a new economic order within Europe, avoiding the danger of a North/South divide.

References

Blazyca, George, Thames Polytechnic, London.

East European Markets, Financial Times Business Information, London.

Economist Intelligence Unit

Financial Times

Fink, Gerhard and Kurt Mauler, *Hard Currency Position of CMEA Countries and Yugoslavia* PlanEcon, Washington, D.C.

East-West Trade 1988-90 Favourable Conditions for Further Growth (Developments in 1988 and Prospects for 1989/90 (November 1988).

Stankovsky, Jan, Institute for Comparative Economic Research, Vienna, September 1989, Report 159.

The Economist

The Independent

Young, David, 'Hungary: Debt Versus Reform', *The World Today* (October 1989).

Chapter 10

Debt policies for an evolving crisis

Michael Hobbs

Introduction

It is difficult to recall an international policy issue that has inspired anything like the outpouring of free advice from financial commentators, legislators and interested bystanders which has been directed at the developing country debt crisis. A Debt Plan scorecard, published monthly in *International Economy* summarised nearly thirty major policy proposals and initiatives as of early 1989, ranging in scope from simple calls for stepped-up lending by the multilateral development banks to Fidel Castro's sublimely unrealistic call for an internationally imposed moratorium on all debt service payments by developing nations to be paid for with offsetting reductions in military expenditures by the creditor nations. It is nonetheless striking how little impact the vociferous public debate over alternative plans has had on the actual conduct of international debt policy, at least until recently. Equally striking is the extent to which the debt strategy has been dominated by US policy initiatives, despite their decidedly mixed results.

International efforts to resolve the debt crisis have evolved through the 1980s, against a backdrop of changing economic circumstances, analytical perspectives and a menu of policy alternatives. The narrative is concerned largely with the commercial bank side of the crisis, and refers less frequently to the involvement of official lenders. This is because commercial banks are the larger source of credit to most of the major debtors, and because the terms of their loans were one cause of the problem. They are usually the 'marginal creditors', the first to bear the consequences of a country's inability to repay. The narrative also focuses somewhat narrowly on events in Latin America. This is not because the debt problem is exclusively a Latin American affair (that it is not is attested by the remainder of this book), nor because the problem has afflicted the Latin American nations more than others (the debt burden has been much more crushing in Sub-Saharan Africa). Rather, it is a reflection of two geo-political facts. One is that debt policy evolved to meet a perceived financial threat to creditor nations, and to the US in particular, which sprang from the absolute magnitude of borrowing by individual debtors. Most of those major debtors were Latin American. The second is that US security interests have lain largely in Latin America. Instances where the discussion is broadened to include other regions reflect more or less the extent to which non-Latin American debtors have figured in the formulation of global debt policy.

Containment policy: chronicle of a debt forestalled

The debt crisis burst upon a stunned banking community following Mexico's suspension of principal payments to its commercial banks in August 1982. In the press and as gauged by official responses, Mexico's inability to keep current on debt repayments was seen as a mortal threat to the international financial system. In fact, the risk to the system from any action that Mexico was likely to take was neither immediate nor acute. There was little doubt that Mexico would eventually continue to service its debt, and arrears on its principal payments threatened neither the value of the loans nor the solvency of the lending banks. Much of the initial shock was due to the fact that the delinquency of such a large and heretofore creditworthy borrower was completely unexpected.

One concern of the banking authorities was that a loss of public confidence in the lending institutions might trigger a run on the banks when Mexico's difficulties became known. It was also true that the banks' large exposures to the developing countries had become a source of systemic risk, one which needed to be carefully contained. Nearly the entire US banking system (by value of assets), as well as almost all of the major European, Canadian and Japanese banks, were deeply involved in lending to the LDCs (less developed countries), and Mexico was not the only sovereign borrower in trouble. For the 171 US banks with claims large enough to warrant reporting to the federal bank regulators, exposure at the end of 1982 to countries classified as 'troubled debtors' amounted to 176 per cent of their primary capital (equity plus general loan-loss reserves). Claims on Mexico alone equalled 34.5 per cent of these banks' capital. For the nine large money-centre banks making up the core of the US banking system[1], exposure to those countries was 233 per cent of primary capital. For some individual banks the exposures were higher still.

The ratio of endangered assets to capital was the critical conduit through which debtor's payment problems threatened the larger financial system. Regulators required banks to maintain capital equal to at least 5 per cent of total assets. Losses on loans are subtracted from capital, so that default or extended arrears on interest by even one or two of its major sovereign debtors would have severely shrunk a bank's capital base. This would have forced it, in turn, to liquidate assets worth up to twenty times the amount of the capital loss, through calling in loans or selling them. Striking all of the major banks at once, it would have caused a huge contraction of credit and a severe economic squeeze.

The debt crisis for the debtors first struck as a liquidity crunch driven by forces in the international monetary system largely outside of their control. It was not seen, originally, as a fundamental development problem. This is not to argue that the highly-indebted middle-income countries (HICs[2]), in particular, had not overborrowed following the first oil price hike and that they continued to overborrow up until 1982. Also most were too slow adjusting to the new realities of a second oil shock and the sharp recession in the developed countries. Despite impressive growth in the 1970s, the developing countries' inward-oriented, statist policies left them with large and sluggish public sectors, particularly vulnerable to adverse external shocks. But it would be equally hard to argue that the LDCs' borrowing behaviour and domestic policies had made a crisis inevitable.

The crisis which did hit was precipitated by a sudden magnification of the LDCs' relative debt burden. A large proportion of the highly-indebted nations' obligations were composed of commercial 'Eurodollar' loans with variable interest rates. The Eurodollar market refers to loans denominated in dollars made by banks operating outside the US, generally in London or one of the offshore banking centres. The rate is usually expressed as a small premium or 'spread' over the London Interbank Offer Rate (LIBOR), which is the rate at which banks lend to each other and which is usually taken to represent the banks' cost of funds. When tight US monetary policy caused dollar interest rates to soar in late 1980, many debtors saw a sharp increase in their nominal debt service due.[3] The recession which followed in the industrial countries drastically reduced demand and prices for developing countries' exports. Caught in a 'scissors' between plummeting foreign exchange earnings and rocketing debt costs, debtors watched their reserves bleed away and debt-servicing capacity shrivel. Banks reacted to the increased riskiness by pulling out of developing countries, calling in loans and refusing to roll over short-term facilities - a rational move for any single bank, but one which was unsuitable when attempted by all of the banks at once.

The initial reaction by banks, governments of the creditor countries, and the International Monetary Fund (IMF) to Mexico's difficulties was swift and decisive. In meetings over the weekend beginning Friday 13th August 1982, Mexican and US officials endorsed a moratorium on principal payments but continued payment of interest, and designed a programme to return Mexico to a regular debt repayment schedule and contain the damage to public confidence in the financial system. A ninety-day 'bridging loan' was immediately floated by the US Federal Reserve.

Over the next two weeks a committee structure was set up to discuss refinancing and new amortisation schedules with the banks. Six weeks later an IMF stabilisation plan calling for austerity and adjustment of the balance was in place. By mid-December, agreement had been reached between Mexico and the committee on rescheduling. In addition to rescheduling the repayment of principal, a 7 per cent increase in funds from the commercial bank lending syndicate was insisted upon by the IMF as a condition for its standby lending provision and supervision.

The 'Mexican Weekend' was only the first in a parade of similar payments emergencies; by the end of the year, thirty-four countries had fallen into arrears. By the end of 1983 some twenty-three countries had rescheduled with the Paris Club (for official creditors), and there had been a further twenty-seven commercial bank reschedulings. Many debtors were involved in both.

From the beginning, the official policy of the banks, multilateral lenders and creditor governments was that, due to the idiosyncracies of each debtor's economic and credit circumstances, countries would be handled on a flexible 'case-by-case' basis. It quickly became apparent, however that the Mexico rescue had set a pattern, and that all countries would be handled using the same skeleton containment plan: IMF adjustment programme and standby agreement, rescheduling and clearing of arrears with both commercial banks and official lenders, an agreement on new lending from the banks, followed by the disbursement of IMF funds. The fact that the containment approach was cobbled together as a first response to the debt crisis did not prevent it from becoming entrenched as the *de facto* debt policy of the US Treasury under Secretary Donald Regan.

In practice, the case-by-case approach meant differentiation only on the portion of the debt to be rescheduled, the amount of new money to be lent, and in the way options, terms and conditions would be hammered out. It meant that the debtors would be divided in negotiation, rather than presenting a unified bargaining front. This was seen as appropriate, because rescheduling and containment of the crisis were understood as a cooperative process between creditor and debtor, not as a source of conflict.

The most crucial component of the strategy was agreement between the debtor government and the IMF on conditions for the extension of a standby line of credit, which would be immediately drawn down by the debtor to repay bridge loans, pay for urgent imports, or to keep current on high-priority payments obligations. This was in keeping with the IMF's traditional role: in return for providing temporary emergency credit to guarantee the short-term external liquidity of its members, the IMF required borrowing countries to take steps to bring the balance of payments into line. By the nature of IMF credit and conditionality, this meant drastic austerity measures aimed at the current account and fiscal imbalances, rather than comprehensive long-run structural adjustment and development strategies. Agreement with the IMF quickly became a prerequisite for rescheduling with the commercial banks, a sort of official seal of approval. Banks saw it as a way to induce debtor countries to adopt policies which would enhance the prospects for loan servicing. Because the actual disbursement of

IMF funds was in turn made conditional upon the conclusion of a rescheduling agreement with the banks, the IMF became in effect the bankers' policeman, forcing liquidity-constrained debtors to the negotiating table and increasing the bank's bargaining power.

Commercial bank loan rescheduling, which in conjunction with an IMF programme, was the centrepiece of the containment strategy, followed a well-defined pattern established during the previous decade for renegotiating loans in the Paris Club. As commercial bankers and official creditors become jealous of each other's burden sharing, rescheduling with the Paris Club became a prerequisite for agreement with the banks, and vice versa. At the beginning of the debt crisis, only the obligations due in a single year were rescheduled at a time. Multi-year rescheduling agreements (MYRAs), covering principal due for several years forward, were introduced in 1984 to save on the costly negotiating process and to reduce the uncertainty over finance faced by national economic planners.

Technically, rescheduling implied only a rearrangement of the pattern of payments on principal, with the same interest rate still charged on the outstanding balances. Only the time profile of repayment was altered, and no addition need be made to the nominal stock of debt. Looked at another way, however, rescheduling was the same as honouring the original agreement plus receiving a 'loan' equal to part of each period's amortisation payment. Since this represented an implicit transfer of financial resources compared to the unrescheduled case, the rescheduling could also be thought of as additional financing in the current period.

Similarly, interest arrears provided in implicit inflow of resources to the debtor nations, in the form of reduced outflows. Arrears represented, in theory, the outcome of the debtor's inability to pay, a 'financing gap', the difference between a country's hard currency resources and current payment obligations, in other words, between its projected net foreign exchange earnings and debt service. In practice they were often actively used as a form of forced lending. Continued timely payment of interest was the overriding goal of the containment strategy, as it allowed the banks to maintain the full book value of their sovereign loans. For that reason, arrears were eventually consolidated as part of the rescheduling process. In most cases, reschedulings also required additional 'new money' to cover the debtor's projected financing gap over the next few periods.

Involuntary lending

The source of new money was to be the commercial banks. This characteristic feature of the containment strategy grew out of IMF insistence that its provision of official funds in standby agreements be supported by commercial bank lending, to avoid a situation in which IMF money simply made a 'round trip' back to the banks as interest payments. The bank advisory committee (BAC) in charge of rescheduling would negotiate, on behalf of the sometimes hundreds of banks in the original lending syndicate, a proportional increase in exposure to be borne by all of the banks. This was in the spirit of the sharing clauses written into the initial syndicated loans, under which all interest or principal received must be apportioned *pro rata* among the lenders. However, individual banks could not be legally forced to cough up additional funds. Smaller banks, in particular, sought a 'free ride' by taking advantage of the repayments received in rescheduling agreements while refusing to provide their share of the new money. The participation of reticent lenders had to be garnered through moral suasion, implicit threats, the extension of favours like access to interbank credit lines, and, at the beginning of the crisis, by charging large front-end rescheduling fees to sweeten the pill. This process was called 'involuntary lending' or 'concerted lending' because collective action was needed to raise funds which individual banks would not have lent voluntarily. In short order it became virtually the only source of commercial bank lending to the troubled debtors. In this manner the IMF also acted as policeman vis-à-vis the lenders, assuring such flows of new money as were forthcoming and reducing the number of free riders.

It is important to realise that 'new money', or net new debt flows, while increasing the nominal value of the debt, was not identical with money available to the borrowers for new investment. The appropriate measure of the benefits or burdens to the debtor of financing arrangements in any given period is the 'net transfer of resources', to the debtor countries. This is defined by the World Bank as net new loans (disbursements less amortisation of principal) minus total net interest payments. The net resource transfer has remained negative despite new money (i.e. the net flow has been outward from the debtors), so that the funds have gone, directly or indirectly, to pay interest. New money has thus in practice been merely an implicit form of interest capitalisation. It is true that new money committed for a high priority project frees up funds for other, lower priority uses. But if the new loans would have simply represented a missed payment, i.e. if new money is no greater than the country's financing gap, then nothing but an unpayable liability has been substituted. In such a case, new financing can add to the debt burden without adding to productive capacity. It simply replaced what would have been arrears; new contractual lending replaces 'extracontractual' lending. New money only augments the economy's productive base to the degree that it reduces the outward resource transfer from what it would have been without the inflow. Thus it is only to the extent that new lending reduces the outward resource transfer that financing can be said actively to help a country grow out from beneath its debt.

On the other hand, new money did not need to add to productive capacity for it to be beneficial, if it kept a solvent debtor from falling into default until its situation improved. It provided a way to avoid the

Table 10.1 Sources of current account improvements

	1982	1983	1984	1985	1986	1987	1988
	Percentage real change						
HIC exports	0.0	5.0	9.3	2.2	0.7	0.4	6.4
HIC imports	−14.1	−20.4	−1.1	−1.6	4.0	−1.7	2.0
HIC investment	−13.1	−21.0	−2.1	4.5	1.9	0.8	−2.9
HIC GDP	−0.4	−2.9	1.9	3.7	3.4	1.7	2.0
Per capita consumption	−2.2	−4.1	−1.7	0.2	2.6	−1.4	−0.6
	US$ billions						
Total external debt	391.0	422	438	454	482	527	529
Net capital inflows	34.6	19.1	13.3	6.0	4.5	6.2	7.6
Net resource transfer	3.7	−9.9	−19.9	−26.5	−25.8	−21.8	−31.1

Source: World Debt Tables, 1988-1989, Table 5. Constant 1980 US dollars, 1988 figures are preliminary estimates

penalties associated with default, such as exclusion from credit markets for a prolonged period and loss of trade credit. Even with the ultimate solvency of the debtor in doubt, it may have been better to provide additional financing than to allow default. The explanation of this riddle is that new lending is a way to protect old loans. Present claims against a debtor represent sunk costs for a bank. The expected rate of return from old plus new loans may thus be greater than the expected return from the old loans alone. As events have shown, if the debtor's bad times last too long, the increase in the debt may become unmanageable. Nonetheless, even with additional debt, the debtor's creditworthiness will improve as long as the growth rate of the debt or the debt service is less than the rate of growth of the economy (exports) plus the relevant rate of inflation (a trade-weighted index of the foreign currency prices of exports). This can occur even though new lending does not add to the productive base, if there is some other impetus to growth or if inflation in the traded-goods index is high.

The connection between the containment strategy which grew out of the Mexico rescue and the characterisation of the debt problem as a matter of temporary illiquidity for the debtors is thus unmistakable. The key assumption of the rescue strategy was that the shocks which had triggered the crisis would be transient: interest rates would fall, commodity prices would return to normal, and exports would revive from their cyclical trough. The debtors' creditworthiness indicators would then improve, and normal lending could resume. Meanwhile, debtors had to be kept plugged in to the lending process, both to allow them to benefit eventually from improved creditworthiness, and to protect the banks from crippling losses.

The containment strategy initially appeared successful. No sovereign debtor fell into default, and the international financial system was spared from potentially fatal shocks. Debtors, under IMF tutelage, wrenched their trade accounts into surpluses to provide foreign exchange earnings for debt service. It eventually became apparent, however that the adverse global economic trends would not be quickly reversed. Despite the recovery in the developed countries, developing countries' terms of trade continued to deteriorate, which meant that debtors faced even higher real rates of interest on their debt, notwithstanding the eventual decline in nominal dollar rates. According to World Bank data, effective real interest rates for LDCs as a whole remained above 12 per cent through 1985, and fell only to 8.1 per cent in 1986, compared with a real rate of 4 per cent in the US in 1985.

At the same time, lower terms of trade meant that countries found it difficult to increase the foreign exchange earnings of their export sectors, despite increases in export volume. The remarkable turnaround in most debtors' balances of trade came therefore from compressing imports, which was accomplished by slashing domestic investment and pushing the economy into recession. The relative importance of import reduction over export performance in the HICs for the period through 1984 can be seen in Table 10.1. The extreme correlation between import restriction and investment levels is also readily apparent. In some countries, the level of investment was so low that it barely covered the depreciation of existing capital stocks.

The shrinking of new money from the commercial banks to the niggardly levels supportable by involuntary lending meant that the net transfer of resources to the developing countries from the lenders fell drastically in 1983 and became an outflow from the countries to the lenders, of steadily increasing magnitude, over succeeding years. With growth rates negative, and what new lending there was flowing back to the banks as interest payments, the relative debt burden increased rather than lessened. By mid-1985, when a slip in oil prices (shortly to become a steep slide) once again made the liquidity problems of Mexico and several other debtors acute, it was evident that the containment strategy had failed to move debtor countries back to creditworthiness, and that to compel their performance on loans through ongoing austerity and economic stagnation was not a sustainable long-run policy.

The Baker Plan: money too tight to mention

A new official approach to the debt crisis, the 'Program for Sustained Growth', was outlined by US Treasury Secretary James Baker III in his address to the Joint Annual Meeting of the IMF and the World Bank at Seoul in early October 1985. The initiative was quickly christened the 'Baker Plan', but in fact it was more like a statement of position on the debt crisis. Put together on relatively short notice for the address, it amounted to a loose global plan for dealing with the debt problem. Subsequent Treasury Department statements targeted fifteen major debtors (all of the HICs except for Costa Rica and Jamaica), although it was understood that the new strategy would provide a framework for the smaller debtors as well.

The initiative incorporated three main elements. First, it emphasised the overriding need for comprehensive economic reform encompassing structural adjustment in addition to the usual IMF stabilisation programme. The structural reforms should give more leeway to the private sector, through trade and financial liberalisation, labour market and tax reform, and increased scope for foreign direct investment. Second, it proposed a greater role for structural adjustment and non-project lending by the World Bank and other regional development banks, with an increase of $3 billion in annual lending for such purposes. Third, it underlined the need for increased commercial bank lending, targeting a level of $20 billion over the following three years, an annual increase (net of repayments) of approximately 2.5 per cent of the banks' outstanding debt. Baker's plan maintained the principles of case-by-case management and full repayment of obligations that had undergirded the previous policy. But it represented a significant shift for the US administration and for the other creditor governments which fell in line behind it, in

1. establishing an explicit policy role for the US government in the crisis,
2. looking at the crisis from the debtors' side as a long-run development problem,
3. calling for sufficient new money to add to the productive stock of the debtors as a spur to growth, and
4. recognising the need to provide official leadership to overcome the problem of free-ridership and give new impetus to stalled commercial bank lending.

The initial response to the Baker Plan, on the part of debtors and creditor banks, was ambivalent. Debtors were wary because the Baker Plan's structural adjustment guidelines were seen as an interference with the country's sovereignty. Hence the reforms were not publicly embraced, even if they were quietly introduced by many of the debtor governments. Banks were wary of making public commitments to substantial new lending in countries which were already in difficulty. Reluctant statements of support by banking groups slowed the momentum of the new plan as soon as it left the starting blocks.

A general weakness of the Baker Plan was that it did not specify any mechanisms by which its targets might be met, either with respect to the lending goals or the debtors' required structural reforms. No concrete incentives were set up for debtors to hold up their end of the plan. Privatisation and greater openness to trade were often resented as the imposition of a peculiarly US style of economic organisation, and were not easy to introduce. Evaluation of the reforms was a highly political matter, as there was no clear system for monitoring the debtors' performance. There were also no incentives for the banks to provide new money, other than the already existing defensive motivations which had led to minimal levels of concerted lending. Additional accounting and regulatory incentives were specifically rejected, as were official guarantees for new lending and early proposals for a trust vehicle operated by the banks which would pool the lending risk and turn the new loans into more liquid securities. The upshot was that the government was left with no means, other than moral suasion, to move the banks from involuntary lending to voluntary provision of new credit. The Baker Plan rested on the notion that pump-priming by the multilateral lending agencies and improved long-term prospects flowing from structural reform would draw in new bank money, but the bankers' scepticism was not so easily overcome.

Lending by the international financial institutions fell short of its planned increment. The shortfall was due largely to the return flow of maturing short-term lending done by the IMF at the outset of the crisis, which was generally not rolled over nor replaced by sufficient World Bank non-project loans. IMF disbursements to the HICs declined after 1984, and were actually negative in each of the years 1986–8, for a total repayment of $2.67 billion according to data from William R. Cline of the Institute for International Economics (IIE). This reflected in turn the reluctance of many debtors to submit to either IMF or World Bank-imposed austerity measures. Many other loans failed to disburse completely when borrowers were unable to keep up with the required adjustment programmes. Disbursements from the Inter-American Development Bank also declined during the period, as infighting between US and Latin American members hampered its ability to raise capital commitments. The World Bank doubled its new lending by 1987, largely in the form of fast-disbursing Structural Adjustment Loans (SALs), but even a continuing 10 per cent annual increase in lending would have been insufficient to cover the concomitant increase in debt service. In all, the multilateral lenders provided an average annual flow of $5.2 billion in new lending, or about three-quarters of its Baker Plan target. But the result, after accounting for the servicing of that debt, was a growing net transfer of resources back to official lenders beginning in 1987, like that flowing to the commercial banks.

On the private side, the Baker Plan simply failed to mobilise *any* appreciable increment in commercial bank funds. The banks' annual net new lending averaged $4.6 billion between 1986 and 1988, which was only two-thirds of its Baker Plan goal. US banks' exposure to the Baker Fifteen actually fell by 8.9 per cent over the period. Aggregate lending figures are misleading. Increases in new money over the pittances that had been provided in previous years were attributable to the increasingly hardheaded negotiating techniques of the major debtors, including their willingness to run up considerable arrears on interest as well as principal and even to declare indefinite moratoria on debt service payments. Mexico's 1986 deal included $7 billion in new money, an expansion of 10 per cent of the banks' Mexican exposure, and almost one-third of the entire Baker Plan quota. But smaller borrowers, who had little bargaining power, were systematically passed over.

Ironically, lending through the Baker Plan turned out to be both too little and too much. It was not enough to clear the supply-side blockages in the debtors' economies caused by shortages of capital goods and imported intermediate inputs, nor to provide for or encourage sufficient new investment. But it augmented the stock of outstanding debt and increased the burden of debt-service payments. By the end of 1988, the debt of the HICs had increased by 34.8 per cent over its level at the start of the Baker programme.

Voluntary debt reduction

The continued failure of concerted lending to generate sufficient new money led Baker to call at the IMF Interim Committee meetings in April 1987 for expanding the 'menu' of lending options to enable banks to tailor their participation to their own circumstances. The announcement amounted to an official benediction for many elements that had already been developed and introduced piecemeal into rescheduling accords with Argentina, Brazil and Mexico. Currency redenomination allowed lenders to switch loans from whatever currency had been lent to their own home currency, take advantage of favourable moves in exchange rates, and avoid future foreign exchange risk. Interest rate options specifying different base lending rates for different lenders in the syndicate would allow lenders to match more closely their domestic cost of funds. On-lending or re-lending permitted banks to allocate their part of new credit to different debtors in the same country, and thereby diversify their project risk, without increasing overall exposure. Banks might also be able to switch from general purpose finance into (presumably) less risky trade credit. Co-financing, the linking of bank loans to lending from the multilateral development lenders, was also suggested, since official development loans were generally held to be implicitly senior to other debt.

Items specifically new to the menu included limited interest capitalisation, in which some of the interest due is simply added to the principal. Because of different accounting regulations, this was attractive primarily to the European lenders. Securitisation was suggested to replace syndicated bank claims with more easily traded assets. New types of participation fees were also proposed.[5]

The most important aspect of the renewed Baker Plan was that it took a small, measured step away from the principle of solving the crisis through continued flows of new finance. Certain of the menu items were designed to offer a way for banks to reduce the amount of debt in their portfolios. These included the expanded use of debt-for-equity swaps, debt buybacks and exit bonds, which are described in greater detail below. These market-based debt-reduction schemes were built around the idea of harnessing the discount at which LDC loans trade in the secondary market. As market transactions, they are characterised by voluntary, bilaterally-negotiated cuts. Thus, they amounted to 'voluntary debt reduction' for those banks willing to absorb the write-offs in face value on assets associated with participation. In principle, the idea of debt reduction seems at odds with a strategy dedicated to encouraging new lending, but it was hoped that in practice it would provide a way to streamline the process of concerted lending by reducing the club of lenders to those who were committed to the debtor nations for the long haul.

Debt buybacks

By 1987 there was already a substantial volume of debt traded on the secondary market. A deceptively simple voluntary debt reduction strategy was for the country to buy back its own debt at the discounted market price and thereby retire the obligation at a fraction of its face value. Buybacks were used extensively to clear up defaults on Latin American bonds in the 1930s, and during the current crisis a significant amount of Mexican private sector debt has been retired in this manner. There are, however two roadblocks to more extensive use of this approach.

One is that the typical syndicated loan agreement prohibits repurchase or prepayment at a discount. Specifically, the mandatory prepayment clause requires that any prepayment be divided among all the banks in proportion to their exposure, and the sharing clause mandates that, likewise, any extra payment be proportionally shared. Modest-sized buybacks have circumvented these requirements by using outside agents or state agencies other than the borrower (e.g. different parastatal companies) to repurchase the debt. But debt reduction on a meaningful scale relying on buybacks would require that the banks unanimously agree to waive the restrictive clauses.

The second roadblock is that buybacks require large amounts of excess reserves of hard currency, precisely the item which is in short supply for countries with debt difficulties. In the two major buybacks which occurred under the latter stage of the Baker Plan, the needed cash represented a windfall to the debtor. Bolivia used outright grants from sympathetic governments and loans from the IMF to be $335 million, or about 40 per cent of its commercial bank debt, at an average price of eleven cents on the dollar, in January 1988. In November, Chile, flush with unexpected reserves from a surge in copper prices, repurchased debt with a face value of $299 million.

A further problem with the debt buyback is that it introduces what economists call a 'moral hazard: by not paying its obligations, a country can drive down the price of its debt until it can be bought for pennies. This strategy was actually followed by the German central bank during the 1930s. If moral hazard can be avoided, the argument for lenders to provide the necessary permission for a buyback depends on the positive incentives that debt reduction can provide to the borrowers. If the positive effects of debt reduction on likely future debt servicing ability are not large, the diversion of funds available for normal debt servicing into buybacks will generally reduce the average amount of funds a country has available for repayment, relative to the debt that remains.

Even if waivers can be obtained and foreign exchange reserves are available, buybacks may not make the best use of reserves. The debtor must compare the 'return' from a buyback, which is the reduction in per-period debt service due on the face value of the debt retired, with the economic return from making the extra foreign exchange available for imports and investment. The buyback will be more attractive, the steeper the discount on the country's debt and the less critical the bottlenecks in its economy from the shortage of imports. It will also be more attractive if the policy disincentives caused by the 'debt overhand', the amount of debt in excess of a country's capacity to service, are great.

During the Baker period no provisions were made to facilitate the use of debt buybacks. A suggestion by John Williamson of the IIE is the Bank Advisory Committee be empowered to grant waivers of the sharing and repayment clauses up to some specified limit, on an annually renewable basis, conditional upon satisfactory debt service by the country. The limit could be determined by the inflow of funds which are sensitive to the debtor's economic policies, such as repatriated flight capital or revenues from new export sectors. These steps would establish incentives for the debtor to avoid depressing the market price of his debt and to follow healthy long-run economic policies.

Exit bonds

Exit bonds are one way to 'defease' existing loans, i.e. to exchange one loan for another, and are sometimes referred to as 'debt-for-debt swaps'. The exit concept underlines that the aim of the new instrument is to decouple the lender from the syndicate, and eliminate any future obligation to participate in concerted lending packages. Because it is a bearer bond without the usual syndication clauses, it will also be more easily sold should the holder wish to liquidate his position entirely. In essence, the exit bond invites potential free-riders to pay a fixed price (a discount from the face value of their original claims) to avoid new money obligations. Generally, exit bonds are given long maturities to break up the future principal repayments, and may include a substantial grace period (an interval during which interest, but no principal, is repaid).

Exit bonds were first introduced into rescheduling efforts under the Baker Plan with the Argentina negotiations in mid-1987. Argentina proposed to trade portions of its debt at par for twenty-five-year bonds paying a 4 per cent fixed interest rate, with a twelve-year grace period. The offering was a rousing failure; only five banks found the exit bonds enticing. A more noteworthy, but only slightly more successful exit bond issue was managed for Mexico by Morgan Guaranty at the beginning of 1988. The arrangement called for bids from the banks on the size of the discount at which they would trade their Mexican loans for twenty-year exit bonds carrying a slightly higher-than-market floating interest rate. Principal repayment on the bonds was guaranteed by the purchase of twenty-year zero-coupon US Treasury bonds (bonds paying only a lump sum at maturity) as collateral. Mexico had hoped to convert up to $10 billion of its debt at large discounts through the bond deal, but the banks' response was lukewarm. Only $3.67 billion was offered at discounts which the Mexican government found acceptable, for an average reduction of 30 per cent. A third exit bond offering, made by Brazil in its rescheduling of late 1988, was more successful, perhaps because it was less ambitious. It converted $1 billion at a fixed 6 per cent rate on twenty-five-year bonds with a ten-year grace period. The Brazilian bonds were limited to a participation of $15 million per bank, in a clear play to induce smaller banks to quit the syndicate.

These cases distinguish between debt service reduction (in effect, a reduction of the interest rate) and reduction of the total debt under a similar interest rate. Interest is usually reduced to a fixed rate, which eliminates any nominal variability in the country's debt service on the bond, but it could also be given as some fixed discount from a floating market rate. From the debtor's viewpoint, reduction in the debt service is what matters, because it determines the net transfer of resources per period; for the debtor the distinction between the two types of reduction is only a formality, since each one implies the other.

For the banks, however the two methods are subject to materially different accounting treatments, and may have very different effects on profits. According to generally accepted accounting principles, banks can keep an asset on the books at face value when the interest rate is reduced, even if it is below market rates or below the bank's cost of funds, as long as the stream of interest plus amortisation payments is greater than the face value of the asset.[6] Although thorough disclosure of such interest reductions is required and the market value of the asset will presumably reflect discounting at a market interest rate, the procedure allows the lender to avoid book losses and corresponding write-offs of reserves or equity capital. In practice, most banks reducing debt have made principal reductions in order to avoid the disclosure requirement, although it is not clear they would continue to do is if the losses involved were very high.

One weakness of exit bonds is that they have a pointed and painful impact on the lender, in terms of book losses or foregone cash flow, in return for a much-diffused effect on the borrower's debt service. There is not much bang for the buck when looking at the *immediate* effects of debt reduction on the debtor's net payments, since the reduction is effective for all future periods. For a 30 per cent discount on a 10 per cent interest rate, the same effect could be had in the first period from new lending of only 3 per cent of the original sum. Of course, the effect of reduction would continue in the resource transfer of future periods, while a lending strategy would require a fresh allocation of 3 per cent every period. Thus an advantage of an exit bond for the debtor is that it locks in the negotiated improvements in cash flow over a long term, while new money must be constantly renegotiated. Moreover, the larger the discount and the interest rate, the more immediate value there is in the reduction given by the exit bond.

A more serious weakness of exit bonds, as is evident from the Mexico/Morgan Guaranty deal, is that the major creditors demand substantially greater security for their assets in return for debt reduction. To compensate for the loss of 'option value', they want assurances for both the principal and interest on the new assets. Guarantees on principal are much less important than security for the interest payments, because the payment of interest is what determines whether an asset is value-impaired, and because interest makes up much more of the payment stream on a long-maturity bond. The problem is that providing collateral for the principal is relatively inexpensive (Mexico's collateral bonds cost only 7 per cent of their face value at maturity), but the cost of collateralising the interest payments would be prohibitive.[7] As a compromise, a small portion of the interest can be collateralised, or collateral can be rolled over to provide security for the interest payments a certain number of years at a time, but the new bonds are then usually rapidly discounted again by the market.

For countries without sufficient extra reserves, uncollateralised exit bonds would require some other form of credit enhancement. One method would be to make the exit bonds senior to existing debt (i.e. to assure that it will be fully serviced before other obligations). This is hardly feasible because the *pari passu* clause in syndication agreements rules out explicit legal subordination of the existing loans. Promises of implicit seniority are unlikely to be credible to holders of the exit bonds because, by taking the exit instruments, they have already signalled to the debtor that their goodwill is less valuable than that of the remaining syndicate members. The other possibility is to enhance the bonds with guarantees from governments or multilateral agencies. Such enhancements were pointedly excluded from the menu options of the Baker Plan, on the grounds that they would have implied a financial commitment by government to bail out the banks.

Debt-for-equity swaps

The most favoured form of debt reduction among the lenders has been the debt/equity swap. The idea was used as early as 1983 (in Brazil) and especially caught on after 1986–7. Debt is bought at a discount in the secondary market by investors, or taken by the original lending bank from its loan portfolio to trade for equity purchases or other local currency investments in the debtor country. In typical cases a bank might trade a private sector debt for an equity share in the borrowing company, or trade public debt for a share in a newly-privatised parastatal company. Debt swaps have also been applied to a wider range of activities in debt countries, from injections of working capital by multinationals, to funding humanitarian projects (debt for-development) or environmental programmes (debt-for-nature).

Once the debt of an eligible type has been obtained by the investor, it is redeemed by the government or central bank for local currency, or for drawing rights on a certain amount of local currency for financial transactions. The conversion rate usually includes some reduction from the local-currency equivalent of the face value of the debt. The investor then uses the local currency funds for his equity investment or other approved purpose. The swap process can occur informally whenever the debtor government is willing to buy back debt using its own currency, but the transactions can affect the money supply, and the resulting investment often requires special treatment under the laws governing foreign ownership of domestic assets. Consequently, most debt/equity swaps operate under special programmes which involve, among other things, obtaining waivers from the lenders for debt purchases and specifying the types of investment activity allowed. If loans are converted at par, all benefit from the secondary market discount goes to the investor, who effectively trades the unsecured loan for a more viable, secured equity asset. Debtor nations can recapture some of the secondary market discount by lowering the conversion price; most recent debt/equity programmes have involved periodic auctions to set the rate of conversion.

When creditor banks themselves acquire equity, the voluntary reduction in asset value they suffer comes only from the conversion discount at which the loan is swapped. At the same time there is a shift in the nature of the risk borne by the bank, from possible non-payment of the loan to variability in profits from the equity investment. More commonly, the commercial banks have been sellers of debt to the businesses which actually undertake the investment. In the latter case the bank's loss is simply the discount at which it rids itself of the loan.

Among debtors enthusiasm for debt/equity swaps has been far from universal. By the end of 1988, programmes had been initiated in most of the HICs, but a number of them had already been suspended, including large-scale programmes in Mexico and Nigeria. One drawback is that swaps put decisions over domestic investment spending priorities into the hands of foreigners. This is a complaint applicable to any policy which encourages foreign direct investment. It is important to the country that the investment attracted by debt/equity swaps be economically valuable, by making use of the country's comparative advantage and generating foreign exchange. The problem can largely be neutralised by selecting which sectors of the economy will be available for swap activity, or by offering better conversion rates for preferred investments. A more critical problem is that by giving foreign investors part of the secondary market discount on the debt, swaps allow them to invest at lower cost and compete unfairly with domestic entrepreneurs. If the investment would have come in anyway, the debt/equity swap offers an unnecessary premium to the foreign investor and displaces an actual capital inflow, which would be a less costly and more flexible contributor to the country's debt management efforts.

The most common criticism of debt/equity swaps is that they distort the country's monetary policy. If financed by monetary emission, a significant amount of swap activity would be inflationary. If the needed local currency is provided instead by government borrowing, it adds to the domestic debt, which usually carries higher rates of interest and is a problem in its own right in most debtor countries.[8] It could also increase domestic interest rates and thereby crowd out domestic investment. The inflationary impact depends upon the scale of debt/equity swaps relative to the amount of underlying monetary growth, and the marginal effect of new money on inflation. It is evident from the success of the Chilean debt/equity programme that the inflation problem can be managed. One way to reduce the monetary side effects is to combine swaps with the privatisation of government-owned enterprises.

Contrary to popular perception, debt swaps do not directly bring new foreign investment flows into the country. The government or central bank issues domestic money to pay for foreigners' investments, in return for the retirement of a foreign currency debt. In essence, a swap is a buyback of the debt in local currency, in which the investment opportunity provides the incentive for the creditor to sell his claim at a discount, and keeps the local currency from being immediately reconverted into foreign currency and taken out of the country. Since there is no actual foreign currency flow from abroad, the debtor's outward resource transfer is not directly affected. Swaps do however reduce the stock of external debt, by enabling the buyback to occur without the use of hard currency reserves. The resulting fall in debt service indirectly improves the resource transfer.

Over the longer run, the debt service reduction will be offset when investors are allowed to repatriate their profits, as profit outflows require hard currency no less than debt payments. As the equity holder is entitled to a residual profit rather than a fixed payment however, a remaining benefit is that the outflow of profits, tied as it is to performance, is presumably better matched to the country's ability to finance it. To a large extent, the relative efficiency of debt/equity swaps as a voluntary debt reduction tool turns on these indirect effects: payment-matching, the ability to encourage investment which otherwise would not occur, and the ability of swaps to encourage additional unsubsidised foreign direct investment, with its infusions of management expertise and technology.

A shifting balance

Voluntary debt reduction was powerfully catalysed by two events in 1987. In February, the largest LDC debtor, Brazil, declared an indefinite moratorium on interest payments on $68 billion of its medium- and long-term debt. The moratorium lasted until the end of the year. Its impact upon the atmosphere at the banks was profound; none of the largest debtors had ever before adopted a confrontational posture. Partly as a response to the Brazilian move, Citicorp announced on 19 May an extraordinary one-time increase in its general loan-loss reserves of $3 billion. Other major US lenders were forced to follow Citicorp's lead. European banks also increased their reserves, although most had already been setting them aside for some time at the behest of their national bank regulating authorities. The reserve increases came out of 1987 earnings and led to the largest losses recorded by US banks since the Great Depression. Ironically, banks' stock prices generally rose, on what was taken to be their belated recognition that LDC loans would never be repaid in full. Among the regional banks, this recognition was signalled by a new willingness to 'take a hit' in order to be rid of developing country debt.

Beginning in late 1987 and picking up in the following year, there was a perceptible tilt toward voluntary debt reduction, especially among the smaller US banks and regionals. This largely accounts for the fall in LDC exposure for the US banks during the Baker period. European banks were more tentative participants. Japanese banks mostly stood to one side, a reflection of their traditionally cautious investment policies and low level of reserves with which to absorb a write-down. Burgeoning demand for debt to swap, especially in Brazil, Chile, Mexico and the Philippines, drove up trading volume in the secondary market to $12 billion in 1987 and an estimated $30 billion in 1988.

In retrospect, putting up reserves effectively poisoned the Baker Plan's lending-based strategy. For the first time, banks reflected on their books some of the thinly-disguised losses they had been taking on the troubled loans. Reserves were a public admission of the banks' growing disinclination to lend to the LDCs. At the same time, the provisions sharply depressed the secondary market indicators of the loans' value. It was clearly going to be more difficult to get banks to throw good money after what was now admitted to be bad. Moreover, by strengthening the banks' balance sheets, the provisions diminished the threat of a cutoff in debt service payments, and enhanced the banks' bargaining position. This made negotiations between the debtors and creditors more difficult. Reserves also magnified the differences between weak and strong banks, making it harder to get agreement on reschedulings and concerted lending packages.

Reserves were only the most obvious evidence of a fundamental shift in balance in the debt crisis, which would lead eventually to a change in policy. Both the containment strategy and the Baker Plan had been designed to guard the stability of the banking system, protect the value of the banks' assets, and ease the borrowers back toward repayment. Mostly because it provided a pretext under which banks could buy time, the Baker policy had provided an opportunity for banks to augment their capital as well as their reserves, and thus to reduce their exposure ratios. For the 171 reporting US banks, the ratio of dollar assets in the troubled debtors to primary capital had fallen to 59 per cent at the end of 1988. By 27 February 1989, *The Economist* could talk credibly of 'the banks' great escape,' and the May 1989 issue of the trade journal *Latin Finance* was announcing retrospectively that '1988 was the year that the major banks declared the debt crisis over.'

The regional surveys in this volume offer sufficient evidence that, from the debtors' point of view, the debt crisis could hardly have been called over at the end of 1988. The Baker Plan had failed to realise its targets for lending from either the multilateral development banks or the commercial banks. Even if it had, Baker had envisioned a new lending level equal to only one quarter of the interest due from the debtors to their commercial and official creditors. As a result, capital continued to drain from the developing countries during the Baker era. The net resource transfer remained profoundly negative, only slightly improved from its 1985 low point. Although this only measures part of the economic picture, the bottom line for the Baker Plan was whether it led to improvement in the growth rates of the Baker Fifteen. Those rates continued to be low, so that by 1987 per capita consumption had once again begun to fall (see again Table 10.1). In most of the major debtors, per capita output was no higher in 1989 than in 1980 - making the 1980s into what several commentators called a 'lost decade'.

If it would have been one-sided or even perverse to claim that the debt crisis was over, it could still be asked in what sense, after nearly seven years, it could be called a 'crisis'. The stability of the international banking system was no longer an issue, and even the survival of the most highly exposed individual banks was not really in doubt. Payments deadlines and rescheduling negotiations continued to provide occasions for displays for political brinkmanship, but for the debtor nations, the problem had long since ceased to be a matter of finding the means to keep up with payments, and had become a question of how to re-initiate development.

Several countries, notably Chile and Colombia, were able to raise small amounts of new loans on a voluntary basis during 1989. But for the remaining debtors, even those like Mexico which instituted wrenching structural reforms, access to credit was as distant as ever. The 'return to normal market lending', for so long the Holy Grail of official debt policy, had in many cases ceased to figure as a goal. Even the meaning of a 'normal market' was changing. Most of the regional banks were pulling out of the international market altogether, and focusing on consolidation in expanding markets in deregulating US and fully-integrating Europe. The banks that remained international players were shifting into fee-based services and merchant banking. They showed little interest in renewed balance of payments lending, preferring to stick to safer sectors like self-liquidating trade lines, collateralized or co-financed project lending, and interbank credit.

The pervasive feeling among policy commentators was that the Baker Plan had begun to wind down. In academic circles, retreat from the Baker Plan was based upon the idea that the debt overhang was itself a part of the problem. It has been debated, with no clear conclusion, whether the excessive debt must inevitably lead either to low investment and stagnation or high inflation and instability. The new argument at its simplest is that debtors have no good reason to follow painful austerity measures if the entire benefit of improved economic performance accrues to creditors through the debtor's increased ability to service the debt. The excessive level of debt thus acts like a high marginal tax rate to create disincentives to economic reform. As has long been recognised in commercial bankruptcies, in their situation, reducing the nominal debt burden should actually increase the amount of debt the debtor will service.

Assessing the alternatives

Between them, these changes in perspective and in circumstance had by early 1988 led to renewed public debate over alternative debt policies. Some of the more important ideas will be reviewed below. The containment strategy and the Baker Plan had been built around maintaining adequate sources of finance to forestall collapse and to spur growth. A few proposals had offered variations in the financing vein, such as guarantees or other enhancements to encourage new lending. But most of the alternative policies involved either more directed and comprehensive debt reduction schemes, or alteration of the way in which risk was shared between debtor and creditor.

Contingent payment schemes: the Bailey and Garcia Plans

The actual onset of repayments difficulties reflects the failure of a debtor's currently available resources to cover his current obligations. The example of a bankruptcy proceeding suggests that one way to eliminate the proximate cause of the crisis would be to arrange each period's payment in line with the availability of resources to the borrower, by matching the country's payments profile to its earnings profile. It requires in short that the range of risks embodied in the loan agreement be shared out differently between borrower and lender.

This idea found expression in a number of the proposals for dealing with the debt crisis. One approach would make the nominal amount of payments specifically contingent upon events related to the debtor's capacity to repay. As early as 1983, Norman Bailey, then Director of

National Security Planning for the US National Security Council, advocated the establishment of a financial instrument called an 'exchange participation note' to replace banks' amortisation schedules with claims on 'some prudent level' of a debtor's foreign exchange earnings. The notes would be issued by the debtor's central bank, which would collect the necessary proportion of foreign exchange and pay it to noteholders on a *pro rata* basis. Variability in the debtor's foreign exchange earnings would thus be translated directly into variability in the creditor's receipts. Bailey's proposal explicitly excluded interest payments, which would still have to be paid on a timely basis from the remaining export earnings. The interest burden has subsequently turned out to be of great importance.

A number of more general contingent-payment schemes have been aired which would cover interest payments as well. Export value is the most common and probably the most relevant measure of the debtor's capacity to repay, but any number of other indices are also possible. Most of the proposals envisage total debt service of around 20 per cent of exports. For the heaviest debtors, interest payments alone are more than 20 per cent, so this range wold mostly rule out principal repayment. In some countries, debt service has required three-quarters or more of export earnings. However, the reduction in the net outward transfer of resources, and corresponding availability of funds for import purchases, to be gained from limiting repayment is somewhat less that the 50 per cent or more that this implies, since it seems likely that new money, at least from commercial banks, would dry up in the event of an extended partial payments moratorium. After accounting for this foregone new lending, a 1985 study by the IIE projected an aggregate net saving to Argentina, Brazil, and Mexico of about 6.5 per cent of exports. This is significant, since it would feed extra growth of approximately 4.5 per cent, but not overwhelming. Because new money flows have tended to go to the largest debtors, however, the savings available to smaller countries would be more substantial. A further issue is whether the payments foregone would simply be forgiven or whether they would be deferred. In the latter case, the capitalisation would increase the nominal stock of debt and in some degree retard progress toward improved creditworthiness.

Calls for limiting debt service to between 15 per cent and 20 per cent of exports were issued in 1984 from both a debtor nations' conference in Cartagena, Colombia and from the meetings of the Latin American Economic System (SELA) in Caracas. Interestingly the contingent-payment scheme has been practically the only broad policy suggestion to emanate from the debtors' camp. Peruvian president Alan Garcia's insistence in his July 1985 inauguration speech that interest payments be limited to 10 per cent of exports was merely a bolder variant of the earlier proposals. Those refusing to accept the limit while concurrently making new loans were threatened with exclusion from any repayment. Presentation of the '10 percent solution' as an ultimatum to the banks may have contributed to the failure of the Latin American debtors to pull together into an effective 'debtors cartel' and their passive acquiescence to policy proposals from the creditor countries. Many debtors sought to distance themselves from Garcia's confrontational rhetoric, especially as abysmal economic policies and retaliation by the banks, in the form of further restricting Peruvian trade credit, made the failure of his strategy apparent.

Mandatory debt forgiveness: the Bradley Plan

The other major alternative to continued financing of a debtor's shortfall is to mandate a reduction in the level of his obligations in each period. One of the first proposals to receive significant popular attention for espousing the principle of outright debt forgiveness was unveiled by US Senator Bill Bradley in a speech in Zurich at the end of June 1986. Bradley's plan was directed at the same fifteen debtors as the Baker Plan, covered the same time interval, and maintained the central Baker principle that participation would be earned by achievement of domestic economic reforms. But instead of piling on new lending, Bradley advocated mandatory interest rate reductions and debt forgiveness. The levels of each would be negotiated country-by-country, but to give the idea shape, Bradley suggested as a benchmark a 3 percentage point cut in the interest rate for three years combined with a 3 per cent annual reduction in principal. These numbers were quickly seized upon for public discussion. The cumulative effects of the cuts would have represented relief of roughly $47 billion from the commercial banks, plus a further $15 billion in forgiveness from official creditors. To some this seemed exceedingly generous, and the Bradley Plan provoked criticism mostly for its prospective high cost to lenders. With loans mostly less than 1 percentage point above LIBOR, the effect of the reductions on cash flow would have eliminated half of the yearly profits of the banks. And at the banks' current levels of exposure, the principal forgiveness implied a capital loss on the order of 6 per cent or more.

A critical omission from the Bradley Plan was its failure to specify a method by which US lenders could be brought to comply with the guidelines and absorb the losses. There is no legal mechanism by which to compel forgiveness by the banks. A number of incentives could be brought to bear, including tax benefits or liabilities, and regulatory requirements such as increased Allocated Transfer Risk Reserves (ATRR) requirements. But even if threats and sanctions induced a bank to write down assets in the books, the bank could retain its claim to full payment and back interest. Borrowers might have to deal with the backlog of principal and interest payments in order to return to the capital markets. And since reduction alone would not provide sufficient financing for recharged growth, there would remain the problem of assuring continued new lending.

A related criticism highlighted the damage the mandatory debt reduction could do to the countries' credit standing. This is a point of some controversy. It has been suggested earlier that insisting upon full repayment as the only way to restore credit market access is a red herring. Most banks are unlikely to lend to developing countries after a debacle like protracted involuntary lending, even if measures of the debtors' creditworthiness eventually improved significantly. There is no appreciable lending even to faithful debtors like Colombia, which has never rescheduled. Historical evidence is also less supportive on this point than is generally maintained. Debtors who fully serviced their bonds in the 1930s had no better access to loans in the succeeding decade and a half than those who defaulted.[9] But even ignoring the potential loss in creditworthiness, some analysts concluded that the benefit to debtors would be small relative to the costs imposed on the creditors. William Cline of the IIE has projected that if the debt reduction could fuel a 10 per cent increase in imports, it would lead in a case like Mexico to additional output growth of only 1 per cent yearly. This estimate is probably too conservative since it ignores the effects of debt reduction on investment and on incentives. But it does underscore the diffuse impact of the debt reduction in any one period.

Centralised debt reduction: the Kenen approach

Credit enhancements such as official guarantees have long figured in alternative proposals as a means of encouraging participation by the creditors. A common form involves the exchange of LDC debts for notes issued by an international debt facility, which would mediate in the crisis. The facility might be either voluntary or involuntary. Barely six months after the onset of the crisis, a centralised plan for debt reduction was aired by Princeton University economics professor Peter Kenen as an alternative to the pattern of case-by case, year-at-a-time rescheduling. Kenen argued for an 'International Debt Discount Corporation' that would exchange its own long-term bonds, guaranteed by creditor-country governments, with the banks for developing country loans at a fixed discount. It would then reschedule the LDC loans over the same long term, using part of the discount for debt or interest rate reduction. While each bank could choose its overall level of participation, the programme would not be strictly voluntary, as the mix of loans to be swapped for the new agency's debt and the timing of the banks' participation would be fixed, to prevent the banks from dumping only their riskiest assets.

A similar proposal, but requiring banks to exchange their loans at the 'underlying value' (defined as the price at which the debt could be fully serviced consistent with normal growth), was proposed in the US Congress by Representative Pease in 1988. The Pease bill would have amended international lending regulations to impose a costly reserve requirement on any bank not participating in the debt exchange.

Other versions of compulsory centralised debt reduction have been proposed by Harvard University economics professor Jeffrey Sachs. He originally suggested, like Bradley, mandatory interest forgiveness for five years for the debtors hardest hit by the crisis. More recently he has supported plans to force bank participation in a Kenen-style facility. Sachs suggests that in addition to regulatory or tax incentives, recalcitrant lenders could be brought to participate by making guarantees on the new debt instruments contingent upon a 'critical mass' of lenders being committed. Also IMF and World Bank disbursements could be decoupled from the achievement of a commercial bank agreement, or disbursement could be allowed while tolerating arrears to the non-participating creditors.

The rationale for compulsory participation in a debt facility (or in any sort of debt reduction) is that voluntary measures cannot assure an adequate level of debt reduction. The required level should be based on an assessment of the budgetary and balance of payments situation of each borrower individually. The voluntary negotiating framework actually inhibits debt reduction because it supports the same free-rider problem as in concerted lending: a sufficient level of debt reduction implies that all remaining claims would be serviced at something closer to their face value. Each participant therefore has an incentive to hold his assets and let other lenders volunteer for the reduction. No single lender will want to take the reduction, so no reduction can occur.

The Rohatyn and Robinson proposals

Notwithstanding the preceding argument, the greater number of proposals involving an international debt agency have conceived of it as a voluntary facility. One of the first to propose a fully voluntary debt relief agency, in early 1983, was Felix Rohatyn of the investment bank Lazard Freres. As in the Kenen proposal, the agency would need minimal funding up front. It would swap its own lower-interest, guaranteed bonds for the debt and carry out a long-term, low-interest rescheduling to reduce the debtors' need for new credit. An important consequence of the plan's being voluntary is that, contrary to the Kenen proposal, the sequence of trades between the banks and the debt agency would establish the relative prices for each country's debt in terms of the agency's bonds.

An updated proposal using the same blueprint was presented by American Express chairman James Robinson in a speech before the Overseas Development Council in March 1988. Robinson's proposed 'Institute of International Debt and Development' - I2D2 for short - was to be jointly operated by the IMF and the World Bank. It was intended to capture the more substantial secondary market discount prevailing on LDC debt as of 1988. While the Rohatyn plan was aimed at interest rate reduction, the Robinson strategy would pass the market discount on to the borrowers as a large, one-time debt reduction.

A more significant difference between the two proposals concerns the treatment of seniority. Rohatyn suggested that debtors commit a dedicated reserve stream from commodity sales or some other source to assure that their reduced long-term obligations to the facility could be serviced 'in an orderly and credible manner'. This would have much the same effect as giving the renegotiated debts seniority over other obligations. Robinson, on the other hand, proposed that the renegotiated bonds be subordinated to all new money deals as a way to encourage banks to re-initiate voluntary lending. Since old and new debt cannot both be given priority, there is obviously a tradeoff to be faced between the terms on which the debt reduction can be done, and the incentives that will be left in its wake for future lending.

Voluntary international debt facility plans along the lines laid down by Rohatyn and Robinson have found many other proponents, including Arjun Sengupta, a director of the World Bank, and investment banker Richard Weinert. They have also formed the basis of bills submitted to the US Congress by Senators Paul Sarbanes and Percy Mistry and by Representative Robert LaFalce. A common feature of the latter proposals is that the debt facility would fund itself in the capital markets by selling its guaranteed bonds directly to investors and simply buying LDC debt from the banks for cash on the secondary market.

It is well known from experience with swaps and buybacks that the cash price in the secondary market will respond strongly to surges in demand due to debt reduction. In the thin and volatile secondary market, there is no presumption that the market price is the best indicator of the true fundamental value of the debt. More likely it is strongly affected by the market power of the major banks. Price volatility also means that voluntary schemes involving a central agency buying up debt with reference to market price may be particularly vulnerable to the moral hazard problem, as countries could try to depress the market price of their debt to maximize the reduction. This could be mitigated by using a price which predates the announcement of the reduction plan as the benchmark.

The Brady Initiative

Against this background - greater resilience at the banks, growing recourse to voluntary debt reduction, legislative calls for comprehensive debt relief, and a general perception that the Baker Plan had run out of steam - the newly-elected administration of US president George Bush undertook in December 1988 a major review of the international debt strategy. It was apparent that certain key principles of the Baker Plan would not be abandoned; Baker himself had been given a more prominent role in the new administration as Secretary of State, and a key architect of his plan, David Mulford, had been promoted to Under-Secretary of the Treasury and had been given much of the responsibility for the policy revision. However, Bush made it clear that it was time for the commercial banks to shoulder more of the burden of achieving a resolution to the crisis.

The new policy was unveiled by Treasury Secretary Nicholas Brady in a speech on 10 March 1989, before a conference of the Bretton Woods Committee. Despite vast differences in personal style, Brady's presentation was in several respects like the launching of the Baker Plan in Seoul three-and-a-half years earlier. It too was prepared on short notice, and was spare on details, especially about the mechanics of gaining cooperation from the banks, and it amounted, like Baker's proposal, to an indicative policy framework rather than a detailed plan. Like the Baker Plan, it embraced a flexible case-by-case approach, relied upon voluntary, negotiated, market-based refinanced options, recognised growth as the essential goal of the debt policy, and demanded proper economic policies within debtor nations as a prerequisite for participation. And, like the Baker speech, Brady's remarks represented a major shift in policy and perspective, in this case from an emphasis on new lending to debt reduction.

Despite disclaimers from the Treasury Department that Brady's speech represented only 'talking points' and not a formal LDC debt plan, his remarks were immediately taken up by the press and public and dubbed the 'Brady Initiative.' The new strategy was built around seven major ideas.

1. First and foremost, Brady said, debtor nations must adopt 'policies which can better encourage new investment flow, strengthen domestic savings and promote the return of flight capital'.
2. In supporting this essential requirement, the creditor community (commercial banks as well as official lenders) must provide a broader and more effective range of financial alternatives. Realism, Brady insisted, indicated that for many debtors improved creditworthiness would only come through debt reduction.
3. At the same time, some voluntary new financing would still be needed; this could be encouraged by differentiating new from old debt.
4. Several steps would help further the process of debt reduction, most importantly a relaxation of the sharing clauses in the lending agreements, perhaps through temporary waivers by banks of those clauses.
5. The IMF and World Bank, besides overseeing debtors' policies and catalysing new lending, would provide funding for debt buybacks, collateral for exit bonds, or guarantees through its policy-based lending programmes.
6. Creditor governments would cooperate to eliminate unnecessary impediments and disincentives to debt reduction from the regulatory, tax, and accounting environments faced by their banks.

7. Finally and critically, the negotiation of debt reduction and new lending transactions, even when involving multilateral agencies as guarantors, must remain in the market place. Thus the new debt strategy pointedly rejected the idea of mandatory or centralised reductions.

The highly indebted countries applauded the shift in policy perspective expressed by Brady, and easily embraced the concept of debt reduction with provision of public funding for guarantees. Those countries qualifying for treatment under the Brady framework on the basis of their domestic policies quickly nominated themselves and seized the opportunity to negotiate under more promising ground rules. There were some sticking points: many debtors objected to US insistence that debt/equity swaps be included in the debt reduction package, and others did not accept the plan's implicit commitment to export-led growth as the model for economic reform. Non-Latin American debtors protested that the new programme discriminated against those who had already imposed difficult reforms in order to keep their debt service current. But debtors realised that the Brady Initiative was the only game in town.

Among the creditor nations, support eventually rallied around the new strategy despite misgivings about the plan's vagueness and about the implicit support it gave to the banks. As the 1989 Spring meetings of the IMF and World Bank, three weeks after the introduction of the initiative, the G-7 ministers issued a statement of tentative support.[10] The amount and the form of application of debt reduction financing by the multilateral lenders was subject to some dispute. Dutch Finance Minister Onno Ruding and British Chancellor of the Exchequer Nigel Lawson expressed concern that the use of official funds to support interest guarantees would leave taxpayers holding the bag for bad commercial bank loans. The IMF and the World Bank executive boards were nonetheless quick to put their shoulders into the task of outlining a policy for the application of their funds. They envisioned allocation of up to 40 per cent of new SALs to debt reduction. Six weeks later the G-7 deputies were able to agree on a formula for applying multilateral funding to interest guarantees. The Bank and the Fund eventually set aside over $20 billion for possible application in debt reduction, and Japan volunteered to ante up $4.5 billion.

At the Spring meetings, Brady also called for individual governments to take action to harmonise regulatory and tax treatment of the debt-reduction instruments. However, reforms of regulatory and tax frameworks did not generate any real momentum, least of all toward actually creating positive incentives for debt reduction. The IMF and World Bank also deflected commercial bank demands for guarantees on new lending, and for cross-default clauses between new bank lending and multilateral loans. Thus the reduction incentives that evolved for commercial banks were limited to the provision of partial interest guarantees. Nonetheless, creditor government support for the initiative continued to solidify. In July 1989, Japan announced provision of a further $5.5 billion for debt relief, and the Brady Initiative received a strong vote of confidence at the G-7 economic summit in Paris.

The initial response from lenders was also supportive of the Brady Initiative's principles, but their enthusiasm for the new strategy cooled quickly. Bankers resisted the proposal to permit waivers of the sharing and pledge clauses, and that idea was shelved in short order. More generally, banks criticised the Brady plan for being hazy and for offering insufficient incentives. The US banks had hoped for significant tax breaks to encourage and soften their write-offs. Instead they were met with an Internal Revenue Service ruling (not directly related to the Brady Initiative) which greatly reduced the tax value of losses on LDC loans. Banks were disappointed, too, with the levels of financial support for debt reduction offered by the IMF and World Bank, which were sufficient to guarantee only small amounts of interest. They also demanded that an equal share of debt reduction be borne by the official Paris Club creditors, including the multilateral development banks. In short, the commercial banks complained that they had been assessed all of the costs of carrying out the new debt policy. Their growing disaffection eventually became clear from foot-dragging over the size and terms of reductions in debt rescheduling negotiations with Mexico.

The Mexican standoff and its implications

In large measure the banks' accusation of haziness in the outline of the Brady Plan was unfair, because it was acknowledged that the Initiative was to be explicitly evolutionary. Bilateral negotiations between debtors and the bank advisory committee would give concrete form to the strategy, because of the insistence upon voluntary and case-by-case treatment. As it had done throughout the crisis, Mexico provided a test case. Its exemplary structural reforms and cooperation with creditors, despite severe austerity, made it a model debtor. Its new president, Carlos Salinas de Gortari, in return for continuing those reforms, had promised his country a significant reduction in the external debt. As negotiations between Mexico and its banks got under way, other countries' bank advisory committees suspended their talks to await a precedent.

The progress of those negotiations augured a difficult road for the new debt initiative. Talks began on 19 April 1989. Mexico, based upon projections of its financing gap over the medium term (projections supported by analysts from the IMF), asked its creditor banks for a 55 per cent reduction in the face value of its debt. This was slightly less than the secondary market discount at the time. Incredulous, the banks responded with a counteroffer of 15 per cent. Six weeks of negotiation, under increasing pressure from the US administration, and including direct appeals to the banks for flexibility from Brady and from the Managing Director of the IMF, Michel Camdessus, produced only a slight narrowing of the gap.

The pace of negotiations quickened when the amount of official money available to Mexico for debt reduction was finalised at $7 billion, but a first deadline at the end of June was allowed to pass, and a second deadline just before the start of the Paris summit was approaching before the two sides reached an agreement in principle on a reduction of 35 per cent with alternative interest rate reduction and new money options. When these talks suddenly ran aground over the timing of disbursements from the multilateral lenders for interest guarantees, and the banks' demand for contingent plans to 'recapture' some of their interest rate and principal concessions, a frustrated Mexico threatened to quit the process entirely.

In a highly dramatic effort to keep the talks on track and avert what threatened to be an embarrassment for his Initiative, Brady made a series of calls from the Paris summit to enlist bank chairmen directly in the negotiating process. But details of the recapture provisions continued to elude solution. On 21 July, in desperation, Salinas set a two-day deadline on the talks. A select group consisting of the chairmen of Mexico's three lead banks, the Mexican finance minister Pedro Aspe and his chief negotiator Angel Gurria, and the highest officials from the US Treasury and Federal Reserve held marathon talks over a second 'Mexican Weekend'. Just before the deadline, on Sunday afternoon, after three months of constant and often bitter negotiation, they finally emerged with a deal.

The Mexican debt-reduction agreement was built around a choice for the banks among three options:

1. Exchange the existing debt at a 35 per cent discount for thirty-year bonds carrying a market interest rate.
2. Exchange the debt for thirty-year par bonds with a fixed below-market interest rate of 6¼ per cent.
3. Keep the existing debt at face value and commit to new loans over the following four year worth 25 per cent of their present exposure.

Principal on the two types of bonds would be collateralised with US Treasury bonds and between eighteen and twenty-four months of interest would be covered by rolling interest guarantees. The extent of coverage available would depend upon the amount and types of bonds selected by the banks. A debt/equity swap programme was included, but limited to $1 billion per year for investment in selected Mexican government privatisations or infrastructure projects. Moreover, a contingency fund would be set up in case oil prices fell below $10 per barrel and a recapture clause allowed banks to reclaim a limited amount of interest concessions beginning in 1996 if oil prices remained above an inflation-adjusted price of $14 per barrel.

In the wake of the hard-won Mexican compromise, bankers were quick to assert that the agreement would not serve, after all, as a prototype for other countries' debt reduction arrangements. European banks in particular, which had already extracted the tax advantages from their high LDC loan loss reserves and saw little to gain from reduction, were reported 'absolutely furious about the Mexican deal, and are saying "never again"'. Reluctance to use Mexico as a model sprang from resentment over the amount of government arm-twisting that had gone into the deal, and from strategic positioning in anticipation of the next showdown. But the bankers' disclaimers could not discourage other eligible debtors from pressing their cases for the next reductions. Venezuela initiated talks by reiterating an earlier demand for a 50 per cent debt reduction, and attempted to apply pressure in support of that cut by selectively withholding interest payments on its commercial bank debt. Less confrontational talks were soon underway with Costa Rica, Morocco and Uruguay.

The fastest mover however was the Philippines. Hardly three weeks after the closing of Mexico's deal - and after only six day of negotiation - the Filipinos had secured a deal of their own. The outlines of the package differed considerably from the Mexican arrangement, a reflection of the vastly different economic and financial circumstances faced by the two countries. With a total $28 billion external debt, of which only $7.1 billion of long-term commercial debt was up for rescheduling, and a yearly financing gap estimated at $1.7 billion, commercial debt reduction had relatively little potential impact on the Philippines' overall payments problem. Even full forgiveness of interest on all of its commercial bank debt would have left the gap yawning at near $1 billion annually. Instead playing to its recent strong growth (above 6 per cent) and good prospects, and taking advantage of the bargaining leverage provided by the Mexican precedent, the Philippines fashioned an agreement relying almost entirely on commitments to new lending. The money was to be provided in the form of a new international bond issue, which reintroduced the aspect of voluntary lending while relying on the creditors' promises to participate in the offering. Estimates of the amount of new money to be provided ranged from $600 million to $1.2 billion. The agreement also provided for a debt buyback option at a price near the secondary market rate of 50 cents on the dollar, as well as an exit option for smaller banks.

Initial impressions were that the Philippines pact, by leaning so heavily on new money, would be contrary to the spirit of the Brady Initiative. But Brady welcomed the accord as a demonstration of the 'versatility' of his debt strategy. The *Washington Post*'s Paul Blustein quoted a Treasury official's argument that the accord justified the Initiative's loose, market-led approach: 'The point was to allow creativity. Brady didn't want to set out a road map. You watch the next couple [of agreements] unfold - you'll see that they'll all be different.'

The actual breakdown between lending and debt reduction in each of the two deals depended upon the options chosen by individual creditor banks. But the outlines of the Filipino package, and public comments by banks on their plans for the Mexican deal suggested that the evolution of the Brady plan into concrete form would result in considerably less debt reduction, and considerably more new lending, than originally expected. The recognition sparked four major criticisms of the Initiative.

1. The banks' refusal to grant general waivers of the restrictive clauses in loan syndications meant that it is not possible to free up the transactions and obtain a market solution. Negotiations degenerate instead into a conflict reflecting the relative market power of the creditors as a group against the individual debtors - a situation of bilateral monopoly.

2. The Brady Initiative fails to squarely face the 'free rider' problem. In the Mexican package, an opportunity to free ride on the debt reduction effort is built in, in the form of the new money option, even though traditional free riding - doing nothing and still collecting payments - has effectively been eliminated. In a debt reduction scenario, giving new money is like free riding, because those lending will expect to be repaid fully for both the old and the new loans, thanks to the loss of those who have accepted the debt reduction. In fact, the problem is all the greater because it is the larger banks who will have the incentive to free ride in this fashion, which smaller banks are likely to grasp the opportunity to exit.

3. The amount of funds provided for guarantees is insufficient. The point of the guarantees is to trade a loss in nominal value for enhanced security. But if the enhancement is not enough to prevent the newly reduced asset from trading at a similar discount, lenders will not be willing to trade for it nor to lend again. It has also been argued that the use of limited enhancement loans to provide rolling interest guarantees is not an efficient use of funds.

4. Guarantees are provided for exit bonds through IMF and World Bank lending even if the amount of debt reduction achieved is not sufficient to improve the creditworthiness of the borrower. By committing the guarantee funds first and leaving the amount of debt reduction to the negotiations between debtor and creditors, the multilateral lenders are underwriting an asset without exercising any control over its value or riskiness. This reduces the incentives to both debtors and creditors to see that reduction reaches meaningful levels.

When the details of recent deals have come clear, it may turn out that these problems have largely been avoided or are insignificant; indeed, the combination of debt reduction by some lenders and new lending by others may be just the right mix to get the developing countries' economies jump-started again. The task, as the new debt initiative reaches a mature stage, will be to monitor the progress carefully and ensure that the process does not get derailed.

Debt policy prospects

The most striking feature of the official (US-led) approach to the LDC debt problem has been its slow metamorphosis from insistence upon full repayment to debt forgiveness. A cynical view would have it that each of the strategies reflects narrow US interests; the focus of policy shifted only when the danger from political instability in Latin America outweighed the financial threat to US banks. A more generous impression is that debt policies have evolved in step with events and with a deepening understanding of the crisis.

Ultimately there are as many scenarios of the debt crisis as there are debtors in crisis. But a general consensus has emerged that the debt crisis resulted from a volatile combination of external shocks, imperfect policies in the borrowing countries, and overlending by the banks. The early response consisted of containing what was perceived as a temporary liquidity crisis. Yet contrary to that initial perception, the crisis once initiated could not simply be undone by a diet of stabilisation policies and elimination of the external shocks. This is partially a reflection that commercial bankers, once burned, were twice shy. As in the 1930s, normal lending may take a decade or more to resume, even to the most conscientious debtors. But it is also a consequence of the inherent hysteresis of economic events. A compounding debt burden, debt fatigue, and decay of the productive base caused by years of austerity have knocked most of the debtor nations off the development course.

If developing country borrowers are to make good their commercial debts, a transfer of resources back to the developed countries is inevitable. But it is the timing and magnitude of such return flows that is the critical development problem. The Baker Plan recognised the need for growth and structural development to take priority over external balance adjustment. But the new money approach was ineffective in generating the required capital flows. Baker's successor Brady embraced what in many circles has been accepted as axiomatic - that the debt was too large to be repaid on the originally agreed terms. The Brady Initiative built upon three vehicles for voluntary debt reduction: debt buybacks, exit bonds and debt/equity swaps. But each of these methods has deficiencies and sticking points, and each requires that a heavy cost be allocated in some way between the debtor and the creditor. Alternative debt policy proposals have by and large been less sanguine about the efficacy of the voluntary market-based approach. Most have suggested ways to shift unilaterally the burden on risk from debtor to creditor or to induce the creditors to reduce substantially their share of the outflow of resources from debtor nations.

Almost all debt policy proposals have recognised that the effectiveness of any financial steps hinges crucially on the debtor's domestic economic reforms. But the political economy of such reforms has been poorly understood. The best motivation for reform is the promise of long-term stability and prosperity. Conditionality is only useful to insure that new lending or debt concessions are not taken as a way of putting off reforms. It is critical to adopt strategies that leave debtor governments with sufficient motivation and political capital to carry reforms through.

All three of the factors which contributed to the crisis - the provision of finance, domestic economic policies and external conditions - will have a place in its resolution. Debt policy itself only addresses the first of these directly, and indirectly, the second. It is equally important that improvements continue in the global macroeconomic variables making up the environment of the debtor countries: lower interest rates, strong growth rates in the developed nations, stable commodity prices, and a reversal of the trend toward greater protectionism.

On the eve of the Brady Initiative, John S. Reed, Chairman of Citicorp and a leader in shaping the banks' debt strategy, predicted in the February 1989 issue of *Latin Finance* that 'the debt situation is going to resolve itself over the new few years'. Reed's optimism may be more warranted than his prescription of *laissez-faire*. The crisis has entered the stage of the end game, in which a series of carefully planned and timed moves could bring it to a final resolution. Above all, the players must avoid blundering into policies that force a stalemate with strings of long negotiations leading to insufficient debt reduction and insignificant amounts of new finance. The amount of pressure required to realise the Mexican agreement destroyed any pretence that creditor governments would not be involved in resolving the debt crisis. Besides moral suasion, leadership may require subsidising positive regulatory, accounting, or tax incentives, or even forcing the participation of lenders to eliminate free ridership and assure adequate levels of relief. The key will be to draw from the widest possible range of policy alternatives for solutions that satisfy the urgent need for renewed development and insure the developing nations' return to true long-term creditworthiness.

Notes

1. The nine money-centre banks are Bank of America, N.A.; Bankers Trust Company; Chase Manhattan Bank, N.A., Citibank, N.A.; Chemical Bank, N.A.; Continental Illinois Bank; First National Bank of Chicago; J.P. Morgan; and Manufacturers Hanover Trust Company.
2. The HICs as defined by the World Bank are: Argentina, Bolivia, Brazil, Chile, Colombia, Costa Rica, Cote d'Ivoire, Ecuador, Jamaica, Mexico, Morocco, Nigeria, Peru, Philippines, Uruguay, Venezuela, and Yugoslavia.
3. The victims were largely Latin American nations, who held an average of 67 per cent of their debt at floating rates, compared to 34 per cent for other debtors. This fact goes part of the way in explaining why the crisis has been so predominant in Latin America.
4. This has provided the means for banks to get around regulatory and accounting rules which do not allow interest to be counted until it is paid (or officially accrued) unless the capitalisation is agreed in advance.

5. For an excellent discussion of the lending menu, see Klaus Regling's 'New Financing Approaches in the Debt Strategy'.
6. The relevant ruling is FASB 15, Financial Accounting Standards Board.
7. To secure all of the interest payments using zero-coupon bonds requires an amount equal to the present value of the whole stream of payments, which is roughly the same as the face value of the instrument being secured.
8. It is worth remembering that many debtors turned to the international capital markets in the 1970s precisely because domestic borrowing costs were significantly higher.
9. For opposing viewpoints on this issue see the articles by Stephen A. Schuker and Barry Eichengreen.
10. The Group of Seven (G-7) are the seven largest industrial, market economies: Canada, France, Italy, Japan, United Kingdom, US, and West Germany. The support of the other G-7 countries was critical since together they controlled the majority of votes in the IMF and World Bank.

References

Bailey, Norman. 'A Safety Net for Foreign Lending', *Business Week*, 10 January 1983.

Bergsten, C. Fred, William R. Cline, and John Williamson, *Bank Lending to Developing Countries: the Policy Alternatives.* Washington, D.C: Institute for International Economics, 1985.

Blustein, Paul, 'Philippine Debt Pact Seeks to Avoid Brady Pitfalls', *Washington Post*, 17 August 1989.

'Brady I or Brady II?', *Latin Finance*, February 1989.

Clarke, Robert, Testimony as Comptroller of the Currency, before the House Committee on Banking, Finance, and Urban Affairs. 5 January 1989.

Cline, William, *Mobilizing Bank Lending to Developing Countries.* Washington, D.C.: Institute for International Economics, 1987.

Cline, William, 'The Baker Plan: Progress, Shortcomings, and Future Evolution', Institute for International Economics mimeograph, 1989.

The Economist, 27 February 1989.

Eichengreen, Barry, 'The US Capital Market and Foreign Lending, 1920-1955', in J. Sachs (ed.), *Development Country Debt and the World Economy.* NBER/University of Chicago Press, 1989.

Feinbery, Richard E., 'How to Reverse the Defunding of Latin America by the Multilateral Lending Agencies', paper presented for the Conference on Financing Latin American Growth, Jerome Levy Institute, Annandale-on-Hudson, New York, October 1988.

Hermann, Robert, Testimony as Senior Deputy Comptroller of the Currency for Bank Supervision Policy, before the House Committee on Banking, Finance, and Urban Affairs, 27 June 1989.

Kenen, Peter B., 'A Bailout Plan for the Banks', *New York Times*, 6 March 1983.

Krugman, Paul, 'International Debt Strategies in an Uncertain World', in J. Cuddington and G. Smith (ed.), *International Debt and the Developing Countries*, Washington, D.C.: World Bank, 1985.

Krugman, Paul, 'Financing Vs. Forgiving a Debt Overhang', *Journal of Development Economics*, 29, 1988.

Kuczynski, Pedro-Pablo, *Latin American Debt.* Baltimore, Johns Hopkins University Press, 1988.

Latin Finance, May 1989.
Regling, Klaus, 'The New Financing Approaches in the Debt Strategy', *Finance and Development*, March 1988.
Rohatyn, Felix, 'A Plan for Stretching Out Global Debt', *Business Week*, 28 February 1983.
Sachs, Jeffrey, 'Making the Brady Plan Work', *Foreign Affairs*, Summer 1989.
Schuker, Stephen A., 'American "Reparations" to Germany, 1919-1933: Implications for the Third-World Debt Crisis', *Princeton Studies in International Finance*, 61, July 1988.
Wertman, Patricia, 'The Baker Plan: A Remedy for the International Debt Crisis?', *Congressional Research Service*, unpublished mimeograph, 1988.
Williamson, John, *Voluntary Approaches to Debt Relief.* Washington, D.C.: Institute for International Economics, 1989.
World Bank, *World Debt Tables, 1986–1987*. Washington, D.C.: World Bank, 1987.
World Bank, *World Development Report, 1987*. Washington, D.C.: Oxford University Press, 1987.
World Bank, *World Debt Tables, 1988–1989* Washington, D.C.: World Bank, January 1989.

Chapter 11

Forecasting the future

Scott B. MacDonald, Margie Lindsay and David L. Crum

One point that this book has tried to emphasize is the wide scope of the phenomenon which falls under the rubric of the global debt crisis. As the various chapters attest, the problem exists in Asia and Africa and even Europe - not just in Latin America.

While the crisis is truly global, its impact is far from homogenous. Portugal and South Korea - which appeared ready to join the rescheduling club - now are being held up as models for other developing countries; export-led growth helped them surmount their particular debt crises. On the other hand, countries which showed such promise at the beginning of the 1980s have been derailed by the debt crisis; there are serious questions, for example, about the future direction of Argentina, Brazil and Nigeria in the 1990s. It can be said however that the debt crisis remains a serious problem for the majority of the developing countries and their creditors in the last decade of the twentieth century.

Responses to this crisis have borne similarities as well as differences directly related to each particular national experience. The export-led growth model, exemplified by the emerging Pacific rim nations, cannot be expected to be duplicated exactly in Sub-Saharan Africa. Nor can countries redraw the global map to duplicate Mexico's strategy of playing the US card. This leaves us with questions about development in the next decade for a number of regions and their particular strategies for escaping the debt trap. Unfortunately there are no panaceas: every proffered 'solution' to the crisis involves allocating the cost to one of the players - the borrowers, the banks, the governments or the multilateral agencies - and none can afford to bear it alone.

With the debt crisis threatening to reach its teens in the 1990s, can it still be labeled a 'crisis'? Although less catchy, perhaps the term 'long-term problem' better captures the nature of the beast. Certainly in the fledgling democracies of Eastern Europe and the impoverished nations of Sub-Saharan Africa, the debt crisis has become just one of many severe challenges which the leaders of the developing world must face.

The balance of this concluding chapter provides the authors' economic forecasts of what the 1990s holds for the major debtor nations. Each forecast includes their thoughts on the scope of the country's debt problem, the potential for economic growth, the welfare of the population, the ability to maintain price stability, and management of external accounts. These forecasts confirm the wide scope of the problem as well as the diversity of the probable outcomes.

Latin America

Argentina

Total external debt (1989)	$60 billion.
Debt management	Problem will ease in early 1990s, but lack of commitment to economic reform will undermine negotiations with creditors over the longer term.
Real GDP growth	Will be uneven throughout the decade, but very little net progress will be made.
Real per capita income	Will show little improvement and may even decline.
Inflation	Will ease in early 1990s, but hyperinflation could return over the longer term.
Current account	Progress will be erratic at best during the forecast period.

Brazil

Total external debt (1989)	$112 billion.
Debt management	Will continue to be a problem, with government vacillating between confrontation and negotiation with creditors depending on the level of domestic political pressure.
Real GDP growth	Dynamic private sector cannot offset effects of bloated public sector, resulting in sluggish overall level of growth.
Real per capita income	Little improvement will be possible.
Inflation	Some improvement will occur in early 1990s, but continued progress depends on government's commitment to economic reform.
Current account	Exports will continue to be most dynamic area of economy, keeping trade surplus healthy.

Chile

Total external debt (1989)	$17 billion.
Debt management	Will be more of a problem than in the 1980s, but major crisis is unlikely.

Real GDP growth	Likely to be less dynamic than in the 1980s, but still positive.
Real per capita income	Likely to improve with efforts focused on more equitable distribution of wealth.
Inflation	Will rise during period, but remain under control.
Current account	Should remain healthy throughout the decade.

Colombia

Total external debt (1989)	$16 billion.
Debt management	Will become more of a problem as earnings from drug traffickers fall off and Colombia pressures creditors for better terms.
Real GDP growth	May be less dynamic than during the 1980s.
Real per capita income	May grow less slowly than during the 1980s.
Inflation	Will remain low throughout the decade.
Current account	Will improve only moderately.

Mexico

Total external debt (1989)	$105 billion.
Debt management	Will be a problem throughout the decade, though US involvement will make creditors more accommodating toward Mexico than other Latin American debtors.
Real GDP growth	Likely to remain relatively sluggish for much of the decade.
Real per capita income	Will show little improvement.
Inflation	Will remain under control by Latin American standards.
Current account	Should improve during the decade, but is largely tied to movements in oil prices.

Peru

Total external debt (1989)	$18 billion.
Debt management	May be less of a problem eventually as Peru decides to rejoin the international financial community, but progress will be rocky and slow.
Real GDP growth	Significant real growth could only resume in the latter part of the decade, at best.
Real per capita income	Little, if any, improvement will be possible.
Inflation	Policies will be instituted by early 1990s to slow

	down hyperinflation, but long-term progress depends on government's commitment to austerity.
Current account	May improve slightly over the period.

Venezuela

Total external debt (1989)	$35 billion.
Debt management	Will be an issue as Venezuela increasingly demands recognition of economic progress from creditors, but confrontation is unlikely.
Real GDP growth	Could improve during the decade if oil prices recover.
Real per capita income	Could improve during the decade if oil prices recover.
Inflation	Should ease to a more moderate level by the early 1990s.
Current account	Could improve during the decade if oil prices recover.

Central America and the Caribbean

Barbados

Total external debt	$621 million.
Debt management	Critical in short term in early 1990s, potential problems mid-decade.
Real GDP growth	Highly foreign exchange earnings dependent economy, will rely heavily on international economic performance.
Real per capita income	Population growth will remain low, hence income will depend on factors mentioned under GDP growth.
Inflation	Will remain low and under tight control.
Current account	Devaluation issue must be faced in early part of decade and will impact competitiveness throughout rest of the 1990s.

Costa Rica

Total external debt	$4.7 billion.
Debt management	Will continue to be most innovative in Central America through debt reduction (buybacks and conversions).
Real GDP growth	Will improve throughout decade and remain

	highly export dependent.
Real per capita income	Will improve throughout decade.
Inflation	Will depend on continued rigidity of monetary policy and that of major trade partners.
Current account	Will register surplus depending on diversification of exports (especially non-traditional exports).

Dominican Republic

Total external debt (1987)	$3.7 billion.
Debt management	Will remain problematic throughout the decade.
Real GDP growth	Will remain low.
Real per capita income	Will also be depressed throughout much of the decade.
Inflation	Will probably fluctuate vigorously.
Current account	Will heavily depend on traditional export performance, i.e. sugar and coffee.

Guatemala

Total external debt (1987)	$2.8 billion.
Debt management	Will continue to depend on commercial borrowing.
Real GDP growth	Will be sporadic because of possible instability of economic policies.
Real per capita income	Will be equally sporadic.
Inflation	Might be contained if domestic policies continue to focus on restraint.
Current account	Be highly dependent on external rather than internal factors.

Guyana

Total external debt (1987)	$1.3 billion.
Debt management	Will improve, arrears will be paid and new financing provided.
Real GDP growth	Steady improvement and development of broader-based economy will occur.
Real per capita income	Will also improve significantly.
Inflation	Will remain under control and relatively low.
Current account	Will make steady progress, shifting from large to small deficits by end of the decade.

Honduras

Total external debt	$3.3 billion.
Debt management	This remains a difficult area, complicated by the economy's overall state of underdevelopment.
Real GDP growth	Will remain heavily dependent on commodity prices.
Real per capita income	In Latin America, will remain one of the lowest.
Inflation	Will remain low.
Current account	Little improvement to be expected.

Jamaica

Total external debt (1987)	$4.4 billion.
Debt management	Tight monetary controls will be continued.
Real GDP growth	Will only grow if the government implements a growth-oriented policy.
Real per capita income	Will continue to be very depressed.
Inflation	At least for the early 1990s, expected to be high, might be controlled.
Current account	Will continue to accrue large deficits.

Nicaragua

Total external debt (1987)	$7.3 billion.
Debt management	Will remain highly problematic and directly related to political developments.
Real GDP growth	Assuming political changes, growth will depend on regaining confidence of international investors.
Real per capita income	Will continue to be very depressed.
Inflation	At least for the early 1990s, expected to be high, might be controlled in earlier years.
Current account	Will continue to accrue large deficits.

Panama

Total external debt (1987)	$5.3 billion.
Debt management	Will remain highly problematic and directly related to political developments.
Real GDP growth	Assuming political changes, growth will depend on regaining confidence of international investors.
Real per capita income	Will grow only marginally.

Inflation	Will remain low.
Current account	Will probably be negative.

Trinidad and Tobago

Total external debt (1987)	$1.8 billion.
Debt management	Conditions will be tight in the early part of the decade, but will improve with structural adjustment measures.
Real GDP growth	Slow growth followed by a faster rate of expansion.
Real per capita income	Will begin to regain lost ground from the severe recession in the 1980s.
Inflation	Will remain relatively low.
Current account	Will gradually improve, shifting to small surpluses by the end of the decade.

Middle East and North Africa

Algeria

Total external debt (1988)	$24 billion.
Debt management	Will be a problem.
Real GDP growth	Likely to continue as dynamic.
Real per capita income	Remains a major problem area due to high birth rate;
Inflation	Will remain low throughout decade.
Current account	Will show improvement.

Egypt

Total external debt	$50.0 billion.
Debt management	Will remain problematic through the decade and dependent on grants and assistance.
Real GDP growth	Will remain low and dependent on the upswing of the regional economy.
Real per capita income	Will remain low under pressure of population growth and will be an ongoing source of social tension.
Inflation	Will remain relatively low.
Current account	Will remain in deficit due to ongoing structural weaknesses in the economy.

Iran

Total external debt	$10.0 billion.
Debt management	Return to markets will be complicated by reluctance of commercial lenders and dependent regime's political moderation.
Real GDP growth	Remains dependent on domestic political environment.
Real per capita income	Has the potential for an upswing by the end of the 1990s.
Inflation	Will remain under control.
Current account	Will remain in moderate deficit with need to modernize infrastructure although exports revenues be dependent on oil price fluctuations.

Iraq

Total external debt	$80.0 billion.
Debt management	Will remain ongoing concern throughout the decade. Some creditors will find payment schedule complicated.
Real GDP growth	Likely to remain on fast pace dependent in part on oil prices.
Real per capita income	Likely to decline in the beginning of decade due to reduction of foreign borrowing, but will regroup at end of decade.
Inflation	Will remain under control.
Current account	Will remain dependent on oil prices as well as ability to handle debt repayment schedule.

Israel

Total external debt	$26.0 billion.
Debt management	Will remain dependent on U.S. largesse and ability to continue structural adjustment of Israeli economy.
Real GDP growth	Will remain relatively low due to fiscal constraints.
Real per capita income	Will remain relatively high due to foreign assistance.
Inflation	Will remain under control, but will be an ongoing concern.
Current account	Will remain in deficit unless substantial structural adjustment programs are undertaken.

Jordan

Total external debt	$5.5 billion.
Debt management	Will remain dependent on health of regional economy especially that of Saudi Arabia, its primary foreign donor.
Real GDP growth	Likely to remain relatively low as structural adjustment takes place.
Real per capita income	Likely to decline beginning of decade and improve later in 1990s.
Inflation	Will remain relatively low.
Current account	Will remain dependent on regional economy and phosphate prices.

Libya

Total external debt	$3.5 billion.
Debt management	Not likely to be major problem.
Real GDP growth	Will remain low until oil prices pick up.
Real per capita income	Will remain an ongoing area of friction within regime.
Inflation	Will remain low.
Current account	Will remain problematic as long as economic reform is lacking.

Morocco

Total external debt	$19.9 billion.
Debt management	Will remain relatively competent and under control.
Real GDP growth	Likely to remain dynamic, but despite diversification phosphate prices are still important.
Real per capita income	Will continue to increase.
Inflation	Will remain low.
Current account	Will remain dependent upon phosphate prices and European Community market access.

Pakistan

Total external debt	$17 billion.
Debt management	Will remain under control.

Real GDP growth	Will remain moderately high and dependent on growth in Persian Gulf and commodity prices.
Real per capita income	Will remain low, but steadily improving throughout decade.
Inflation	Will remain relatively low.
Current account	Will remain dependent on Persian Gulf economy as well as commodity prices.

Syria

Total external debt	$4.9 billion.
Debt management	Will remain problematic, but under control.
Real GDP growth	Will remain low and dependent on structural adjustment.
Real per capita income	Will be impacted by pressing need for economic reform.
Inflation	Will remain relatively low.
Current account	Will be highly problematic due to the need for structural reforms especially in the trade regime.

Tunisia

Total external debt	$6.7 billion.
Debt management	Will remain relatively competent throughout decade.
Real GDP growth	Will remain moderately high.
Real per capita income	Will make gradual improvements throughout decade.
Inflation	Will remain under control and moderately low.
Current account	Will remain under control.

Sub-Saharan Africa

Angola

Total external debt (1987)	$3.8 billion.
Debt management	Will continue to be a problem.
Real GDP growth	Will stay negative as long as civil war continues to disrupt economy.
Real per capita income	Will continue to shrink.
Inflation	Could be spurred by a needed currency devaluation.
Current account	Will remain in deficit and oil dependent.

Cameroon

Total external debt (1987)	$4 billion.
Debt management	Will be a concern.
Real GDP growth	Will remain slow or negative.
Real per capita income	Will remain high for the region.
Inflation	Will remain low.
Current account	Will remain in deficit with reliance on oil and other commodities.

Congo

Total external debt (1987)	$4.6 billion.
Debt management	Will remain a problem due to relative size and large non-concessional component.
Real GDP growth	Will shrink with low oil prices.
Real per capita income	Relatively high due to oil revenue.
Inflation	Will remain low.
Current account	Will remain in deficit.

Cote d'Ivoire

Total external debt (1987)	$13.6 billion.
Debt management	Will remain a problem due to size and large non-concessional element.
Real GDP growth	Will remain negative.
Real per capita income	Will be under pressure without renewed growth.
Inflation	Will remain moderate.
Current account	Will remain in deficit despite some diversification away from cocoa and coffee exports.

Ethiopia

Total external debt (1987)	$2.6 billion.
Debt management	Will be a problem.
Real GDP growth	Will remain slow or negative, complicated by regional conflict and refugees.
Real per capita income	Will remain the world's lowest.
Inflation	Will remain low.
Current account	Will remain in deficit despite some improvement in exports.

Gabon

Total external debt (1987)	$2.1 billion.
Debt management	Will remain a problem due to debt stock and non-concessional nature.
Real GDP growth	Will be constrained by oil market and austerity economic program.
Real per capita income	Will remain relatively high.
Inflation	Will be low due to tight policies and link to Franc Zone.
Current account	Will remain in deficit with oil market weak despite higher production.

Ghana

Total external debt (1987)	$3.1 billion.
Debt management	Will remain a concern despite economic reform.
Real GDP growth	Will remain positive led by gold mining.
Real per capita income	Will show slow growth.
Inflation	Will remain a problem due to currency devaluation and wage pressures.
Current account	Will remain in deficit.

Guinea

Total external debt (1987)	$1.8 billion.
Debt management	Will be a problem.
Real GDP growth	Will remain moderate under IMF guidance.
Real per capita income	Will remain slow.
Inflation	Has been a problem.
Current account	Over-reliant on exports of bauxite and other mining products.

Kenya

Total external debt (1987)	$6.0 billion.
Debt management	Will be a concern particularly if foreign investment does not offset steep debt service schedule.
Real GDP growth	Will slow with IMF austerity package and without a recovery of tea and coffee prices.

Real per capita income	Will be negative due to high population growth rate.
Inflation	Will remain moderate.
Current account	Will remain in deficit with most tourism gains already realized.

Liberia

Total external debt (1987)	$1.6 billion.
Debt management	Will be a problem with IMF and World Bank arrearages continuing.
Real GDP growth	Has been negative and could be hurt by domestic political tensions.
Real per capita income	Will be negative.
Inflation	Will remain low.
Current account	Will remain in rough balance as long as US aid continues.

Madagascar

Total external debt (1987)	$3.4 billion.
Debt management	Will remain a problem with further relief and rescheduling.
Real GDP growth	Will remain moderate.
Real per capita income	May turn positive with sufficient western aid in support of market-style reforms.
Inflation	Will remain a problem especially in near term if currency is devalued to re-enter the Franc Zone.
Current account	Will remain in deficit.

Mozambique

Total external debt (1987)	$3.2 billion.
Debt management	Will remain a problem.
Real GDP growth	Dependent on foreign aid and curbing South African involvement in the civil war.
Real per capita income	Will remain reliant on foreign aid.
Inflation	Will be fueled by belated price liberalization under IMF auspices.
Current account	Will remain in deficit.

Nigeria

Total external debt (1987)	$28.7 billion.
Debt management	Will remain a problem.
Real GDP growth	Growth will remain moderate without a recovery in the oil sector.
Real per capita income	Will remain lower with weak oil prices.
Inflation	Price stability will be under pressure from effects of currency unification and debt swap program.
Current account	Poor export price prospects will bring about a deficit despite rescheduling and continued austerity.

Senegal

Total external debt (1987)	$3.7 billion.
Debt management	Will remain a problem.
Real GDP growth	Will remain slow, dependent on agricultural production, especially of groundnuts.
Real per capita income	Will be slow.
Inflation	Will remain low, helped by Franc Zone link.
Current account	Will remain in deficit.

Somalia

Total external debt (1987)	$2.6 billion.
Debt management	Will remain a problem.
Real GDP growth	Will be slow or negative due largely to internal conflict and political concerns.
Real per capita income	Will be compounded by population growth.
Inflation	Will remain a problem.
Current account	Will remain in deficit.

Sudan

Total external debt (1987)	$11.1 billion.
Debt management	Will be a continuing problem.
Real GDP growth	Will be slowed by effects of civil war with crop output the determining variable.
Real per capita income	Will continue to shrink.
Inflation	Will remain a problem.
Current account	Will remain in deficit and reliant on aid.

Tanzania

Total external debt (1987)	$4.3 billion.
Debt management	Will be a problem.
Real GDP growth	Will remain slow.
Real per capita income	Will remain slightly positive.
Inflation	Will remain a problem exacerbated by currency devaluation.
Current account	Will remain in deficit.

Zaire

Total external debt (1987)	$8.6 billion.
Debt management	Will continue to be a problem.
Real GDP growth	Will remain slow.
Real per capita income	Will remain one of the lowest despite wealth amassed by the elite.
Inflation	Will remain a problem.
Current account	Will stay negative without a recovery of copper.

Zambia

Total external debt (1987)	$6.4 billion.
Debt management	Will remain a problem complicated by arrears accumulated during a self-imposed payments cap.
Real GDP growth	Will remain slow or negative.
Real per capita income	Will continue to decline.
Inflation	Will remain a problem worsened in short term by price decontrol.
Current account	Will remain negative with no current alternative to exports of copper, reserves of which are being depleted.

Zimbabwe

Total external debt (1987)	$2.5 billion.
Debt management	Will be a concern although mitigated by a moderating debt service schedule.
Real GDP growth	Will remain slow, boosted by any bumper crop years.
Real per capita income	Will continue gradual rise.
Inflation	Will remain a problem.

Current account	Will remain in rough balance.

Sources: Economist Intelligence Unit, *World Outlook 1989, January 1989* (London: The Economist Intelligence Unit, 1989). United Nations Development Programme - The World Bank, *African Economic and Financial Data* (Washington, D.C.: The World Bank, 1989). World Bank, *World Development Report 1989* (New York: Oxford University Press, 1989).

South Africa

South Africa

Total external debt (1989)	$23.4 billion.
Debt management	Will remain complicated by the political cost of apartheid.
Real GDP growth	Will continue to be low due to monetary constraints related to anti-inflationary measures as well as political uncertainty through the decade.
Real per capita income	Is likely to be an ongoing problem because of the skewed nature of income distribution inherent in the apartheid structure.
Inflation	Although high by South African standards, will be controlled, but at the cost of low GDP growth.
Current account	Will be kept at a surplus, but the size will remain dependent on commodity prices, political change and the ability to circumvent anti-apartheid sanctions.

Asia

China

Total external debt	$42.0 billion.
Debt management	Will remain under control, but increasing concern over access to international markets due to the potential for political change.
Real GDP growth	Likely to remain moderate throughout decade.
Real per capita income	Will continue to improve.
Inflation	Need for price reforms could engender inflationary pressures.
Current account	Will remain totally dependent on ability of government to manage trade liberalization.

India

Total external debt	$57.5 billion.
Debt management	Will be problem of growing concern especially in early 1990s.
Real GDP growth	Will remain around the 5 per cent mark through the decade except during bad monsoon years.
Real per capita income	Will remain skewed between the poor and the middle class and remain a source of social tension.
Inflation	Has the potential to be a problem if economic liberalization reform continues.
Current account	Will be impacted by trade liberalization and increased interest payment on foreign debt.

Indonesia

Total external debt	$52.6 billion.
Debt management	Will remain highly competent especially within the working relationship with the Inter-Governmental Group for Indonesia (IGGI).
Real GDP growth	Will remain moderately high.
Real per capita income	Will gradually improve.
Inflation	Will remain under control.
Current account	Will remain under control.

Malaysia

Total external debt	$20.5 billion.
Debt management	Will continue to be highly competent with considerable potential for debt reduction.
Real GDP growth	Will continue to improve.
Real per capita income	Will continue to improve.
Inflation	Will remain under control.
Current account	Will remain under control and most likely in surplus for majority of decade.

Philippines

Total external debt	$29.4 billion.
Debt management	Will continue to be a concern, although Brady Plan will help in better controls.

Real GDP growth	Will remain relatively moderate although fluctuating as structural reform takes place.
Real per capita income	Will continue to improve although large differences will exist between lower- and upper-most tiers.
Inflation	Will remain under control although a point of concern.
Current account	Will remain in deficit throughout much of decade due to structural reforms.

South Korea

Total external debt	$37.2 billion.
Debt management	Will remain highly competent with shift from net debtor to creditor probable.
Real GDP growth	Will remain relatively high depending on economic behavior in the US and Japan.
Real per capita income	Will continue to increase substantially.
Inflation	Will remain under control.
Current account	Will continue to be in surplus throughout most of decade.

Thailand

Total external debt	$20.5 billion.
Debt management	Probably will continue to avoid problems although may bear watching.
Real GDP growth	Will remain dynamic throughout decade as Thailand becomes the next 'Asian tiger'.
Real per capita income	Will continue to improve throughout decade.
Inflation	Will bear watching although likely to remain under control.
Current account	Will continue to improve throughout decade through strong export-led economic growth.

Southern Europe

Greece

Total external debt (1988)	$24.5 billion.
Debt management	Will remain problematic due to the political nature of the budget and the size of the external debt.

Real GDP growth	Will remain low until later in decade when integration with European Community addresses structural problems.
Real per capita income	Problems with external debt will be balanced by EC assistance and programs. By end of 1990s, advances are likely.
Inflation	Will remain a problem area through most of the decade until later years due to budgetary problems. Likely to fall at end of 1990s because of EC pressure to reduce it to be more in line with the rest of the Community.
Current account	Will continue in deficit.

Portugal

Total external debt (1988)	$19.5 billion.
Debt management	Will continue to be responsible.
Real GDP growth	Will remain relatively high by EC standards, between 3-5 per cent through most of the 1990s.
Real per capita income	Will continue to improve.
Inflation	Not a major problem.
Current account	Will be an initial widening of deficit due to EC membership and liberalization of the economy. By mid-decade improvements likely.

Turkey

Total external debt (1988)	$42.3 billion.
Debt management	Will continue to be a concern, but likely under control.
Real GDP growth	Slow growth at beginning of decade, but will regain momentum by 1993 and continue through to 2000.
Real per capita income	Will remain problematic, but will improve substantially by end of decade, especially in the western part of the country.
Inflation	Will remain problematic, but under 100 per cent. Efforts will be made to reduce it by end of decade due to EC membership bid.
Current account	Will fluctuate between small deficits and small surpluses through decade.

Yugoslavia

Total external debt (1988)	$20.8 billion.
Debt management	Problematic in the early 1990s due to political complications, but will be back on track by mid-decade and potentially under control by 2000.
Real GDP growth	Will slowly regain dynamic growth, but only after political changes that provide central authorities with decision-making powers for entire country.
Real per capita income	Will suffer from political turmoil and economic uncertainty until mid-decade.
Inflation	Major problem in early 1990s, but measures will be undertaken to bring it under control.
Current account	Will maintain a surplus, but will vary in size due to initial difficulties with trade liberalization and a recovery in export performance in early 1990s.

Eastern Europe

Albania

Total external debt (1988)	$0.2 billion.
Debt management	Debt is minimal, but increased borrowing may be necessary as a component of needed modernization.
Real GDP growth	Updating of industrial base necessary for sustained improvement.
Real per capita income	Needs to be accompanied by improvement in supply of food and consumer goods.
Inflation	Any modernization policy including price reform and currency devaluation poses an inflationary risk.
Current account	In order to modernize economy with imports from western countries, Albania will continue to relax its 'no debt' stance and allow modest deficits.

Bulgaria

Total external debt (1988)	$10.8 billion.
Debt management	Payment difficulties will lead to rescheduling; IMF membership should help to introduce acceptable payment programme.
Real GDP growth	Reform from a planned economy will help in medium term, but difficult short term adjustment period must be completed first.
Real per capita income	Will be problematic.

Inflation	Price reform and currency devaluation pose the risk of serious inflation.
Current account	With exports slumping, deficits will be a problem area.

Czechoslovakia

Total external debt (1988)	$5.2 billion.
Debt management	Relatively low debt will aid in reform process; project-related financing will increase. Some sovereign borrowing will accompany move towards currency convertibility.
Real GDP growth	One of the strongest economies in the region will serve as a good base for reforms leading towards a market economy and away from a concentration in heavy industry.
Real per capita income	Initially will drop as reform proceeds, but should gradually increase towards 1995.
Inflation	Price reform and currency devaluation pose the risk of serious inflation.
Current account	Will need to import capital goods in order to modernize industrial sector, may have short-term trade deficits as switch from socialist to competitive Western markets is made.

East Germany

Total external debt (1988)	$19.1 billion.
Debt management	Given strength of economy, debt is not excessive. Monetary union will put control firmly in the hands of West Germany's Bundesbank.
Real GDP growth	Difficulties of implementing reforms will be mitigated by strong economic base and financial assistance from West Germany.
Real per capita income	Will improve as a result of overall growth and moves towards unity, although there will be in the initial phase some fall in living standards.
Inflation	Price reform and currency union should not lead to serious inflation problems as the Bundesbank in West Germany will be eager to control such a problem.
Current account	Will come under some pressure from capital imports, but West German assistance will reduce resulting debt and financing costs.

Hungary

Total external debt (1988)	$17 billion.
Debt management	With the highest per capita debt in the region, Hungary can avoid a rescheduling in the 1990s only by successfully undertaking rapid economic reform and severe austerity measures. Rescheduling and/or debt relief is a more likely prospect.
Real GDP growth	Austerity, needed to avoid debt rescheduling and to comply with IMF programmes, will minimize growth prospects.
Real per capita income	Will be constrained as a result of slow economic growth.
Inflation	Tight economic policies will help offset the effects of price reform and currency devaluation on inflation, but at the beginning of 1990 inflation was already running ahead of projected estimates.
Current account	Hungary faced with the dilemma that a current account surplus is needed to avoid debt rescheduling, but at the cost of foregoing the imports needed to update its industrial base.

Poland

Total external debt (1988)	$28.7 billion.
Debt management	Rescheduling in place by early 1990 but debt relief will be needed as Poland's debt problems continue.
Real GDP growth	Will suffer while economic reforms are pursued and the foreign debt burden is brought under control.
Real per capita income	The combination of growth prospects and IMF demand control policies, will further constrain personal incomes.
Inflation	Expected to be kept under control as first indications show the radical 'big bang' reform programme introduced in January 1990 was showing some success by mid 1990.
Current account	Planned deficit (with IMF blessing) is intended to boost imports in short term so industry can be competitive in future.

Romania

Total external debt (1988)	$3.1 billion.
Debt management	Success of Ceausescu's debt reduction priority gives new regime some flexibility but money needed for restructuring industry and needed imports for both consumers and industrial sectors.
Real GDP growth	Difficulties inherent in economic reform will be mitigated by end of Ceausescu fixation on improving external accounts.
Real per capita income	Suffered with emphasis on debt repayment under Ceausescu, but improvement here should be a priority of new government.
Inflation	Price reform, currency devaluation and pent-up consumer demand pose the risk of serious inflation.
Current account	Improvements under Ceausescu were made at the expense of economic health of domestic economy. Imports must be increased to repair damage to economy and to modernize industrial base.

USSR

Total external debt (1988)	$40.1 billion.
Debt management	Debt not excessive given size of economy and natural resource export potential.
Real GDP growth	Gradual economic reform policies will make improvement difficult unless radicalisation pursued in early 1990s.
Real per capita income	Constraints on economic growth will be balanced by greater emphasis on consumer sector.
Inflation	Price reform, currency devaluation and pent-up consumer demand pose the risk of inflation.
Current account	Given export potential and small size of foreign trade relative to the overall economy, management of the external accounts should not be a problem in the long term, despite a likely rise in capital goods and consumer imports.

Appendix

Total Debt and Organization Membership Data

Latin America

Country	External debt	Membership
Argentina	$60,000 million	IMF, IBRD
Brazil	$112,000 million	IMF, IBRD
Chile	$17,000 million	IMF, IBRD
Colombia	$16,000 million	IMF, IBRD
Mexico	$105,000 million	IMF, IBRD
Peru	$18,000 million	IMF, IBRD
Venezuela	$35,000 million	IMF, IBRD, OPEC

Source: Author's estimates

Central America and the Caribbean

Country	External debt	Membership
Bahamas	$232.7 million	IMF, IBRD, IDB, CARICOM
Barbados	621 million	IMF, IBRD, IDB, CARICOM
Costa Rica	4,727 million	IMF, IBRD, IDB, CARICOM
Dom. Rep.	3,695 million	IMF, IBRD, IDB
El Salvador	1,762 million	IMF, IBRD, IDB, CACM, CABEI
Guatemala	2,825 million	IMF, IBRD, IDB, CACM, CABEI
Guyana	1,285 million	IMF, IBRD, IDB, CARICOM, CDB
Haiti	804 million	IMF, IBRD, IDB
Honduras	3,303 million	IMF, IBRD, IDB, CABEI
Jamaica	4,446 million	IMF, IBRD, IDB, CARICOM, CDB
Nicaragua	7,291 million	IMF, IBRD, IDB, CACM, CABEI
Panama	5,324 million	IMF, IBRD, IDB
Suriname	71 million	IMF, IBRD, IDB
Trinidad/Tob.	1,801 million	IMF, IBRD, IDB, CARICOM, CDB

Source: World Bank Debt Tables, except Suriname, Inter-American Development Bank

(CARICOM: the Commonwealth Caribbean Common Market; IDB: the Inter-American Development Bank; CACM: Central American Common Market; CDB: Caribbean Development Bank; OECS: Organization of Eastern Caribbean States; CABEI: Central American Bank for Economic Investment.

Middle East and Africa

Country	External debt	Membership
Algeria	$24,850 million	IMF, IBRD, OPEC
Bahrain	N/A	IMF, IBRD, OPEC
Egypt	$49,970 million	IMF, IBRD
Iran	$10,000 million	IMF, IBRD, OPEC
Iraq	$80,000 million	IMF, IBRD, OPEC
Israel	$26,000 million	IMF, IBRD
Jordan	$5,532 million	IMF, IBRD
Kuwait	$7,930 million	IMF, IBRD, OPEC
Lebanon	$499 million	IMF, IBRD
Libya	$3,500 million	IMF, IBRD, OPEC
Morocco	$19,900 million	IMF, IBRD, OPEC
Oman	$2,940 million	IMF, IBRD
Pakistan	$17,010 million	IMF, IBRD
Qatar	N/A	IMF, IBRD, OPEC
Saudi Arabia	N/A	IMF, IBRD, OPEC
South Yemen	$1,927 million	IMF, IBRD
Syria	$4,890 million	IMF, IBRD
Tunisia	$6,672 million	IMF, IBRD
Yemen (North)	$2,052 million	IMF, IBRD
United Arab Emirates	$8,740 million	IMF, IBRD, OPEC

Sources: Debt figures are from the World Bank for 1988 except for Iran, Iraq and Yemen (author's estimates); Israel (Economist Intelligence Unit [EIU]); Kuwait (EIU for 1987); Libya, South Yemen and United Arab Emirates (EIU for 1986).

Sub-Saharan Africa

Country	External debt	Membership
Angola	$3,800 million*	IMF, IBRD
Benin	$1,133 million	IMF, IBRD
Botswana	$518 million	IMF, IBRD
Burkina Faso	$861 million	IMF, IBRD
Burundi	$755 million	IMF, IBRD
Cameroon	$4,028 million	IMF, IBRD

Country	External debt	Membership
Cape Verde	$131 million	IMF, IBRD
Central African Republic	$585 million	IMF, IBRD
Chad	$318 million	IMF, IBRD
Comoros	$203 million	IMF, IBRD
Congo	$4,636 million	IMF, IBRD
Cote d'Ivoire	$13,555 million	IMF, IBRD
Djibouti	$181 million	IMF, IBRD
Equatorial Guinea	$193 million	IMF, IBRD
Ethiopia	$2,590 million	IMF, IBRD
Gabon	$2,071 million	IMF, IBRD, OPEC
Gambia	$319 million	IMF, IBRD
Ghana	$3,124 million	IMF, IBRD
Guinea	$1,784 million	IMF, IBRD
Guinea-Bissau	$424 million	IMF, IBRD
Kenya	$5,590 million	IMF, IBRD
Lesotho	$241 million	IMF, IBRD
Liberia	$1,618 million	IMF, IBRD
Madagascar	$3,377 million	IMF, IBRD
Malawi	$1,363 million	IMF, IBRD
Mali	$2,016 million	IMF, IBRD
Mauritania	$2,035 million	IMF, IBRD
Mauritius	$755 million	IMF, IBRD
Mozambique	$3,200 million*	IMF, IBRD
Niger	$1,679 million	IMF, IBRD
Nigeria	$28,714 million	IMF, IBRD, OPEC
Rwanda	$583 million	IMF, IBRD
Sao Tome and Principe	$87 million	IMF, IBRD
Senegal	$3,695 million	IMF, IBRD
Seychelles	$119 million	IMF, IBRD
Sierra Leone	$659 million	IMF, IBRD
Somalia	$2,567 million	IMF, IBRD
Sudan	$11,126 million	IMF, IBRD
Swaziland	$293 million	IMF, IBRD
Tanzania	$4,335 million	IMF, IBRD
Togo	$1,223 million	IMF, IBRD
Uganda	$1,405 million	IMF, IBRD
Zaire	$8,630 million	IMF, IBRD
Zambia	$6,400 million	IMF, IBRD
Zimbabwe	$2,512 million	IMF, IBRD

Sources: Unless asterisked (*), data is from the United Nations Development Programme - The World Bank, *African Economic and Financial Data* (Washington, D.C.: The World Bank, 1989), p. 89. Otherwise they are from the Economist Intelligence Unit, *World Outlook 1989, January 1989* (London: The Economist Intelligence Unit, 1989). Figures are for total external debt at end-1987.

South Africa

Country	External debt	Membership
South Africa	$23,400 million	None

Asia

Country	External debt	Membership
Bangladesh	$10,219 million	IMF, IBRD
Brunei	None	IMF, IBRD, ASEAN
Burma [Myanmar]	$4,321 million	IMF, IBRD
Cambodia	$503 million	IMF, IBRD
China	$42,015 million	IMF, IBRD
India	$57,513 million	IMF, IBRD
Indonesia	$52,600 million	IMF, IBRD, ASEAN, OPEC
Laos	$824 million	IMF, IBRD
Malaysia	$20,541 million	IMF, IBRD, ASEAN
North Korea	$3,500 million	
Nepal	$1,164 million	IMF, IBRD
Papua New Guinea	$2,270 million	IMF, IBRD
Philippines	$29,448 million	IMF, IBRD, ASEAN
Singapore	$2,250 million	IMF, IBRD, ASEAN
South Korea	$37,156 million	IMF, IBRD
Sri Lanka	$5,189 million	IMF, IBRD
Taiwan	$1,500 million	
Thailand	$20,530 million	IMF, IBRD, ASEAN
Viet Nam	$7,700 million	IMF, IBRD

Sources: Debt figures are from the World Bank for 1988 except for Taiwan (Economist Intelligence Unit [EIU] estimate for 1988). Singapore (EIU for 1987), Viet Nam (EIU for 1986), and Cambodia and North Korea (EIU for 1984).

Southern Europe

Country	External debt	Membership
Greece	$24,500 million	IMF, IBRD, EC, NATO
Portugal	$17,168 million	IMF, IBRD, EC, NATO
Turkey	$42,300 million	IMF, IBRD, NATO
Yugoslavia	$21,684 million	IMF, IBRD, NATO

Sources: Debt figures are from the World Bank for 1988 except for Greece and Turkey (author's estimates for 1988).

Eastern Europe

Country	External debt (gross, $bn)	Membership
Albania	0.2	
Bulgaria	7.2 (end 1988)	applied to join IMF, IBRD
Czechoslovakia	6.6 (end 1989)	applied to join IMF, IBRD
East Germany	20.6 (end 1989)	unity will lead to *de facto* membership
Hungary	20.0 (end 1989)	IMF, IBRD
Poland	38.0 (end 1989	IMF, IBRD
Romania	0.350 (first quarter 1989)	IMF, IBRD
Soviet Union	49.5 (end 1988)	application expected

Albania

Total external debt (gross): $200 m (estimate).

Debt management: At the beginning of the 1990s, Albania was still constitutionally unable to borrow money from the West, although some trade-related credits were being used. There were no debt payments problems, as most hard currency deals were transacted on a cash basis.

Real GDP growth: minimal growth was expected to continue, but with little or no attempt to modernise and restructure industry, relative to the rest of the world, growth was expected to fall during the 1990s.

Real per capita income: remained steady, although austerity measures introduced by the Government at the beginning of 1990 could lead to a fall in real wages.

Inflation: officially there is no inflation; hidden inflation was estimated to be around 2–3 per cent. If a price reform were undertaken, inflation would initially be high as supply and demand balanced.

Current account: balanced. Albania was beginning to use trade credits at the start of 1990, but limited these. Most imports were on a barter basis or cash basis.

Bulgaria

Total external debt (gross): $7.2 bn (end 1988).

Debt management: problems were expected with a possible rescheduling sometime in 1990. Applied to join the IMF. Economic policies were expected to move the country towards a market economy, but short-term trade prospects with the West were considered poor in early 1990s; a substantial investment from the West would be needed in order to make industry competitive. At the same time, the country needed to aim more of its trade to hard currency markets (at the beginning of 1990, over 80 per cent of foreign trade was conducted with non-convertible currency area).

Real GDP growth: falling and possible negative growth in the first half of the decade as the country pursued long-term economic reforms.

Real per capita income: falling in the first half of the 1990s following the introduction of a market reform package; expected to rise slightly towards the end of the decade, if economic policies are successful.

Inflation: still low at the beginning of 1990 but high rates expected when price reforms introduced.

Current account: deficit on 1989 trade and poor prospects for the first years of the 1990s. Depending on economic policies and interest of western investors, Bulgaria could continue to have problems throughout the decade.

Czechoslovakia

Total external debt (gross): $6.6 bn (end 1989).

Debt management: small debt at the beginning of the decade, with no problems of payments. Increased borrowing expected, but most financing will be projected related. Few saw any long-term worries. IMF membership should aid sensible borrowing policies.

Real GDP growth: falling and expected to be low in the first half of the 1990s as the country restructures and modernises its obsolete industrial base and expands the private sector.

Real per capita income: falling and expected to fall in the first two to three years of the decade as economic reforms tighten domestic money supply.

Inflation: low at the beginning of 1990, but expected to be kept to single digits, even though a substantial price reform is planned.

Current account: deficit at the end of 1989 and problems expected in the early 1990s unless foreign trade sector is liberalised and monopoly control ended.

East Germany

Total external debt (gross): $20.6 bn (end 1989).

Debt management: no problems on repayments. If, as seems likely, the country is reunified with West Germany, no significant problems with debt repayments are expected.

Real GDP growth: falling in 1990 as the political and economic uncertainty and poor productivity continues; depending on the speed of reunification, slow growth was expected in light of the economic reforms necessary.

Real per capita income: falling in the beginning of the 1990s as the currency was devalued and savings eroded by economic reforms.

Inflation: expected to rise in the first year-and-a-half of the decade, but should be brought under control relatively quickly.

Current account: deficit at the end of 1989 with no change expected for 1990. As foreign trade liberalised, export performance to hard currency area expected to improve and strengthen.

Hungary

Total external debt (gross): $20.0 bn (end 1989).

Debt management: Problems expected, but rescheduling should be avoided, as the country struggles against a very high debt service ratio. A comprehensive IMF package together with a Paris Club refinancing could help the country make it through the first half of the 1990s.

Real GDP growth: expected to be 2–3 per cent in 1990 and could fall even lower in the first few years of the decade as a new, freely elected government comes to terms with introducing a market economy.

Real per capita income: continued falling in 1990 and expected to make only marginal improvement in the first half of the decade. If economic restructuring successful, incomes could begin to rise in the second half of the 1990s.

Inflation: expected to be in low twenties in 1990 and could rise rapidly in the first half of the decade if budget imbalance continues. An austerity programme, with IMF backing, could bring inflation down to reasonable levels by the end of the decade.

Current account: deficit in 1989 expected to be continued in 1990, but at a lower figure. IMF programme expected to give surplus by mid 1990s.

Poland

Total external debt (gross): $38.0 bn (end 1989).

Debt management: following an IMF agreement in early 1990 and Paris Club long-term rescheduling, the country should be able to manage repayment in the short term. A debt reduction programme was expected to be introduced in the first half of the decade. If economic reforms are successful, the country could be on the way to real economic recovery by the late 1990s.

Real GDP growth: falling in 1990, but expected to pick up as monopoly state dismantled, western investment increases and private sector expands.

Real per capita income: falling in 1990 as austerity measures are pursued, but expected to begin to pick up by earliest 1992 and later.

Inflation: measures introduced at the beginning of 1990 were aimed to curb hyperinflation. If they work, the government expects inflation to be around 10 per cent a month by the end of 1990 and by mid-1990s back to acceptable West European levels.

Current account: good balance. Significant rescheduling and potential debt relief should mean a more healthy current account suplus by the mid-1990s.

Romania

Total external debt (gross): $350 m (first quarter 1989).

Debt management: at the beginning of 1990, no real debt, but high borrowing expected as the country restructures. Unless export potential expanded, debt repayment could be a problem by the end of the decade.

Real GDP growth: no accurate figures for the 1980s; predicting 1990 difficult as country's revolutionary government unsure of economic policies. Long-term prospects are thought to be good, if a sensible economic reform programme, aimed at a free market, is introduced with IMF backing.

Real per capita income: no growth recorded at the beginning of 1990, but given the low average, substantial increases are expected by the mid-1990s, with a return to normal average European growth rates by the end of the decade.

Inflation: beginning in 1990, with the free pricing for agricultural goods, there was concern that inflation could run out of control without firm economic policy measures. Expected to be under control by the end of the decade.

Current account: surplus at end of 1989, but forecast for the first half of the decade is for deficit as the country borrows in order to re-equip and restructure industry starved of capital investment during the Ceasuscu years.

Soviet Union

Total external debt (gross): $49.5 bn (end 1988).

Debt management: no problems at the beginning of 1990, but some concern if hard currency exports (primarily oil) continue to decline.

Real GDP growth: expected to be low for the first half of the 1990s. If significant economic reforms are implemented, including price reform and privatisation, growth could pick up in the second half of the decade; if policies remain ideologically weighted, negative growth could characterise the end of the 1990s.

Real per capita income: rising with no corresponding increase in productivity. If economic reforms are implemented, incomes could fall in the first half of the decade.

Inflation: rising and could leap to hyperinflationary levels if no measures are undertaken to soak up the excess money supply caused by severe shortages of consumer goods and few investment opportunities for the general public. If significant price reform implemented, inflation could be a real problem throughout the 1990s.

Current account: in deficit with the hard currency area at the end of 1989, and no improvement expected in 1990. Unless significant changes are made to industrial export structure, reliance on raw material export to earn hard currency could cause real problems by the mid-1990s.

Index